Multinationals in India

Multinationals in India

FDI and Complementation Strategy in a Developing Country

Amar K.J.R. Nayak

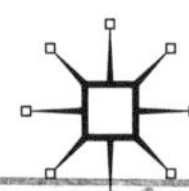

First published 2008 by
PALGRAVE MACMILLAN
Houndmills, Basingstoke, Hampshire RG21 6XS and
175 Fifth Avenue, New York, N.Y. 10010
Companies and representatives throughout the world

PALGRAVE MACMILLAN is the global academic imprint of the Palgrave Macmillan division of St. Martin's Press, LLC and of Palgrave Macmillan Ltd. Macmillan® is a registered trademark in the United States, United Kingdom and other countries. Palgrave is a registered trademark in the European Union and other countries.

ISBN-13: 978–0–230–20269–6 hardback
ISBN-10: 0–230–20269–1 hardback

This book is printed on paper suitable for recycling and made from fully managed and sustained forest sources. Logging, pulping and manufacturing processes are expected to conform to the environmental regulations of the country of origin.

A catalogue record for this book is available from the British Library

Library of Congress Cataloging-in-Publication Data

Nayak, Amar K. J. R.
Multinationals in India : FDI and complementation strategy in a developing country/Amar KJR Nayak.
p. cm.
Includes bibliographical references and index.
ISBN 0–230–20269–1 (alk. paper)
1. International business enterprises—India. 2. Business enterprises, Foreign—India. 3. Investments, Foreign—India. I. Title.
HD2899.N39 2008
338.8'8854—dc22

2008011804

10 9 8 7 6 5 4 3 2 1
17 16 15 14 13 12 11 10 09 08

Printed and bound in Great Britain by
CPI Antony Rowe, Chippenham and Eastbourne

Contents

List of Charts

List of Figures

List of Tables

List of Abbreviations

ATC	American Tobacco Company
BAT	British American Tobacco
CBR	Case-Based Research
CEEC	Central and Eastern European Countries
CMIE	Centre for Monitoring Indian Economy
ED	Enforcement Directorate
EPZ	Export Processing Zone
FDI	Foreign Direct Investment
FEMA	Foreign Exchange Management Act
FERA	Foreign Exchange Regulation Act
FPI	Foreign Portfolio Investment
GDP	Gross Domestic Product
GDR	Global Depository Receipt
GOI	Government of India
HLL	Hindustan Lever Limited
HUL	Hindustan Unilever Limited
IBD	International Business Division
IDBI	Industrial Development Bank of India
IIC	Indian Investment Centre
ILP	Industrial Licensing Policy
ILTD	Indian Leaf Tobacco Development
IMF	International Monetary Fund
INR	Indian Rupee
ITC	ITC Limited
MNE	Multinational Enterprise
MRTP	Monopolies & Restrictive Trade Practices
MUL	Maruti Udyog Ltd
OGL	Open General License
OLI	Ownership–Location–Internationalization paradigm
PAT	Profit after tax
PBDIT	Profit before depreciation, interest & tax
SMC	Suzuki Motor Corporation
UNILEVER	Unilever PLC
WTO	World Trade Organization

Terms used alternatively

BAT/ITC Ltd
Foreign Firms/Foreign Companies/Multinational Enterprises
Joint Ventures/Collaborations
SMC/MUL

Preface

The year 1991 herarlded the onset of large-scale liberalization of the Indian economy. It was an exciting time to watch the cautious entry and re-entry of several Multinational Enterprises (MNEs), the corresponding confusion among the Indian firms, the conflict among policy-makers on the extent and degree of liberalization so as not to jeopardize their control over the economy and the scepticism in the minds of the intellectuals over the suitability of it all to a developing country such as India.

Poor performance of the multinational enterprises and slow growth of the Indian economy were being attributed to the policy framework of the country including the policies on trade and foreign investment in India. MNEs like General Motors, Ford Motors and IBM, among many others, divested from India in the 1960s and 1970s because they perceived that it was not profitable to operate in India under the existing policy framework. Against this backdrop, I was curious to find out if all foreign companies in India failed to perform under the general policy framework of the 1960s and 1970s or were there some who had succeeded in the same circumstances. Intuitively, I felt that there were some companies that would have done well during the same period. This hypothesis triggered my research and has resulted in this book.

One of the biggest challenges in this was to identify foreign MNEs that have survived and thrived, presumably under an inhospitable policy environment. It compelled me to master the art and science of sampling for case selection appropriate to a research question. The process also helped me to undertake and appreciate contextual and multilayered analyses in case research. Whether it was the sampling process or case analysis, the power of triangulation has been evident in this work. However, as the study progressed, the most important aspect has been the possibility of developing a theory of management (Ghosal and Moran 2005) in FDI strategy that augurs well for both an investing firm and the host country.

In its analyses, the book establishes that the key determinants of the success of a foreign firm in India lie in the internal strategy of the firms and not in the external policy framework of a host country. More than a myopic strategy to seek resources, markets or efficiency that most MNEs adopt in India, a holistic investment strategy including investment in the main business, complementary businesses, priority sectors, and local equity were critical to the consistent performance of individual firms. Most importantly, the book argues that the investments in complementary businesses contribute significantly to the financial performance and success of MNEs in a developing host country context.

While three cases have been analysed in detail to make the argument, it has not been my intention to portray these companies as role models and examples of perfection. Many of the management decisions made by each of these companies might have been out of necessity or by accident. The outcomes in retrospect, however, provide insights to a winning strategy in international business and foreign direct investment in a developing country context, a strategy that is worth emulating.

Amar K.J.R. Nayak

Acknowledgements

This book is based on my doctoral thesis and it belongs as much to the teachers who guided me through it as it does to me. I shall always be grateful to Professor Tetsuya Kuwahara for choosing me as his research scholar despite the fact that I knew little of both the subject and the skills of research. In his quiet and non-intrusive style, he has shaped my thinking as well as my way of doing research. I would also like to thank my supervisors. Professor Kalyan Chakravarti who saw the point of this research even before I had finished describing it to him. Professor Prabina Rajib drilled into me the discipline of writing. Professor G.S. Sanyal advised me to condense my thesis to a mathematical equation. His support, and the innovative and critical comments from Professors Kalyan Guin, A.N. Sadhu, and P.K.J. Mohapatra, ensured the analytical and methodological rigour.

I would like to thank ITC Ltd, Hindustan Lever Ltd, and Maruti Udyog Ltd for giving me access to their print resources and their senior and top executives who shared their valuable and unique experiences. Fr. E. Abraham, s.j. has been the person most supportive and appreciative of this work. I thank him from the bottom of my heart. I also thank Arthur Monteiro for editing the first draft of this work. Sashmi, my wife has been closely associated with me in this work. Without the encouragement and support of my family the work wouldn't have materialized.

Finally, I would like to thank the commissioning team at Palgrave Macmillan, especially Virginia Thorp, for her eagerness to publish this work and for her valuable suggestions. My thanks to Ann Marangos and Emily Bown for their excellent editorial support. Lastly, it would only be fair to say that the mistakes and shortcomings of this book, if any, are all mine.

Amar K.J.R. Nayak
Bhubaneswar

Introduction

The Globalization Process in developing countries has been the most notable phenomena during the last two decades. The cross-border transaction of mere commodity trading of natural resources since the 1850s has snowballed into high volumes of direct investment in high value products in the recent years. The number of multinational enterprises the world over has increased substantially over the last one hundred and fifty years and their presence in the developing countries in particular has been significant in recent times.

Regulatory frameworks concerning international trade and investment in the developing countries have also undergone transformation during the last few decades. From little restriction to international trade in the nineteenth century, barriers to trade first appeared towards the end of the First World War. In the 1950s, many of today's developing countries were free from colonial rule and barriers to cross-border transactions began to appear and intensified by the 1970s. While some freely opened up their economies, others cautiously guarded their economies only to open up under pressure in the 1990s.

In the overall globalization process, India as a host country has been significant since the early nineteenth century and the interest of multinational enterprises in India has been prominent for a longtime. As a major force of change both in economic and social transactions, the phenomenon of globalization and multinational enterprises in India during the last two decades has given rise to a variety of complex issues for discussion.

We however, may broadly classify these issues into two broad areas, namely macroeconomic issues of host country and firm level issues of foreign firms. The macro level issues such as appropriateness of liberalized investment policies, impact of such policies on Indian industry and economy, pressures of global forces on India in the World Trade Organization (WTO) regime have grappled the policy makers and civil society in the country. At the micro-level, performance levels of foreign firms and the appropriateness of their business strategy in the Indian context have been significant. Although firm-level business strategies form the foundation for a sustainable growth of both the firm and the host country and the long term success of cross-border investments, this aspect has not been discussed sufficiently.

This book squarely puts on the table the FDI strategy that has worked successfully in a developing host country context, a strategy that questions both the policy framework in the developing host context and the logic of foreign multinational enterprises seeking greater economic liberalization for better firm level performance. In essence, the book analyses the key determinants of successful direct investment strategy by foreign firms in India. The direct investment strategy of three successful foreign firms, namely British American Tobacco, Unilever, and Suzuki Motor Corporation have been elaborated to emphasize the point.

In the analyses, the book establishes that the key determinants of success of foreign firms in India lay in the internal strategy of the firms. More than a myopic strategy to seek resources, markets or efficiency, a holistic investment strategy including investment in main business, complementary businesses, priority sectors, and local equity were critical to consistent performance of individual firms. Most importantly, the book argues that the investments in complementary businesses of their respective industries contributed significantly to the financial performances of firms. Through the analyses and findings, the book raises some important questions. Whether host government policies prior to the 1980s have been obstacles for success of multinational companies and growth of Indian economy – an issue that has forced India to liberalize its FDI policies for higher efficiency of both the host country and the multinational companies. Whether the success of a firm is solely determined by externalities or largely determined by the internal strategy of a firm in a given context? The results of the analysis in the book provide important cues to multinational enterprises in India and other developing countries on how to invest strategically in these host countries for the benefit of the company and the host country.

The book has been organized into eight chapters. It begins with the ongoing debates on Foreign Direct Investment (FDI) and multinational enterprise strategy and goes on to enrich the context by discussing the story of FDI in India. It then sets the analytical framework through which the book put forth its central argument. The argument has been developed by analysing the strategies adopted by three highly interesting multinational enterprises in India and the findings from these case studies have been verified statistically before the concluding chapter is reached.

Chapter 1 presents the various debates on FDI. Among the many areas of studies in FDI, it outlines the four major areas of research arising out of the two key agents of FDI, namely the investing foreign company and the host country. The discussion of these four major research areas of FDI provide the backdrop for the theme of the book and bring to the fore the relevance of the argument made in the context of the various viewpoints on FDI in India.

Chapter 2 describes the evolution of FDI in India during the 1900s–2000. This chapter consists of two main sections, namely (a) studies of different periods, namely 1900s–1918, 1919–42, 1943–61, 1962–77, 1978–90, 1991–2000 and (b) major characteristics of FDI in India and the periodization of FDI history in India. Although direct investment in India has been significant since the 1930s, there are no studies that link the developments of FDI in India during the last 75 years. Some studies relate to developments in the 1930s, while some to the 1960s and 1970s, and many relate to post-1991. By providing a review of the evolution of FDI, this chapter bridges the gap that exists in the current literature on FDI in India. A critical understanding of the history and characteristics of FDI in India also provides a sound background to understanding the context of globalization in India in which the main argument of the book has been placed.

Chapter 3 discusses the key hypotheses around which the book has been organized. It explains in detail the conceptual framework and the methodologies adopted in its investigation and analyses of firm level business strategies. The three hypotheses being, first, successful foreign firms in India have made *holistic investment* across the various market functions of their respective industries in India. Secondly, direct investment by foreign firms in *complementary businesses* of their respective industries contributed significantly to their success in India. Thirdly, determinants of success for foreign firms have been similar for successful companies across all industries in India.

The chapter also provides a detailed explanation on how the sample cases were selected and how each case was studied. The cases for detailed study have been sampled by two methods, namely (a) *five step sampling process* and (b) *hierarchical clustering technique*. It discusses how each case was analysed using a variety of primary and secondary documents like company annual reports, case histories, memoranda of understanding, company prospectus, annual speeches of CEOs and interviews with a few past and present senior and top executives in the companies. The various statistical techniques used for analyses have also been explained in this chapter.

Chapter 4, 5 and 6 deal with the analyses of three cases, namely British American Tobacco (1906–2004), Unilever (1932–2004), and Suzuki Motor Corporation (1982–2004). Each case has been analysed to explain how the company made investment in its main business, in complementary businesses, in priorities areas in the host country, and in local equity.

Chapter 7, through the various *confirmatory statistical tests* compares the effect of different investments on the financial performance of each company. Further, using Multiple Linear Regression and Artificial Neural Networking Analysis on aggregate data, the chapter presents the impact of different investments on financial performance at an aggregate level. The chapter finally provides the equations that show the nature and degree of relationship between the different kinds of investments and sales and profit after tax (PAT) separately for individual MNE and then at an aggregate level taking all the three MNEs from different industries. The intuition developed from the qualitative discussions in the three cases have been triangulated with the statistical findings.

Chapter 8 discusses the core FDI strategy that is unique to developing countries. It argues that complementation is the winning strategy in a developing country context. It establishes the significance of investment in complementary businesses on financial performance in each case studied and at an aggregate industry level. Through its empirical evidence of strategy and success at firm level and aggregate industry level, this chapter raises several questions on the current strategies and policies of host governments and multinational enterprises in the developing countries. The chapter provides a fresh perspective to effective business strategies of foreign multinational companies investing in developing countries. Finally, the chapter outlines some directions for future research that can enhance the field of international business and strategy.

1
Debates in FDI Studies

This chapter presents the various debates on FDI. Among the many areas of studies in FDI, it outlines the four major areas of research arising out of the two key agents of FDI, namely the investing foreign company and the host country. The discussions of these four major research areas of FDI provide the backdrop for the theme of the book and brings to the fore the relevance of the argument made in the context of the various viewpoints on FDI in India.

FDI depends upon two key agents, namely a firm that desires to invest in another country, i.e. investing foreign firm, and a country open to foreign investment, i.e. the host country. The interplay between these two agents determines the factors that effect the flow of FDI and the subsequent relationship between these two agents generates varied outcomes for each. Most of the available literature on FDI can accordingly be classified into four major areas of study, namely (a) determinants or motivations of FDI for investing firm, (b) host country policies to attract FDI, (c) impact of FDI on the host economy, and (d) performance of investing firm in the host country (see Table 1.1).

This simple classification, however, does not include all studies from the vast literature on FDI, international business and multinational enterprises as they are beyond the scope of the present discussion. Multinational enterprise strategy and its performance in a developing host country, one of the above four research areas, is the focus of this book.

A brief discussion of these four major research areas will provide a backdrop to the questions that have been raised in this study and will also bring to the fore the relevance of potential areas suggested in this book for further research.

Table 1.1 Classification of FDI studies

	Determinants of/policies for FDI	*Strategy/performance of FDI*
Foreign firm	1 Resource Seeking Market Seeking Efficiency Seeking OLI Paradigm	4 New Area of Research
Host country	2 Liberalization Privatization Globalization	3 Heterogeneous Impact

Determinants of the investing firm

Literature on the factors that motivate foreign firms to invest in host countries, especially industrially developing countries, is expansive. The motivational factors identified in these studies have been discussed with reference to the country of origin of the investing firm, which in most cases are from the industrially developed countries of America, Europe, and Japan, and the host countries, which are usually from the developing countries. Foreign firms have been motivated to invest in the developing host countries primarily because of availability of resources and markets in the host countries. Foreign firms have also been motivated by lower factor costs for production in the developing countries. Further, locational advantage and ownership advantage have been key driving factors for foreign firms to invest in host countries.

The 'Ownership–Location–Internalization' (OLI) an eclectic paradigm of Dunning (1988) includes the motivations of resource seeking, market seeking, efficiency seeking, and strategic asset seeking. Later Dunning (1998) reasoned that MNEs invested in a host country only when they found both ownership advantage and location advantage. He has advanced his argument that location advantage is an increasingly important determinant. Indeed, many of the previous studies have used Dunning's framework to explain factors that have motivated firms to undertake FDI.

It is contended that internalization is the cornerstone of the OLI paradigm and hence the OLI paradigm is an extension of internalization as expounded by Oliver E. Williamson. However, Dunning (1998) counter argued that internalization of Williamson only explains the existence and growth of multi-activity firms and not the character of

MNEs. However, MNEs internalize cross-border markets based on the comparative cost and benefit between the two locations, i.e. in the home economy and the host economy of the MNE.

Looking for resources in the host countries has been a major driving force behind FDI in the late 19th and early 20th century. In a study on the history of FDI, Jones (1996) found that towards the beginning of the 20th century the initial motivation for firms to engage in FDI was to find resources in foreign markets, and he notes that by the end of the Second World War many of the world's natural resources were in the hands of large multinational enterprises. Dunning (1998) and Rugman and Verbeke (2001) also identify 'resource seeking' among many other factors as a motivation for firms to move outside their home markets. Recent studies of Chandrapalert (2000) and Park (2003) with reference to FDI from USA in Thailand and FDI from Japan in USA, respectively provide empirical evidence to the resource-seeking factor behind FDI.

Large unexplored markets have been another factor for FDI by foreign firms in the developing countries. Vernon's (1966) discussion of international product life cycle highlighted this phenomenon. Foreign firms had to move out of their home markets, which had matured, to new markets in the less developed and developing countries to sell their products. Milner and Pentecost (2001) discussed American firms that invested directly in UK owing to the large market size of UK. Similarly, Park and Lee (2003) show that the American firms invested in China to take advantage of the potential market in China. Anand and Delios (1996) showed that the Japanese firms were motivated to find markets in India.

Yet another motivation for firms to engage in FDI has been to take advantage of the low cost of production in the host countries. Vernon (1966) explained FDI of American firms in UK and Canada on this basis. Increased FDI in developing countries in Asia in the last two decades have been largely explained from this point of view. Vertical integration of US MNEs in a host country as per Tang (2002) was induced by the comparatively low labour cost in the host economy. Similarly, Walkenhorst (2004) argues that FDI in Poland was determined by lower capital cost in Poland. Yang *et al.* (2000) found that favourable interest rates and wage rates influenced foreign companies to invest in Australia.

Some have also argued that host country's path and pace of structural reforms and openness to trade have influenced firms on FDI decisions. Resmini (2000) found that the path and pace of structural reforms was a crucial factor in attracting FDI in the Central and East European countries (CEEC). Galego *et al.* (2004) imply that potential market demand, openness to world trade, and lower relative labour compensation levels were responsible for the flow of FDI into CEEC. Chakrabarti (2001), in his sensitivity cross-country regression, found that a host country's openness to trade has a better correlation with its inward flow of FDI than with other variables like tax, wage, exchange rate, tariff, growth rate of GDP or trade balance.

Political instability, low intra-regional trade and the small size of national markets in the Balkans region have been cited as reasons for low FDI by Slaveski and Nedanovski (2002). Ok (2004) provides a similar explanation to the lower amounts of FDI in Turkey. In another case Zhao and Levary (2002) found that flow of FDI in the retail industry was dependent upon the risk and uncertainty in the economic and political climate in a host country. Sara and Newhouse (1995) interpreted openness in trade and business as a part of efficiency seeking measures of foreign firms. They asserted that firms seek locations that economize bounded rationality and minimize losses from opportunism. While a fair legal system and friendly government policies in the host country can economize bounded rationality, a stable and unambiguous commercial code to protect against dishonest local agents minimizes losses from opportunism.

Gaining ownership of strategic assets and location advantage has been shown to be other key factors for foreign firms while deciding on whether or not to invest in a host country. Cieslik and Ryan (2002) showed that FDI from Japanese firms in East European countries has been largely motivated by scopes for greater ownership in the host country. It is observed that more of the Japanese firms chose wholly-owned subsidiaries over minority-owned joint ventures while entering the East European host countries. On a similar argument, Choe (2000) discussed Japanese FDI in the Electrical Machinery and Appliances industry in the United States. He argued that Japanese firms were motivated to invest in USA because of ownership advantage over knowledge-based assets and locational advantage of agglomeration economies and skilled labour in the host economy. Anand and Delios (1996) show that Japanese firms were motivated by location specific productive resources while entering China.

Ownership structure favourable to foreign direct investors has been a significant motivator in luring initial FDI. Ellis and Fausten (2002) indicated this trend in their comparative study of Japanese, Korean and American firms. Rajib *et al.* (2003) also indicated that many foreign firms in India moved from efficiency seeking to ownership seeking in the recent years after 1991 (see Table 1.2 for a summary of these studies).

The approach of this strand of research seems to explain a general business behaviour and tries to provide theoretical explanation to the

Table 1.2 Determinants of the investing firm

Focus of study	*Author (year)*
1. Resource seeking	Dunning (1988, 1998), Jones (1996), Rugman & Verbeke (2001), Chandrapalert (2000), Park (2003)
2. Market seeking	Anand & Delios (1996), Vernon (1966), Milner & Pentecost (2001), Park & Lee (2003)
3. Efficiency seeking	
(a) Low production cost	Vernon (1966)
(b) Low labour cost	Tang (2002)
(c) Lower capital cost	Walkenhorst (2004)
(d) Favourable interest rates and wage rates	Yang *et al.* (2000)
(e) Path & Pace of Structural Reform in CEEC	Resmini (2000)
(f) Market demand, openness to world trade, and lower relative labour compensation levels in CEEC	Galego *et al.* (2004)
(g) Host country's openness to trade	Chakrabarti (2001)
(h) Political stability, intra-regional trade and size of market with regard to Balkan region and Turkey	Slaveski & Nedanovski (2002), Ok (2004)
(i) Risk and uncertainty in the economic and political climate	Zhao & Levary (2002)
(j) Openness in trade and business	Sara & Newhouse (1995)
(k) Gaining ownership of strategic assets and location: Japanese firms in East European countries	Cieslik & Ryan (2002)
(l) Japanese FDI n the electrical machinery and appliances industry in USA	Choe (2000)
(m) Location specific productive resources: Japanese firm in China	Anand & Delios (1996)
(n) Ownership structure	Ellis & Fausten (2002)
(o) Move from efficiency to ownership	Rajib *et al.* (2003)

motivation of MNEs to invest directly outside their home economies. All the studies relating to determinants of FDI have been looked at from the perspective of firms seeking direct investments in foreign countries. It is assumed that once FDI is established in a host country, the host country will invariably benefit, and therefore the determinants of FDI are sacrosanct to the growth of FDI worldwide.

The determinants of FDI for multinational enterprises are seen from a global perspective of the enterprise's operation and not in terms of the MNE's business unit in the host country. In other words, the MNE's headquarters seem to look at the overall performance of its global operation rather than the performance of individual business units in respective host countries. All the major determinants like those of resource seeking, market seeking or efficiency seeking have been seen from the viewpoint of multinational enterprises. In other words, multinational investments have been seen as a one-way process and have ignored that direct investment in a foreign host country is very different from making investments in the domestic market of the multinational enterprise.

Here, it is useful to look at the context of a host country. Developing countries are usually characterized by weak industry infrastructure, lack of ancillary and support industry and several institutional deficiencies that are required for a multinational enterprise from an industrially advanced country to start their operations in a developing host country. The governments of such developing countries are not in a position to meet all these requirements of a foreign multinational enterprise. In the above context how does an MNE formulate its investment decisions in a developing country? How do we see the determinants like resource seeking, market seeking, and efficiency seeking achieve successful FDI in a developing country? Apparently, there seem to be some contradictions in the determinants of FDI and the characteristics of a developing host country context.

Host-country policies

Host countries have invited FDI with the hope that it would bring along with it an increase in industrial productivity, growth in trade and commerce, and overall economic development. Much research has been done on the policies of the host countries that help attract FDI. Most of this research suggest that the host economies in the developing countries should liberalize their economy, privatize business and globalize in order to achieve a share of FDI in their respective countries.

In order to invite FDI, less developed nations have been advised to provide unique, non-replicable and created assets to MNEs interested in investing in their economics. Host governments that provide complementary created asset-based location-specific advantages are considered to be successful in attracting FDI. Further, the host countries have to provide good governance along with the right kind of immobile assets and allow mobile investments to be locked into these assets as in Narula and Dunning (2000).

Host government's policies and incentives are integral to the internalization theory of FDI. Wage subsidies, training grants, relaxation of industrial relations laws, direct subsidy, sales tax exemption, subsidized building, subsidized transportation, subsidized loans, subsidized equity, guarantee against expropriation and attract FDI (Brewer, 1992). Incentives like direct tax grants, employment grants and training allowances, subsidies on land and building purchase, interest subsidies, tariff protection, exemption from imports and exports duties, exemption from income tax, dividend and capital gains, guarantee for currency conversion, guarantee for profits and capital repatriation can attract FDI (Pradhan, 2000).

It has also been suggested that host countries can be successful in finding FDI if they provide investment support package to the MNEs. Host countries are to first target the appropriate MNEs and then tailor-make an appropriate package of incentives for those MNEs as in Mudambi (1999). Host countries should pay attention to the political system, the quality of democracy and rule of law to make them desirable to MNEs as in Oliva and Batiz (2002). There has been a proliferation of incentives offered by competing host countries to allure MNEs to invest in their economics. Rolfe *et al.* (1993) showed that 51 different types of incentives were being offered by the developing countries to attract FDI.

The policy prescriptions to developing countries for attracting FDI look like the wish list of MNEs to reduce cost and increase profits. It appears from the above two stands of FDI research that if the policies of the host country can reduce the cost of investment, then FDI can be easily attracted. A major problem with these studies is that policies suggested to host countries for attracting FDI have been derived from factors that motivate MNEs to engage in FDI. While this may look logical, the efficacy of such measures can be evaluated only after looking at the outcome of FDI for both the host country and the investing foreign firms in that host country. There are indeed a number of studies that argue that the government of the host country have to be alert to the liberal polices for free global trade and investments (Trivedi, 2004). See Table 1.3 for a summary of relevant literature pertaining to host country policies on FDI.

The studies in this strand of research seem to emanate from the arguments placed in the previous stream of study, namely determinants of FDI. These studies look like persuasive suggestions to facilitate the firms from the saturated markets to make investments in the developing

Table 1.3 Host-country policies

Focus of study	*Author (year)*
1. Good governance along with the right kind of immobile assets and allow mobile assets to be locked into these assets	Narula & Dunning (2000)
2. Wage subsidies, training grants, relaxation of industrial relations laws, direct subsidy, sales tax exemption, subsidy building, subsidized transportation, subsidized loans, subsidized equity, & guarantee against expropriation	Brewer (1992)
3. Incentives like direct tax grants, employment grants and training allowances, subsidy on land and building purchase, interest subsidies tariff protection, exemption from import and export duties, exemption from income tax dividend from capital gains, guarantee for currency conversion, guarantee for profits and capital repatriation	Pradhan (2002)
4. Tailor-made investment support package of incentives for MNEs	Mudambi (1999)
5. Improve the political system, the quality of democracy and rule of law	Oliva & Batiz (2002)
6. Identified 51 different types of incentives that one being offered by host countries	Rolfe *et al.* (1992)
7. Host countries need to be alert to the liberal policies for free global trade and investments	Trivedi (2004)

countries. The differences in the market structures in the developed, developing and poor countries have not been considered. Further, the concerns of the developing countries in terms of employment generation or enhancing productivity in their respective local economy have been ignored. The policy prescriptions have been visualized only in terms of those factors that will motivate foreign firms to invest in a developing host country.

While foreign firms find it convenient to operate in a host country that provides good infrastructure and several incentives; good infrastructure in a host country lends lesser opportunity to a foreign firm to ground itself in such a host country and it can play only a limited role there. For instance, several hundred firms operated in India prior to 1990, but only the few firms that committed to invest deeply in their respective businesses emerged to be market leaders in their respective businesses in India.

Impact of FDI on the host country

Literature on the impact of FDI on the host country highlights that FDI has had a heterogeneous effect on host countries over time and across the world. While some studies show that FDI has benefited a host country, many other studies show that they have either had a negative impact or no impact on host countries. Wilkins (1994) argued that FDI had different outcomes in different host countries depending on the host country conditions. Zhang's (2001) study asserted that FDI promoted income growth in the coastal regions of China. Ng and Tuan (2002) also suggested that the upsurge of FDI in China has made a profound contribution to the country's income and asset formation. Ramirez's (2000) study on the impact of FDI in Mexico points out that the increase in lagged foreign investments have had a positive and significant effect on the rate of labour productivity growth. Ericsson and Irandoust (2001) found that FDI has had a positive impact on economic growth in Norway.

The impact of FDI on India as a host country has been well covered in the literature. It provides arguments on both the positive and the negative aspects of FDI. Johri (1983), by studying the business strategies of foreign multinational companies in the drug and pharmaceutical industry, showed that domestic companies benefited greatly by the investments of foreign pharmaceutical companies in India. N. Kumar (1990) showed that the Indian companies benefited from the operations of multinational companies in India. Similarly, S. Kumar (1996) projected that domestic companies benefited from FDI in India. Myneni (2000) and Debroy (1996) argued that the free flow of investments and trade were beneficial for the country.

A number of highly compelling studies show that FDI has not been beneficial to host countries. Nair-Reichert and Weinhold (2001) studied the impact of FDI on over 24 countries in different stages of development and found that FDI had a heterogeneous impact. Country specific analyses of host countries show that FDI has not helped them in meeting their national objectives. Trevino *et al.* (2002) argued that FDI inflows by trade liberalization and privatization have not helped to optimize the economic goals of Argentina, Brazil, Chile, Mexico, Peru, and Venezuela. These countries together draw 85% of FDI in Latin America. A similar observation has been made with respect to FDI in some Scandinavian countries. Ericsson and Irandoust (2001) reported that a relationship between increasing FDI inflow and economic growth could not be established in the case of Finland and Norway.

Host countries have looked for the transfer of technology from foreign companies to domestic companies by inviting FDI. Some studies show that even though FDI has had a positive impact on economic growth it has not been able to bring about a technological spillover to the host country. Technological joint ventures too have not generated spillover effects in most cases. Malairaja and Zawdie (2004) show that FDI with technology transfer constituted a very small portion of total FDI in Malaysia. The local partners in such cases were relegated to activities that hardly involved the challenge of innovation. Deolalikar and Evenson (1989), however, found that purchasable foreign technology has brought about greater adaptive research and development in India.

With respect to impact of FDI on India, Kidron (1965) and Kurian (1966) asserted that FDI had a severe negative impact on the Indian economy. Lall (1999) argued that the nature of exportable items from India were low technology and low valued products and hence not competitive in the world market. The trends of foreign exchange reserves of India have also fluctuated severely as can be seen in database of the Reserve Bank of India (2003). Sharma (2000) showed that the growth in exports during 1970–98 from India was not as a result of increased FDI to India but because of a favourable rupee–dollar exchange rate. K. Kumar (2003) shows that the large Indian companies had failed to generate enough foreign exchange despite the imports of foreign technology.

It has been inferred that trade liberalization policy of the Indian Government did have a positive impact in the short run but on the whole FDI in India tends to displace labour (Chakraborty and Basu, 2002). It has also been shown that FDI had a lesser positive elasticity coefficient than exports when compared with gross domestic product (GDP) and Industrial productivity (Sahoo and Mathiyazhagan, 2003). Empirical studies showed that while FDI had positive association with exports and import substitution during 1955–75, it had a negative association with import substitution in the period after 1979–2000 (Nayak, 2003). Further, FDI on the whole in India has neither been effective for India nor for the foreign companies in India (Nayak, 2002, 2004, 2005a).

Despite growing FDI across the world, there have been severe doubts about the impact of FDI on host countries. Vernon (1971) feared that foreign companies could be the conduits for exercising control over the host country by foreign governments. Chang (2003) criticized developed countries for imposing policy of a free trade and investment on developing countries. He argued that developed countries had themselves adopted protective measures when they were in developing stage. Similarly, Stiglitz (2002) remonstrated that globalization as pursued by

USA and other developed countries had led to wider global discontent as it failed to deliver what it promised. Yaffe (2003) saw globalization as being pursued by the industrially advanced countries as an introduction to a new world-order of imperialism. Vernon (1971) explained how the sovereignty of nations was at risk with the expansion of multinational companies.

While the studies on determinants of FDI for foreign firms clearly identified the factors that motivate foreign firms to invest in a host country, the studies on policies of developing host countries on FDI showed various incentives that can attract FDI. Despite this understanding FDI in general has had a mixed impact on host countries. Although, Wilkins (1994) pointed out that the difference in impact is as a result of the nature of a host country, she omits the role of foreign firms in the success or failure of both the host country and foreign firm due to FDI. The current literature on FDI has focused on the above three strands of research on FDI. However, unless equal focus is given on the conduct and performance of foreign firms in the host country situation, it is difficult to obtain a clear picture of the dynamics of FDI in general (see Table 1.4 for a summary of these studies).

The impact of FDI across the world has appeared to be heterogeneous in nature. In some countries the impact has been positive but in some negative. Some studies have been carried out over a specific period of time or for a specific aspect or for a small economy. It is hard to generalize based on such studies. Correlation coefficients in some of the studies have been seen as cause and effect phenomena *vis-à-vis* the degree of association.

Strategies and performance of foreign firms in the host country

In the light of the three strands of literature that have been discussed in this chapter, we also need to look at one of the most important aspects of FDI; strategies and performance of foreign firms in the developing country context. Although, this aspect is critical for the success of firms in the situation where several foreign firms are operating in a host country context, the importance of studying this aspect has been realized only in the last decade. This strand of literature brings in the firm perspective to explain the factors that help in the success of a firm in a host country. Performance of foreign firms in a host country has been seen from the internal strategy of a firm rather than from the policy and environmental framework in the host country.

Table 1.4 Impact of FDI on host country

	Focus of study	*Author (year)*
1.	FDI promoted income growth in the coastal regions of China	Zhang (2001)
2.	FDI has had profound contribution to the country's income and asset formation	Ng & Tuan (2002)
3.	FDI had a positive and significant effect on the rate of labor productivity	Ramirez (2000)
4.	FDI had a positive impact on economic growth Irandoust (2001)	Ericsson &
5.	FDI has had positive impact	Johri (1983)
6.	Indian companies have benefited from the operation of MNEs in India	Kumar (1990), Kumar (1996)
7.	Free flow of investment and trade are good for the host country	Myneni (2000), Debroy (1996)
8.	Purchasable foreign technology has brought about greater adaptive research and development	Deolalikar & Evenson (1989)
9.	Heterogeneous outcomes depending on the host country	Wilkins (1994)
10.	FDI has had a heterogeneous impact	Nair-Reichert & Weinhold (2001)
11.	FDI inflows by trade liberalization and privatization have not helped to optimize the economic goals of host countries	Trevino *et al.* (2002)
12.	Relationship between increasing FDI inflows and economic growth could not be established	Ericsson & Irandoust (2001)
13.	Technology transfer constituted a very small portion of total FDI	Malairaja & Zawdie (2004)
14.	FDI has had a severe negative impact	Kidron (1965), Kurian (1966)
15.	Nature of exportable items from India were of low technology and low value	Lall (1999)
16.	Growth in exports has not been because of FDI but because of favourable rupee–dollar exchange rate	Sharma (2000)
17.	Large Indian companies have failed to generate enough foreign exchange despite imports of foreign technology	K. Kumar (2003)
18.	Trade liberalization policy led to displace labour	Chakravorty & Basu (2002)
19.	FDI had a lesser positive elasticity coefficient than exports when compared with GDP and Industrial productivity	Sahoo & Mathiyazhagan (2003)

(*Continued*)

Table 1.4 (Continued)

Focus of study	*Author (year)*
20. FDI has had in different time periods. Positive impact in a regulatory regime of the host country and had negative impact in the de-regulated period	Nayak (2003)
21. FDI on the whole has neither been effective for the host country nor for the investing foreign subsidiary	Nayak (2002, 2004, 2005a)
22. Foreign companies could be conduits of foreign governments exercising control over the host country	Vernon (1972)
23. Developed countries generally impose policy of free trade and investment on developing countries	Chang (2003)
24. Globalization as pursued by USA and other developed countries have led to a wider global discontent	Stiglitz (2002)
25. Sovereignty of nations was at risk with the expansion of multinational companies	Vernon (1971)

Characteristics and organizational structures of multinational enterprises have been identified to be critical for higher performance of these enterprises (Birkinshaw and Morrison, 1995; Birkinshaw and Hood, 2000; Hennart, 2000; Barlett and Ghosal, 2002). Vernon (1966) explained the process by which large American firms expanded their operations in Europe and less developed countries. However, research on the factors that determine good performance of foreign firms in a host country is still in the early stages. The determinants of success and failure of firms in a host country situation as a fundamental issue in business strategy has been highlighted by Rumelt *et al.* (1994) and more recently by Rangan and Drummond (2004). With reference to India as a host country, the success of the Suzuki Motor Corporation has been attributed to its holistic investment strategy (Nayak *et al.*, 2005b).

The success of foreign firms in a host country situation has been attributed to factors like timing of entry, length of operation, distance of foreign firm from a host country, host government policies, technological intensity, and a combined factor of local partner and conduct of foreign firms and host government.

The timing of investment has been argued as being critical for the success of foreign firms in a host country (Rivoli and Salori, 1996). Using the concept of timing, Luo (1998b) showed that early entrants outperformed late ones in terms of local market expansion and asset turnover. Early entrants into FDI achieved superior asset efficiency but were inferior in terms of the accounting performance in the first three years.

The length of operation of a foreign firm in a host country has been contended as being a factor for success of foreign firms in the host countries. Carlsson *et al.* (2005) through their survey research, showed that the length of operation has been crucial to the performance of Scandinavian firms in China.

The distance of foreign firm from host country has been explained as an important determinant of entry as well as a factor of success of foreign firms in a host country. Ghemawat (2001) argued that different kinds of distances – : cultural, administrative, geographic, and economic distance – between the investing company and the host country affected the performance of foreign firms in a host country.

Patronage from the host government has been identified as another key to success of foreign firms in a host country. In his historical study of private investments in India during 1900s–1939, Bagchi (1972) pointed that strong political patronage helped British companies to flourish and grow in India. Encarnation (1989) demonstrated that in the 1970s the strong alliance of local firms, state financial institutions, and regulatory authorities in India reduced the bargaining power of multinationals there. Bjorkman and Osland (1998) attributed the success of foreign companies in China to maintaining a good relationship with the Chinese Government.

The success of an MNE has been seen in terms of appropriate defence strategy, political strategy and staffing in the host country (Poynter, 1986). Poynter suggested that a global firm may have state of the art technology, exports, and intra-MNE sourcing as its defence strategy. Giving lower priority to the host country may be its political strategy. And, short term technologically oriented staffing may be its staffing strategy. A multi domestic MNE may introduce new products as a defence strategy. A good understanding of the local political dynamics and a continuous interaction with the local political leaders can help a company to strategically appoint executives to deal with the local dynamics of business – a factor important for success in a host countries.

The traditional idea that the success of a foreign firm depends on having a successful relationship with the host government has been confirmed by others. Moon and Lado (2000) suggested that the bargaining power of a multinational enterprise lay in its technological intensity, advertising intensity, intra-MNC sourcing, export intensity, staffing policy and product diversity. They argued that the performance of the MNE will depend on exercising these bargaining powers.

Taking the success of foreign firms in India as vital to competence of the British firms, Tomlinson (1989) displayed that the short-term structures created by British expatriates and multinationals to generate immediate success limited their options for future evolution after 1950s.

The concept of a resource based view has been adopted to show empirically the success of foreign firms in a host country. Andersson *et al.* (2001) observed through their research on Swedish firms in the US market that technology embeddedness was critical for success. Taggart (1999) in another survey showed that active involvement of the subsidiary in the local host firm improved the performance of the subsidiary. Chen (1999) showed that the international performance of multinational firms depended on firm specific assets and the type of ownership with which they entered the host country. Franko (1989) observed that the US companies accepted minority ownership in the host countries. Often the 'second rank oligopolists' adopted this strategy. He reasoned that success of these MNEs depended on a variety of factors like the kind of local partner, MNE conduct and host government (see Table 1.5).

In the above research, several issues like timing, length of operation, ownership by investing firm, asset specificity of foreign firm, distance of investing firm from the host economy, political patronage of the host government toward the investing firm, have been identified as being factors for the success of a foreign firm in a host country. While each of these factors may be critical to a particular company in a specific host country situation, the study by Nayak *et al.* (2005b) presented a holistic investment pattern for the success of foreign firms in a developing host country situation. However, more country-specific studies, especially involving different industries, need to be studied to enrich the understanding of the success of foreign firms in a host economy.

Summary and gaps in past research

From the above study of the existing literature on FDI there are many potential areas for research. However, there are also a few aspects of the strategy and performance of foreign companies that needs to be looked into. First, the factors like early entry, longer stay, specific asset advantage, distance, and good rapport with host country can provide an edge to a foreign firm in a host country. However, whether these conditions by themselves are sufficient for the success of a foreign firm remains to be examined. Further, whether the above factors *per se*, or the processes

Table 1.5 MNE Strategy of FDI

Focus of study	*Author (Year)*
1. Highlight the importance of studying the determinants of success and failure of firms in host country situation	Rumelt, *et al.* (1994), Rangan & Drummond (2004)
2. Foreign firms in a developing host country situation can succeed by adopting a holistic investment pattern	Nayak *et al.* (2005b)
3. Timing of investment has been critical for success of foreign firms in host country	Rivoli & Salori (1996)
4. Early entrants outperformed late entrants in terms of local market expansion and asset turnover	Luo (1998)
5. Length of operation of foreign firms in a host country is critical for its success in the host country	Carlsson *et al.* (2005)
6. Distances in terms of culture, administrative, geographic, economic between investing company and host country affect performance of investing firms	Ghemawat (2001)
7. Patronage from host government has been crucial for high performance of foreign firms in host country	Bagchi (1972), Encarnation (1989)
8. Managing good relationship with the Chinese Government	Bjorkman & Osland (1998)
9. Appropriate defence strategy, political strategy and staffing in host country	Poynter (1986)
10. Multinational enterprise manages the host government better using its bargaining power of advanced product technology, advertising intensity, export intensity, staffing policy and product diversity	Moon & Lado (2000)
11. Short-term structures of British firms resulted in their limited success in India	Tomlinson (1989)
12. Technological embeddedness was critical for success of Swedish firms in the US market	Andersson *et al.* (2001)
13. International performance of multinational firms depended on firm specific assets and the type of ownership	Chen (1999)
14. Factors like the kind of local partner, MNE conduct and host government were critical for success of second rank US oligopolies	Franko (1989)

by which a foreign firm implements its strategy, hold the key to success, need examination.

Secondly, many of the previous studies have used surveys as a means of research. Given the complexities of carrying out research on the strategy and success of foreign firms in a host country, it needs to be investigated whether survey methods capture the realities of the situation. Buckley and Casson (2001) have expressed similar concern on methods of research used in international business and have suggested researchers seek new methods of research.

In the developing country framework, most of the industries have been in an early stage while some have been in an emerging stage. Each host country may have some characteristics that may be different from the other host countries. The nature of economy, industry, and infrastructure will be specific to a host country. Within the same host country, some industries may be in a developing stage while some others may be in an emerging stage and some others may be in a developed stage. The FDI strategy for success will therefore be highly contextual. Hence, research studies relating to FDI strategy have to be sensitive to the methodology of research.

Thirdly, though there have been a number of case studies on performance of multinational enterprises, these case studies have been based on convenient sampling. Comparison of the cases across industries has not been done. Hence, whether the findings of these studies can be used to understand strategic pattern of investment for success in host country situation is a point of concern.

More studies in the above research strand, namely strategies and performance of foreign firms in a host country context is vital as these will refresh the existing literature in the other three areas of FDI research as pointed out earlier. An interaction of ideas of these different areas will help understand the complex issues involved with FDI and its success for both the host country and investing foreign firms. In the present circumstance, there are a number of issues to be explored in several contexts of foreign firm and host country.

Areas for future research

From the analysis of the four major research areas in FDI, there seems to be a huge scope for understanding and explaining issues relating to the determinants of successful FDI strategy, especially with reference to the developing economies. There are at least six research areas in FDI that could be potential areas of research.

First, the FDI strategy of successful foreign firms in other developing economies in Asia, Africa, Eastern Europe and South America can be explored. If the argument is also proved in other countries, it will help build a theory of FDI strategy that is beneficial to both the investing firm and the developing host countries.

Secondly, the investment strategy of foreign firms that failed in some of the host economies can be examined. This will help in establishing the causality of investment strategy and sustainable performance of a foreign firm in a developing host country as has been argued in this book.

Thirdly, whether the holistic FDI strategy (Nayak *et al.*, 2005b) suggested with reference to a developing country like India holds true for the success of foreign firms in industrially developed countries can be investigated.

Fourthly, finding out whether successful FDI strategy in the manufacturing industry differs from the non-manufacturing industry or whether they are similar. Service industries such as the mobile phone industry in the large developing countries like India, China, Brazil and Russia provide a good basis for study.

Fifthly, the firm specific impact of an individual successful foreign firm on a host economy can be studied. This would remove several myths about the role of a multinational enterprise in a host country situation.

Sixthly, FDI strategies of MNEs from the developing countries investing in other developing countries can also provide interesting insights into the FDI strategies that work best. Here the strategies of firms from India, China and Russia can be looked into. The large number of Chinese MNEs investing in Africa could be a rich research field in the above context.

2
Evolution of FDI, 1900s–2000

This chapter describes the evolution of FDI in India during the twentieth century. This chapter consists of two main sections, namely (a) studies of different periods, i.e. 1900s–1918, 1919–42, 1943–61, 1962–77, 1978–90, 1991–2000 and (b) major characteristics of FDI in India and the periodization of FDI history in India. By providing a review of the evolution of FDI, this chapter bridges the gap that exists in the current literature on FDI in India. A critical understanding of the history and characteristics of FDI in India also provides a sound background to understanding the context of globalization in India in which the main argument of the book has been placed.

Though FDI[1] started in India in the early 1900s, literature on it is scanty. Barring a few time zones such as 1948–61, 1971–78, and 1991 onwards, the other periods are inadequately covered. Also, more often than not data in secondary sources do not agree with each other. Most of the studies have either focused on the amount of flow of FDI or its impact on India. Recent literature focuses on the flow of FDI to India since 1991 and its impact on the Indian economy. Wilkins (1994) indicated the flow of FDI during 1921–29. Athreye and Kapur (1999) estimated the flow of FDI during 1971–78. Some studies have discussed the impact of FDI on India during 1948–61 (Kidron 1965; Kurian 1966).

A few studies have dealt with the performance of foreign firms in India. Bagchi (1972) argues that British firms succeeded in the early decades of the twentieth century because of their nexus within the government. Tomlinson (1989) argues that British firms failed after 1947[2] because of their short-term operational structures. Encarnation (1989) holds that foreign firms failed in India because of the nexus among local firms, local financial institutions, and the Government of India. Attributing performance of foreign firms in India to the local government as in the above studies appears to be rather weak.

To take stock of the overall development of FDI in India before outlining any hypothesis about the performance of foreign firms in India, the present chapter makes a critical review of the history of FDI during the period 1900s–2000. A long-term view of the progress of FDI would result in a better perspective than observations focusing on short intervals.

This sketchy history of FDI in India primarily relies on empirical data pertaining to the period 1901–2000 collated and triangulated from various university archives, company archives, public libraries, and the National Archive of India and Japan. The sources included secondary data, published reports of the British Government in India prior to 1947, the Government of India and a few foreign companies. These secondary data were supplemented and updated with unpublished data of the Government of India and a few foreign companies in India.

This chapter consists of two sections, namely (a) FDI history of different periods, i.e. 1900s–18, 1919–42, 1943–61, 1962–77, 1978–90, 1991–2000 and (b) findings and analysis, which includes periodization of FDI history in India and the major characteristics of FDI during the different periods. These characteristics include (1) trends of FDI in manufacturing *vis-à-vis* non-manufacturing industries, (2) trends in countrywise amounts of FDI, (3) trends in countrywise number of joint ventures, and (4) firm-level response of foreign companies to the policies of the Government of India from time to time.

FDI in different periods

Each period study focuses on three issues, i.e., overall socio-economic and political situation in India, industrial and FDI policy in the country, and the nature and pattern of FDI.

1901–18

India was an agriculture-based economy during this period. The main commercial crops were cotton, tea, and jute. In terms of domestic business the number of joint stock companies increased from 1550 in 1904–1905 to 2668 in 1917–18 (DCIS[3] 1924).

The industrial policy in India was not clearly articulated and there seemed to be little barrier to foreign investments in the country as was the case in other parts of the world. However, as India was a colony of the United Kingdom during this time, British investments dominated foreign trade and investment in India. About 14 per cent of British investments came to India and other Asian countries during 1865–1914 (Bagchi 1972). India ranked eighth as host to foreign investment in 1914 (Wilkins 1994). British Managing Agents were the predominant enterprises that invested in India. There were several Managing Agents such as Andrew Yule & Company, Bird & Company, Williamson, Magor & Company, Shaw Wallace & Company, Duncan Brothers, Begg, Dunlop & Company, Octavius Steel & Company, among many others. The Managing Agents held as many as 15–20 different types of companies engaged in tea, jute, sugar, and coal, and also had interests in timber, paper, insurance, shipping, indigo, etc. (Bagchi 1972). Japanese trading firms had also made some investments in India during this period. Mitsui Bussan set up a trading office in Bombay in 1893 and subsequently many Japanese companies started trading in raw cotton and yarn with India in the late nineteenth and early twentieth centuries (see Tables 2.1 and 2.2).[4]

There were also a few manufacturing companies from UK, Switzerland, Netherlands, Germany, USA, and Japan engaged in trading and manufacturing activities. About eleven manufacturing companies from UK, Europe, USA and Japan traded their products in India. British manufacturing companies like Unilever, ITC, Glaxo, ICI, GEC, Goodlass Nerolac, and Britannia Biscuits imported from their parent companies in Europe for trading in India. Chicago Pneumatics and Ludlow Jute from USA, Margarine from Netherlands, and Denso from Japan operated in India during this period (see Tables 2.3–2.5).

1919–42

By the end of World War I in 1918 Britain's position in India had weakened. The freedom movement was effervescent. Also, the United States of America and Japan emerged as powerful nations. These political developments had some bearing on the pattern of foreign investment. The number of registered local manufacturing companies grew from 111 in 1923 to 365 by 1940 (DCIS 1929, 1931, 1939, 1941, and 1951).

Among American companies starting their operation in India during this period were General Motors, Ford Motors, and Colgate–Palmolive. General Motors started assembling passenger cars in Bombay in 1928. Ford started its assembling unit in Madras (1930), Bombay (1931) and Calcutta (1931). Colgate–Palmolive started its toothpaste business in India in 1937.

By 1928, Japan emerged as one of the largest cotton trade partners of India. With better quality and competitive prices[5] the Japanese textile companies outperformed the British textile companies in India. Japan

Table 2.1 Japan's total raw cotton imports from India, 1928–42

Year	*World*			*India*			*% from India*
	Quantity (tonne)	*Value (Yen)*	*Unit price (Yen)*	*Quantity (tonne)*	*Value (Yen)*	*Unit price (Yen)*	
1928	1,302,023	549,942	0.42	613,857	232,267	0.38	47
1929	1,438,610	573,016	0.4	634,863	231,108	0.36	44
1930	1,276,421	362,047	0.28	630,059	147,038	0.23	49
1931	1,487,577	296,273	0.2	641,100	113,262	0.18	43
1932	1,698,688	447,401	0.26	365,312	91,747	0.25	22
1933	1,665,277	604,847	0.36	530,304	163,797	0.31	32
1934	1,807,314	731,423	0.4	772,318	252,435	0.33	43
1935	1,637,832	714,262	0.44	694,805	259,037	0.37	42
1936	2,028,156	850,451	0.42	836,926	315,061	0.38	41
1937	1,835,322	851,163	0.46	935,498	363,635	0.39	51
1938	1,259,461	436,835	0.35	412,811	113,331	0.27	33
1939	1,335,127	462,007	0.35	448,320	120,997	0.27	34
1940	1,026,248	504,072	0.49	312,358	115,374	0.37	30
1941	785,892	391,783	0.5	283,937	94,064	0.33	36
1942	269,375	224,306	0.83	2,910	1,574	0.54	1

Source: The author has compiled these from the All Japan Cotton Spinners Association (1949) and Cotton Statistics of Japan, 1903–49.

exported 57 per cent of its cotton yarn and 28 per cent of its finished cotton garments goods to India in 1932. It also imported 47 per cent of its raw cotton requirement from India in 1928, which increased to 51 per cent in 1937. While the Japanese firms procured raw cotton from India at a unit price lower than the unit price in the world market, these firms sold the finished cotton products at a unit price higher than at which they could sell in the world market (see Tables 2.1 and 2.2).

India was still attractive for British investments. Between 1930 and 1945, 28 manufacturing British subsidiaries started their operations in India (Tomlinson 1989). With the continued interest of British investments and the additional interest of American, Japanese and other European countries, the total inward FDI was about US$1.0 billion by 1929. India ranked third among the favourable hosts to FDI in 1929 (Wilkins 1994).

In 1935, under local and international pressure, the British Government in India passed the Government of India Act, which allowed the Indian legislators to have a say in the legislation of the country. With this new power, the Indian legislators lobbied in favour of Indian businesses. The British Government in India, under the pressure from local

Table 2.2 Japan's exports of cotton yarn to India, 1918–42

Year	*World*			*India*			*% from India*
	Quantity (tonne)	*Value (Yen)*	*Unit price (Yen)*	*Quantity (tonne)*	*Value (Yen)*	*Unit price (Yen)*	
1918	168,605,067	162,789,759	0.97	31,770,667	34,998,715	1.1	19
1919	92,134,800	121,636,927	1.32	1,901,200	2,930,475	1.54	2
1920	121,970,000	154,981,805	1.27	19,016,133	30,252,515	1.59	16
1921	116,904,400	80,563,002	0.69	14,865,600	11,991,354	0.81	13
1922	157,624,800	114,723,255	0.73	27,327,867	20,666,783	0.76	17
1923	99,329,867	78,511,961	0.79	23,574,934	20,511,834	0.87	24
1924	108,144,267	109,610,952	1.01	32,336,133	35,954,637	1.11	30
1925	124,321,067	123,116,965	0.99	34,863,667	33,716,812	0.97	28
1926	82,220,400	70,716,335	0.86	23,913,333	23,086,163	0.97	29
1927	47,062,400	38,794,408	0.82	21,895,200	20,010,131	0.91	47
1928	28,662,400	25,894,905	0.9	6,991,099	9,131,071	1.31	24
1929	26,960,667	26,755,702	0.99	11,055,600	13,443,308	1.22	41
1930	23,846,400	15,032,819	0.63	8,015,733	6,576,936	0.82	34
1931	12,690,267	8,510,607	0.67	6,479,467	5,592,234	0.86	51
1932	35,842,133	21,546,681	0.6	20,313,133	14,343,000	0.71	57
1933	19,322,133	15,712,038	0.81	7,372,800	7,605,372	1.03	38
1934	25,937,733	23,484,505	0.91	9,727,333	11,111,917	1.14	38
1935	38,633,200	35,873,277	0.93	17,953,133	20,093,092	1.12	46
1936	44,209,733	38,344,845	0.87	16,870,400	18,050,783	1.07	38
1937	51,892,267	54,905,696	1.06	14,754,233	19,845,595	1.35	28
1938	42,106,000	39,355,054	0.93	18,823,899	29,591,750	1.57	45
1939	82,838,339	71,089,521	0.86	23,430,957	23,953,631	1.02	28
1940	60,950,331	57,975,942	0.95	12,795,151	16,017,440	1.25	21
1941	45,100,000	52,973,763	1.17	5,493,100	9,590,522	1.75	12
1942	2,943,560	5,789,137	1.97	–	–	–	–

Source: The author has compiled these from the All Japan Cotton Spinners Association (1949) and Cotton Statistics of Japan, 1903–49.

legislators, introduced import duties[6] in order to protect local industries. The introduction of import duty seems to have activated the foreign companies to make direct investments in product manufacturing in India. As many as 30 foreign companies registered in India during this period (1919–42) as compared to only seven during the previous period, 1901–18 (Centre for Monitoring Indian Economy 1989–2002).

FDI in Indian manufacturing industries started in the true sense during the 1930s. Many British and Dutch companies, hitherto engaged in trading activities, started to invest in local manufacturing in the 1930s. Unilever invested heavily in local manufacture of bath soap, washing soap, and cooking oil/fat. Hindustan Vanaspati Manufacturing Company started manufacturing vanaspati (hydrogenated cooking oil) in 1932 at Sewri, Bombay. Lever Brothers India started manufacturing soap at Sewri in 1934. Metal Box started to manufacture tin containers in 1934. J & P Coats began to manufacture under the name Acme Thread Company in 1935 (Hunter and Keir 1969). Dunlop started tyre manufacture in 1936. ICI set up Alkali and Chemical Corporation of India in Rishra, West Bengal in 1939. See Tables 2.3–2.5 for a sample list of foreign companies from the UK, Europe and USA that operated in India during this period.

In 1942 the Quit India Movement started by the Indian National Congress greatly disrupted foreign business in India and British business, in particular. The increasing conflict within India and the competition among the British textile industry, the Indian textile industry and the Japanese textile industry halted the huge textile trade transaction that Japan enjoyed with India in 1942. See Tables 2.1 and 2.2 for data on trade of cotton and cotton yarn between Japan and India.

1943–61

Although the British Government formally transferred power to Indians on 15 August 1947 the policies on FDI were largely dictated by the local business houses and politicians from around 1943. Between 1943 and 1945, 14 foreign companies were registered in India. Direct investment by foreign companies, activated in the 1930s, was enhanced and encouraged by both the Indian business houses and by the newly formed Government of India during this period. Local industries had felt the need for foreign technology and foreign capital by 1942. This trend was maintained in the subsequent years until 1961 when another 27 foreign companies were registered.

The post-independence government was faced with a myriad of problems concerning economic and industrial development of the country. Industries considered strategic for the country (power, oil and petroleum, mining, insurance, airlines, etc.) were nationalized. A system of five-year plans was adopted for planned industrialization and development. To strengthen the public sector enterprises the government sought financial and technical support from the Soviet Union, Germany and the United Kingdom to set up large-scale industrial projects. Public sector enterprises were promoted in areas like steel, oil, power, defence, and telecommunications. Private sector investment was encouraged in areas like chemicals, light industries, personal care, and consumer goods.

Having experienced global competition, the Indian textile and textile-related businesses had been looking for foreign technology and foreign capital by the end of 1930s (Bagchi 1972). With the entry of more foreign companies during the 1930s and 1940s, domestic competition also

Table 2.3 British companies with investments in India

Year of investment	*Parent company*	*Indian company*
1767	Forbes	Forbes Gokak
1843	Parry & Co.	Parry & Co.
1876	Binny & Co.	Binny & Co.
1911	ITC	ITC Ltd
1911	GEC	GEC (India)
1918	Associated Biscuits	Britannia Biscuits
1920	Burmah Oil Co.	Tinplate Co. (India)
1921	Burner Mond & Co.	Burner Mond & Co. (India)
1921	Ingersoll & Rand Ltd	Ingersoll & Rand (India) Ltd
1924	H.J. Foster & Co.	H.J. Foster & Co.
1924	Glaxo Industries	Glaxo (I) Ltd
1926	Joseph Nathan & Co	Joseph Nathan & Co.
1929	ICI	ICI (India)
1930	VST	VST Industries
1931	GKN	Guest, Keen, Williams
1931	Lever Brothers	Hindustan Vanaspati Mfg Co
1933	United Traders	United Traders
1933	Lever Brothers	Lever Brothers India Ltd
1933	Metal Box	Metal Box (India)
1934	Turner Newall	Asbestos Cement
1934	Eveready Industries	Eveready Industries India Ltd
1935	BOC	Indian Oxygen
1935	J&P Coats	Acme Thread Co. Ltd
1936	Philips	Godfrey Philips (India)
1936	Dunlop	Dunlop (India)
1937	ICI	Alkali & Chemicals Corporation
1947	Greeves	Crompton Greeves Ltd
1948	British Leyland	Ashok Leyland
1948	Cadbury	Cadbury India Ltd
1948	Rallis Ltd	Rallis India Ltd
1949	TI	Tube Investment (India)
1951	Reckitt & Coleman	Reckitt & Coleman of India Ltd
1953	ICI	Indian Explosives
1956	Unilever	Hindustan Lever Ltd
1958	Horlicks Ltd	Hindustan Milk Food Manufacturers
1961	ICI	Chemicals & Fibres
1961	Lucas	Lucas-TVS
1963	B P L (Instruments)	BPL India
1974	J&P Coats	Madura Coats
1984	Beecham	Eskaylab
1985	SBG International	BSL India (SBG India Ltd)

Source: The author has compiled these from Bagchi (1972), Tomlinson (1989), Hines and Jones (1989), and individual company history.

Table 2.4 European companies with investments in India

Year of investment	*Parent company*	*Indian company*	*Country*
1923	Swedish Match AB	Wimco Ltd	Sweden
1930	Philips	Philips Electricals (Co.) Ltd	Holland
1937	Swedish Match AB	Vulcan Trading Co.	Sweden
1944	Knoll, AG	Knoll Pharmaceuticals Ltd (Now Abbot Laboratories)	Germany
1956	Hoechst Marion Russel Ltd	Hoechst Marion Russef Ltd	Germany
1957	BASF, AG	Bayer (India) Ltd	Germany
1957	Siemens	Siemens India Ltd	Germany
1959	Nestle	Nestle India Ltd	Switzerland
1959	Ursus	Escorts Ltd	Poland
1960	Electrolux	Whirpool of India Ltd	Sweden
1961	Swedish Match AB	Alfa Laval	Sweden
1962	Clariant	Clariant (O) India	Switzerland
1964	Secheron Ltd	Emco Transformers	Switzerland
1968	Watsila Oy	Watsila NSD India Ltd	Finland
1971	Continental, AG	Modi Rubber Ltd	Germany
1972	Piaggio	LML Ltd	Italy
1974	Heinrich Schmid, AG	IFB Industries Ltd (Indian Fire Blank Ltd)	Switzerland
1979	Philips	Philips India Pvt Ltd	Holland

Source: The author has compiled these from Individual company history and individual company home pages.

peaked and the pressure to upgrade technology increased among the Indian companies. The government itself faced the need for foreign technology and foreign capital for industrial growth and foreign exchange to meet the burgeoning imports of essential commodities. Facing a severe foreign exchange problem in 1957–58, the Government of India encouraged FDIs, so that it could increase its foreign exchange reserves. The liberal policies on foreign investment in the First Plan (1951–55) and Second Plan (1956–61) reflect this thinking.

The government also informally invited the large companies, both foreign and domestic, to invest in a few core industries to promote economic and social development in the country. Glaxo, Unilever, ICI, General Motors, Ford Motors, Pepsi Drinks, etc. were informally asked to invest in new ventures. They were also asked to include local equity in their investments in India (Fieldhouse 1978; Davenport *et al.* 1992).

Table 2.5 American companies with investments in India

Year of investment	*Parent company*	*Indian company*
1910s	Ludlow Jute Co.	Ludlow Jute Co.
1928	General Motors	General Motors
1930	Ford Motors	Ford Motors
1937	Colgate–Palmolive	Colgate–Palmolive (India) Ltd
1950	Pfizer	Dumex Pvt Ltd
1950	Coke	Coke
1951	Vicks Product Inc.	Vicks Product Inc.
1951	IBM	IBM India
1956	Pepsi	Pepsi
1958	Parke-Davis	Parke-Davis (India) Ltd
1962	Cummins	Cummins India Ltd
1963	Mansfield Tire & Rubber Co.	MRF Ltd
1967	E. Merck	E Merck (India) Ltd
1979	Castrol	Castrol India Ltd
1985	Procter & Gamble	P&G India (by acquiring Richardson Vicks Inc.)
1987	Timken Inc.	Tata Timken
1989	Hewlett Packard	Hewlett Packard India

Source: The author has compiled these from Individual company history and individual company home pages.

Many large foreign companies found this request unpalatable and hence quit India. For instance, General Motors and Ford enjoyed monopolistic position in India for more than twenty years, but closed their operations in 1953. Pepsi Drinks, unwilling to abide by the government regulation to include local participation in its equity, ceased its operation in India in 1961.

The popular perception is that government policies to nationalize companies in certain industries and the informal government pressures on foreign companies to increase local equity participation reduced the flow of FDI into India. This study finds, however, that FDI during this period actually rose and peaked in 1961. From 1948 to 1961, FDI stock grew from INR2558 million (Indian Rupee) to INR5285 million, an increase of nearly 143 per cent. The number of joint ventures increased from 34 in 1951 to 464 in 1961, a 14-fold increase within 11 years.

Over one hundred American companies entered India during 1959–61 (US Department of Commerce 1961; see Tables 2.6–2.8). These

Table 2.6 American companies with investments in India, 1961

US firm	*Indian subsidiary or affiliate*
Abbot Universal Ltd	Abbot Laboratories (India) Pvt Ltd
American Cyanamid Co.	Lederle Laboratories (India) Pvt Ltd
American Express Co. Inc.	American Express Co. Inc.
American Home Products Corp.	John Wyeth & Brothers, Ltd; Wyeth (India) Pvt Ltd
Amerin Trading Companies	Malabar Fisheries Corporation
California Texas Oil Co.	Caltex Oil Refining (India) Ltd
Caltex Corporation	Caltex (India) Ltd
The Carborundum Co.	Carborundum Universal Ltd
Colgate–Palmolive Co.	Colgate-Palmolive (India) Ltd
Corn Products Refining Co.	Corn Product Co. (India) Pvt Ltd
Dayton Rubber Co.	Premier Tyres Ltd
Dorr-Oliver Inc.	Dorr-Oliver (India) Ltd
Dow Chemical Co.	Polychem Ltd
The Firestone Tire and Rubber Co.	The Firestone Tire & Rubber Co. of India Pvt Ltd
Geophysical Service Inc.	Geophysical Service International, S.A.
Goodyear Tire & Rubber Co.	Goodyear Tire & Rubber Co. of India Pvt Ltd
IBM World Trade Corporation	IBM World Trade Corporation
Johnson & Johnson Inc.	Johnson & Johnson Ltd
Kaiser Aluminum & Chemical Corp	Hindustan Aluminium Corp. Ltd
Kaiser Engineering Overseas Corp	Mysore Cements Ltd
Mr F. S. Kerr	F. S. Kerr & Co. Pvt Ltd; Cochin Co.
Ludlow Jute Co.	Ludlow Jute Co. Ltd
Otis Elevator Co.	Otis Elevator Co. India Pvt Ltd
Parke-Davis & Co. Ltd	Parke-Davis & Co. Ltd
Parsons & Whittemore South Asia Co. Inc.	Mandya National Paper Mills Ltd
Philips Petroleum Co.	Phillips Carbon Black Ltd
Radio Corporation of America	Photophones Equipment Pvt Ltd
Remington Rand Division	Remington Rand of India Ltd
Standard Vacuum Oil Co.	Standard Vacuum Oil Co.
Steel Improvement Forge Co.	Republic Forge Co. Ltd
Union Carbide Corporation	Union Carbide (India) Ltd
Von Kohorn International Corp.	India Rayon Corporation Ltd
Westrex Corporation	Westrex Co. (India)
Willey's Overland Export Corporation	Mahindra & Mahindra Ltd

Source: US Department of Commerce, 1961.

Table 2.7 American companies with licensing or other agreements with Indian firms, 1961

US firm	*Indian firm*
American Chemical Paint Co.	Imperial Chemical Industries (India) Ltd
Bahnson Co.	C-Doctor and Co. Pvt Ltd
Bancroft, Jos., and Sons Co.	Standard Mills Co. Ltd
Bogen, David, Co. Inc	Electronic Ltd.
Buell Engineering Co. Inc	Associated Cement Companies Ltd
Burgess Battery Co.	Estrela Batteries Ltd
Bush Manufacturing Co.	American Refrigerator Co.
Byron Jackson Pumps Inc	Greeves Cooton & Co. Ltd
Carrier Corporation	Voltas Ltd
Chrysler Corporation	Premier Automobiles Ltd
Dark Electronic Laboratories	Automatic Electric Devices Co. Ltd
Cluett-Peabody & Co. Inc	Serampur Cotton Mills Ltd
Colgate–Palmolive Co.	Colgate–Palmolive (India) Pvt Ltd
Combustion Engineering Inc.	Textile Machinery Corporation Ltd
Davis & Lawrence Co.	Geoffrey Manners & Co. Pvt Ltd
Ebasco Services Inc.	Tata Hydro-Electric Co. Ltd
The English Mica Co.	Governor of Rajasthan
Firestone Tire & Rubber Co.	Automobile Products of India Ltd
Gould-National Batteries Inc.	Amco Batteries Ltd
Hackett Brass Foundry	Tata Iron & Steel Co. Ltd
Kinney, S.P. Engineers Inc.	Tata Iron & Steel Co. Ltd
Koppers Co. Inc.	Tata Iron & Steel Co. Ltd
Kullian Corporation	Damodar Valley Corporation
Nielson Chemical Co.	Addition Paints & Chemicals Pvt Ltd
Rayon Consultants Inc.	National Rayon Corporation Ltd
Sawyer's Inc.	Patel (India) Ltd
Skonandoa Rayon Corporation	National Rayon Corporation Ltd
Snell, Foster D. Inc.	Swastic Oil Mill Ltd
Squibb, E.R. and Sons	Sarabhai Chemicals Ltd
Studebaker Packard Corporation	Hindustan Motors Ltd
United States Air Conditioning Corp	Electronics Ltd
United States Vitamin Corp	American Products Co. Ltd
Wayne Pump Co.	Mercantile & Industrial Development Co. Ltd
Willys Motors Ltd	Mahindra & Mahlndra Ltd
Zonite Products Ltd	Geoffrey Manners & Co. Pvt Ltd

Source: US Department of Commerce, 1961.

Table 2.8 American companies with investments in India, 1961

US firm	*Indian subsidiary or affiliate*
Armco International Corp.	Armco (India) Pvt Ltd
American Bureau of Shipping	American Bureau of Shipping
American Export Lines Inc.	American Export Lines Inc.
American Foreign Insurance Association	American Foreign Insurance Association
American International Underwriters Corp.	American International Underwriters (India) Pvt Ltd
Associated Press	Associated Press of America
Chase Manhattan Bank	Chase Manhattan Bank
Cheseborough-Pond's Inc.	Cheseborough-Pond's Inc.
Coca-Cola Export Corporation	Coca-Cola Export Corporation
Columbia Broadcasting System	Columbia Broadcasting System
Columbia Pictures Intl. Corp.	Columbia Films of India Ltd
The Chicago Pneumatic Tool Co.	Consolidated Pneumatic Tool Co. Ltd
Dodge & Seymor Ltd	Dodge & Seymor (India) Pvt Ltd
Eli Lilly Intrernational Corp.	Eli Lilly and Co. of India, Inc.
First National City Bank of New York	First National City Bank of New York
Gerdau India Corporation	Gerdau India Corporation
Getz Brothers & Co.	Getz Brothers & Co.
Grant Advertizing Inc	Grant Advertizing Inc
Gulf Oil Corporation	Gulf Oil (India) Ltd
International Business Consultants Ltd	Iboon Private Ltd
Indamer Co. Pvt Ltd	Indamer Co. Pvt Ltd
Ingersoll-Rand Co.	Ingersoll-Rand (India) Pvt Ltd
International Chemical Co. Inc.	International Chemical Co. Ltd
International General Electric Co.	International General Electric Co. (India) Pvt Ltd
Isthmian Lines Inc	Isthmian Steamship Co.
Kuljian Corporation	Kuljian Corporation
Loew's International Corporation	Metro-Goldwyn-Mayer India Ltd
Loew's International Corporation	Metro Theatre Bombay Ltd
McGraw-Hill International Corporation	McGraw-Hill International Corporation
Monsanto Chemical Co.	Monsanto Chemical Co.
Muller & Phipps (Asia) Ltd	Muller & Phipps (India) Pvt. Ltd
National Cash Register Co.	Picker International Corporation
Pan American World Airways Inc	Pan American World Airways Inc
Paramount International Films Inc	Paramount Films of India Ltd
Ralph M. Parson Co.	Ralph M. Parson Co.
Pepsi-Cola	Pepsi-Cola
Picker X-Ray Corporation	Picker International Corporation
RKO Radio Pictures	RKO Radio Pictures (Private) Ltd
Republic Pictures International Corp	Republic Pictures of India Ltd

(*Continued*)

Table 2.8 (Continued)

US firm	*Indian subsidiary or affiliate*
Edward T. Robertson and Sons	Edward T. Robertson and Sons
L D Seymour & Co. Inc	L D Seymour & Co. (India) Pvt Ltd
Singer Sewing Machine Co.	Singer Sewing Machine Co.
The Stanley Works	The Stanley Works
J- Walter Thompson Far Eastern Co.	J. Walter Thompson Co. Pvt Ltd
Trans World Airlines Inc	Trans World Airlines Inc
20th Century-Fox Intl Corp.	20th Century-Fox Corp. (India) Pvt Ltd
United Artists Corporation	United Press Association
Universal Pictures Co. Inc. (Production)	Universal Pictures India Pvt Ltd
Van Reekum-Gepacy Paper Inc.	Van Reekum-Gepacy Paper Pvt Ltd
Warner Brothers	Warner Brothers, First National Pictures Inc.
Westinghouse Trading (Asia) Ltd	Westinghouse Trading Co. (Asia) Ltd

Note: The above investments have been primarily in office equipment, stores, stocks and spare parts.
Source: US Department of Commerce, 1961.

were largely marketing companies or entering companies into license agreements or were largely in the business of office equipments, stores and spare parts. Most of these companies, however, sought markets in India and had little interest in direct investments in India. Nevertheless, the share of FDI by American companies in India increased from 4.4 per cent in 1948 to over 13 per cent by 1961. German and Swiss companies increased their investment modestly. Japan hardly had any investment in India from 1942 to the middle 1950s. Investments in trade and plantation steadily declined to 37 per cent by 1948, 23 per cent by 1961 and 5 per cent by 1991. At the same time, investment in manufacturing increased to over 60 per cent by the end of this period.

British investments grew due to the deeper commitment of British companies in India prior to 1947. In addition, there were new entrants such as Cadbury Chocolates, Tube Investments, Reckitt & Coleman, and Horlicks. New entrants from the US were Pfizer, Parke Davis, Otis Elevator, Coke, Pepsi, and Vicks Products, among others. Nestle, Siemens, Pharmacia, Hoechst, BASF and others came from Europe. Tables 2.2–2.4 present a sample list of foreign companies from different countries that came to India during this period. Although Japanese trading firms had stopped cotton and cotton yarn trading in 1942, a few Japanese manufacturing companies like Asahi Glass, Shimada Glass, Nippon Chemicals, Hitachi, and Nichimen came to India in this period.

1962–77

Earlier, the Government of India had been suggesting informally to the foreign companies to include Indian equity. During the period 1962–77 these issues were formalized through legislation. The Foreign Exchange Regulation Act (FERA),[7] which put curbs on foreign equity, came into force in 1973. Foreign companies also came under the Monopolies and Restrictive Trade Practices (MRTP)[8] Act, 1969, during this period. The Act curtailed the size of business operations and pricing policies of products and services.

Foreign companies that found the FERA legislation unduly cumbersome decided to cease operations in India. As many as 54 companies applied to wind up their operations by 1977–78 and nine companies applied to wind up their operations in 1980–81 (RBI Annual Reports, 1977–78 and 1980–81). The closure of Coca Cola (1977) and IBM (1978) are notable cases.

The amount of FDI and the number of foreign joint ventures declined drastically between 1962 and 1968 and showed an erratic trend from 1969 till 1977. The number of foreign collaborations declined from 464 in 1961 to 131 in 1968. Nevertheless, some of the larger foreign companies consolidated their market positions. For instance, Unilever invested in Modern Foods, Indexport Ltd, and Hind Lever Chemicals. ICI set up Chemical and Fibres of India Limited in Thane in 1963 to manufacture polyester staple fibres; started manufacturing fertilizer in Panki near Kanpur in 1969; and set up the ICI Research and Technology Centre in Thane in 1976. Some of these companies also invested in export activities as the Government of India provided incentives for exports by setting up two Export Processing Zones at Kandla in 1965 and Santa Cruz in 1972. The new entrants in India during this period were British companies like BPL, American companies such as Cummins, Frick, E Merck, Precision Gears, and Singer Machine, European companies such as Continental AG, Heinrich Schmidt AG, Piaggio, Wartsila Oy, and from Japan Kokoku Wires, Mitsubishi, Yuken, Sankyo, and Daikin.

1978–90

In a new phase of liberalization and globalization, the government's Industrial Policy Statement, 1977 announced relaxation in remittances of profits, royalties, dividends and repatriation of capital by foreign companies. The Industrial Policy, 1980, further set the tone of liberalization in a slow but steady pace. Industrial licensing was streamlined and made easier. Provisions in the MRTP Act (1970) were modified to simplify business transactions. Export and import norms were also changed to encourage FDI in India. Hitherto most of the imported items were routed through the State Trading Corporation, leaving only a few items that were inconsequential to the total outflow/inflow of foreign exchange in the list of Open General Licence (OGL). In 1978 the government transferred most of the imports to OGL. Nearly 350 importable items were liberalized in two years (1984–85) and many more were subsequently added to the list of OGL.

The government also reduced import restrictions and reduced tariffs in general by nearly 25 per cent and in some cases between 5 and 10 per cent. To boost exports the government provided special facilities and tax privileges to foreign companies to set up 100 per cent export-oriented units. Four additional export processing zones were also set up. All these policy changes led to greater liberalization of foreign trade.

The number of joint ventures increased steadily from 1978 until 1984–85, decreased for some time, and showed signs of recovery during 1989–90. The largest numbers of joint ventures during this period were from USA; Germany ranked second. The share of British companies in the number of joint ventures declined noticeably. The share of other countries including those from Europe increased gradually.

The amount of FDI fluctuated greatly, especially from the USA and Germany. FDI from Japan increased in 1982–83, slowly declining until the end of 1990. FDI from the UK declined dramatically. However, the liberalization process initiated in this period resulted in more than doubling the number of foreign companies registered in India during this period from only 62 during 1962–77 to 128. The number of joint ventures also increased from 307 in 1978 to 703 in 1990. Similarly, the amount of FDI rose from INR89 million to INR1238 million, an increase of over 13 times.

1991–2000

In 1990 India faced a critical foreign exchange crisis. The International Monetary Fund (IMF) and the World Bank agreed to provide loans on condition that it would make major changes to liberalize trade and investments. With the Industrial Licensing Policy (ILP), 1991, industrial licensing was abolished except for 18 industries. FDI up to 51 per cent foreign equity was allowed in 34 high-priority industries and the concept of phased manufacturing was removed. The tariffs on imports have steadily been reduced in every budget since 1991. In 1999 Foreign Exchange Management Act (FEMA) replaced FERA, 1973. The objectives of FEMA have been to facilitate external trade and payments and to promote orderly development and maintenance of foreign exchange market. It is meant to facilitate and not regulate foreign trade and investment (Roy 2000).

Automatic approval of FDI has been allowed in all sectors except banking, civil aviation, petroleum, real estate, venture capital funds, investing companies in infrastructure and service sector, atomic energy, defence, agriculture and plantation, print media, broadcasting and postal services.

The ILP resulted in an all-time high flow of FDI into India. In addition to thousands of foreign collaborations 145 foreign companies registered in India between 1991 and 2000. Companies like General Motors, Ford Motors, and IBM that had divested from India in the 1950s and 1970s re-entered. A large number of Asian companies like Daewoo Motors, Hyundai Motors and LG Electronics from South Korea and Matsushita Television and Honda Motors from Japan invested in India during this period.

The number of foreign collaborations increased from 976 in 1991 to 2144 in 2000. The amount of FDI increased from INR5156 million to INR373,722 million. While the share of FDI from the UK declined to about 10 per cent and the share of FDI from USA also decreased, the share of other countries including South Korea, Malaysia, Australia, and other countries from Asia and European Union constituted over 65 per cent of the FDI during this period.

Periodization of FDI in India, 1900s–2000

FDI to India has been there for a long time even before the twentieth century. From being a favourable destination of FDI in the early part of the twentieth century, it ran out of favour in the 1970s and 1980s and has regained importance since the 1990s. It is rather interesting to see the evolutionary process of FDI in India; the drivers of change, the driving forces, major sources of investment, nature of investments and the stages of evolution.

During the first stage (1900s–1918), there were hardly any restrictions on the nature and type of foreign investments. Cross border transactions occurred rather freely as was the case in the rest of the world. However, investments were largely from the United Kingdom in trade and finance. British firms were the dominant investors during this period and they invested largely through the British Managing Agents.

Foreign investments in the form of direct investments actually originated during the second phase (1919–42). The introduction of import duties during this period 'stimulated' many British companies to invest in the Indian manufacturing sector to protect their businesses in India. Although Japanese companies increased their share of trade with India during this period, the British firms remained the dominant investor.

During the third phase (1943–61), the flow of FDI into India increased significantly. During this period Indian companies and the government realized the need to import technology and finance from foreign companies. This led to 'ambitious' investments by many companies from countries like the UK and the USA.

The fourth phase (1962–77) marked the Indian Government's regulatory regime that imposed severe restrictions to control foreign exchange, type of FDI and ownership of foreign companies in India. These restrictions led to a 'controlled' flow of FDI. Nearly 80 companies divested from India during this period.

The fifth phase (1978–90) witnessed liberalization in imports and exports. The roots of economic liberalization of the 1990s actually lie in this period, when a number initiatives were taken by the Government of India to encourage foreign investments into the country. Although, the amount of FDI increased by over 13 times during this period, foreign firms were cautious to invest in India.

In the final phase (1991–2000), the liberalization process was accelerated at the behest of the IMF and the World Bank. This phase witnessed very high growth in the amount of FDI and the number of joint ventures. FDI flowed from across the world, resulting in a globalized structure of FDI.

In summary, FDI in India evolved through six stages: free flow (1900s–1918), stimulated flow (1919–42), ambitious flow (1943–61), controlled flow (1962–77), cautious flow (1978–90), and globalized flow (1991–2000). Table 2.9 summarizes the periods, the policy framework, the nature of investments, the sources of investments and the stages of evolution.

Major trends in FDI

Non-manufacturing vs manufacturing

Most of the investments in the first 50 years were in trade and finance with focus on plantation and mining industries like tea, jute, and coal. By 1948, the share of FDI in trade and finance was 64 per cent. However, by 1991–99 this had dropped to 12 per cent and the share in manufacturing had grown to nearly 88 per cent. The share of FDI in the manufacturing and non-manufacturing sectors during the twentieth century replicates an 'X' structure (see Figure 2.1).

Amount of FDI

Despite the fluctuations in the economic and political circumstances the average annual amount of FDI to India steadily rose during the period 1921–2000 (see Figure 2.2 and Table 2.10). Contrary to the general perception, the annual average of FDI to India has increased over the years.

Table 2.9 History of FDI in India, 1900s–2000

Characteristics/ period	*Drivers of change*	*Driving forces*	*Major sources of investments*	*Nature of investments*	*Stages of evolution*
1900s–1918	UK	No restriction in FDI	UK	Trading & finance	Free flow phase
1919–42	UK, Japan and Local textile companies	Introduction of import duties	UK and Japan	Trading, finance & manufacturing	Stimulated phase
1943–61	Government of India	Demand for foreign technology & capital in manufacturing sector	UK and USA	Manufacturing, sales & services	Ambitious phase
1962–77	Government of India	MRTP (1970), FERA, (1973), and Investments in public sector companies	USA, Germany and UK	Manufacturing	Controlled phase
1978–90	Government of India, WTO and Indian Companies & Business Houses	Liberalization of imports and exports	USA and Germany	Manufacturing	Cautious phase
1991–2000	IMF, World Bank, WTO and Indian Business Houses	Acceleration of liberalization and globalization of FDI	Globalized	Manufacturing, trade & financial service	Globalized phase

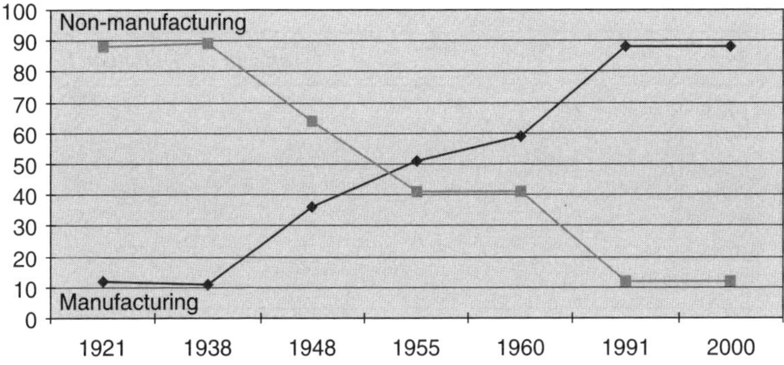

Source: Compiled by the author using data from Tomlinson (1989), Kurian (1966), Ganesh (1997), India Investment Centre (GOI), Centre for Industrial and Economic Research, International Investment Position of India (2003), and Ministry of Finance, GOI.

Figure 2.1 Sectoral share of FDI, 1921–2000

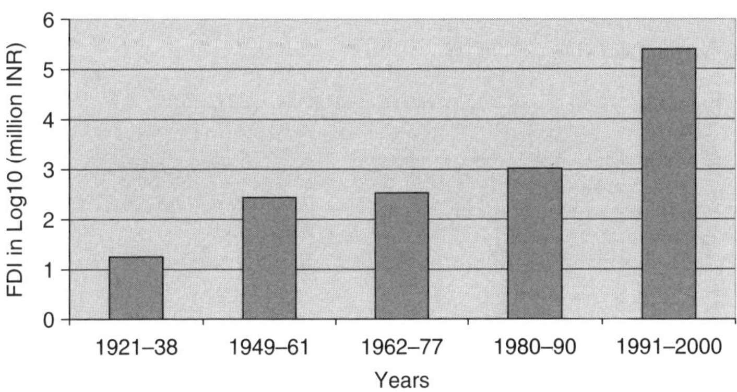

Note: The amount for the period 1991–2002 is the amount approved by the GOI and not the actual amount invested.

Source: The author has compiled these figures from Tomlinson (1989), Wilkins (1994), India Investment Centre Monthly Newsletters (1967–70), Kurian (1996), and India Investment Centre FDI Data, 1991–2000.

Figure 2.2 Annual average FDI in India, 1921–2000

It is most striking to see that the flow of FDI to India did not decrease even during 1942–61, the period during which India fought tooth and nail for India's freedom from the United Kingdom, a major FDI investors in India prior to this period.

Over the years, share of FDI from different countries have also changed. FDI from UK constituted over 85 per cent until 1964–65. Japan was a

Table 2.10 Total amount of FDI in India, 1921–2000

Year	*Amount of FDI (billion INR)*
1921	2.03
1921–38	0.32
1949–61	3.55
1962–68	2.20
1970–79	3.53
1980–90	11.50
1991–2000	2,474.00

Sources: The author has compiled this from Tomlinson (1989), Wilkins (1994), Monthly Newsletters: (1967–70) India Investment Centre, GOI, Kurian (1996), *Industrial Data Book* (1986), *Industrial Data Book* (2000–2001), and FDI data (1991–2000), India Investment Centre (Government of India). The amounts for the period 1991–2002 are amounts approved by the GOI and not the actual investment.

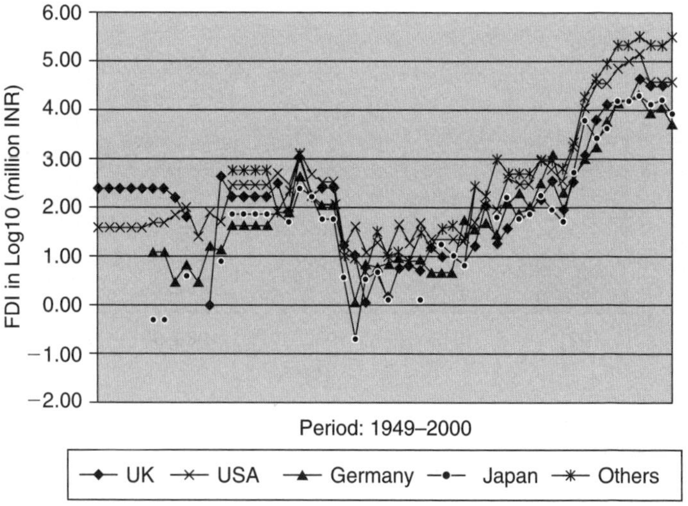

Source: India Investment Centre.
Figure 2.3 Amount of FDI in India, 1949–2000

major trading partner during 1919–41. The USA and Germany became the lead investors during 1965–90. In the recent decade, countries from the European Union and Asia have greatly increased their share, from 52 per cent in 1991 to 86 per cent in 2000 (see Figure 2.3 and Table 2.11).[9]

Table 2.11 Country-wise amount of FDI in India, 1949–2000 (million INR)

Year	*UK*	*USA*	*Germany*	*Japan*	*Others*	*Total*
1949*	240.8	37.8	0.0	0.0	n.a.	278.6
1950*	240.8	37.8	0.0	0.0	n.a.	278.6
1951*	240.8	37.8	0.0	0.0	n.a.	278.6
1952*	240.8	37.8	0.0	0.0	n.a.	278.6
1953*	240.8	37.8	0.0	0.0	n.a.	278.6
1954	252.0	49.0	12.0	0.5	n.a.	313.5
1955	252.0	49.0	12.0	0.5	n.a.	313.5
1956	157.0	71.0	3.0	0.0	n.a.	231.0
1957	63.0	105.0	7.0	4.0	n.a.	179.0
1958	0.0	25.0	3.0	0.0	n.a.	28.0
1959	1.0	76.0	16.0	0.0	n.a.	93.0
1960	427.0	50.0	14.0	8.0	n.a.	499.0
1961	163.7	286.3	42.75	71.75	564.5	1,091.3
1962	163.7	286.3	42.75	71.75	564.5	1,091.3
1963	163.7	286.3	42.75	71.75	564.5	1,091.3
1964	163.7	286.3	42.75	71.75	564.5	1,091.3
1965	314.0	522.0	82.0	72.0	83.0	1,073.0
1966	94.0	286.0	75.0	49.0	178.0	682.0
1967	956.0	1,283.0	450.0	232.0	1,045.0	3,966.0
1968	0.0	472.0	156.0	171.0	163.0	769.0
1969	241.0	331.0	112.8	58.1	263.6	1,007.1
1970	241.0	331.0	112.8	58.1	263.6	1,007.1
1971	16.6	15.8	11.4	3.7	10.9	58.4
1972	10.8	40.9	1.1	0.2	9.2	62.3
1973	1.2	12.0	7.0	3.3	4.8	28.2
1974	5.2	19.4	6.0	4.7	32.0	67.1
1975	1.5	12.0	6.9	1.3	10.1	31.8
1976	5.6	44.7	9.8	0.0	12.6	72.7
1977	6.7	18.2	7.5	0.0	7.7	40.0
1978	5.0	47.3	8.6	1.3	32.0	94.1
1979	14.8	22.2	4.4	0.0	15.0	56.4
1980	9.7	21.7	4.7	17.0	35.2	88.3
1980	9.7	22.0	4.7	10.2	42.4	89.0
1981	7.1	22.5	54.2	6.5	18.7	109.0
1982	16.5	50.3	35.3	251.1	274.8	628.0
1983	98.0	138.9	48.4	160.8	172.9	619.0
1984	18.1	89.5	28.4	61.5	932.5	1,130.0
1985	37.0	400.0	118.0	157.0	495.0	1,207.0
1986	77.0	294.0	202.0	56.0	441.0	1,070.0
1987	85.0	295.0	99.0	69.0	529.0	1,077.0
1988	139.0	970.0	310.0	174.0	805.0	2,398.0
1989	335.0	622.0	1,203.0	88.0	919.0	3,167.0
1990	91.0	345.0	195.0	50.0	602.0	1,283.0

(Continued)

Table 2.11 (Continued)

Year	*UK*	*USA*	*Germany*	*Japan*	*Others*	*Total*
1991†	313.0	1,749.0	376.0	520.0	2,207.0	5,165.0
1992	1,177.0	11,383.0	965.0	6,102.0	18,388.0	38,015.0
1993	6,227.0	34,730.0	1,754.0	2,574.0	43,333.0	88,618.0
1994	12,991.0	34,881.0	5,694.0	4,009.0	84,298.0	141,873.0
1995	17,259.0	70,448.0	13,395.0	15,143.0	208,579.0	324,824.0
1996	15,246.0	100,549.0	15,375.0	14,882.0	215,447.0	361,499.0
1997	44,907.0	135,698.0	21,548.0	19,064.0	327,687.0	548,904.0
1998	32,008.0	35,619.0	8,538.0	12,828.0	218,642.0	307,635.0
1999	29,630.0	35,755.0	11,430.0	15,947.0	190,903.0	283,665.0
2000	4,121.0	41,398.0	5,938.0	8,275.0	313,990.0	373,722.0

Notes: * Average figures; † The amounts for the period 1991–2002 are amounts approved by the GOI and not the actual investment.
Source: The author has compiled these figures from Centre for Industrial Economic Research (1986 and 2001), *Industrial Data Book* (1986), *Industrial Data Book* (2000–2001), (1991–2000), Indian Investment Centre, (1967–90), Monthly News Letters, and India Investment Centre (1991–2000), FDI Data.

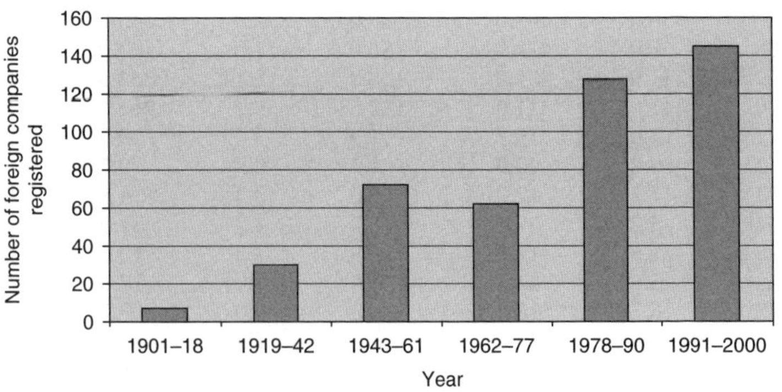

Source: Centre for Monitoring Indian Economy.
Figure 2.4 Number of Foreign Companies Registered in India, 1901–2000

Number of investing companies

The number of foreign companies registered in India has increased over the years. Except for a slight drop in the numbers of foreign firms during 1962–77, there has been a steady rise in numbers during 1901–2000 (see Figure 2.4). The number of foreign collaborations with the Indian companies has also steadily increased during 1951–2000. However, there was a significant shift in the country-wise number of foreign collaborations (see Figure 2.5 and Table 2.12).

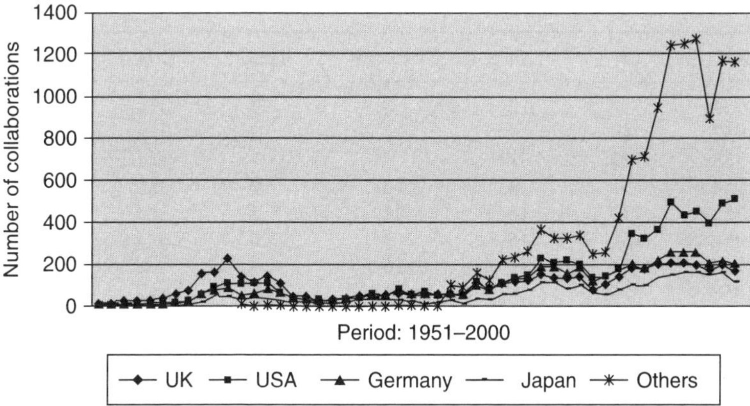

Source: India Investment Centre.

Figure 2.5 Trends in country-wise number of foreign collaborations, 1951–2000

Summing up

While there were virtually no restrictions on FDI during the period 1901–18, until the end of World War I, foreign investment in India was dominated by British companies. Trading and services were their major areas of operation. Manufacturing companies also operated as traders of their products imported from the mother companies.

During 1919–42, while UK became vulnerable, USA and Japan emerged as powerful nations. American and Japanese companies entered the Indian market in a big way during this period. Japan's trade with India reached an all-time high and by the end of 1942, it touched rock bottom due to various developments in this period. The representation of Indians increased in legislative matters. Local businesses pressed for the protection of local industries, leading to the introduction of import duties. This set in a new shift in the composition of foreign investment in India as many foreign companies directly invested in manufacturing activities in India. Indeed, this period marked the beginning of FDI in India.

During 1943–61, the amount of FDI and the number of foreign joint ventures in India increased significantly. Many British manufacturing companies increased their investments. Companies from other countries, especially from USA, entered India in large numbers. There was also a qualitative change in the nature of FDI, with the share of FDI in manufacturing sector increasing significantly.

The period 1962–77 clearly marks a shift in the government's FDI policy. FERA (1973) was the culmination of the manifestation of the

Table 2.12 Country-wise number of collaborations in India, 1951–2000

Year	*UK*	*USA*	*Germany*	*Japan*	*Others*	*Total*
1951	17	12	3	2	n.a.	34
1952	19	9	1	2	n.a.	31
1953	29	7	4	1	n.a.	41
1954	31	14	5	0	n.a.	50
1955	30	15	11	2	n.a.	58
1956	39	16	7	6	n.a.	68
1957	57	19	15	4	n.a.	95
1958	75	29	21	6	n.a.	131
1959	160	58	61	15	n.a.	377
1960	161	93	73	50	n.a.	464
1961	226	108	85	45	n.a.	337
1962	141	103	54	29	10	337
1963	118	110	59	44	1	332
1964	143	112	80	37	5	377
1965	108	65	60	31	3	267
1966	44	42	41	18	0	145
1967	50	34	24	21	2	131
1968	19	36	22	12	0	89
1969	34	18	28	17	2	99
1970	39	33	36	15	0	123
1971	55	43	42	35	1	176
1972	38	62	49	27	1	177
1973	53	48	60	36	2	199
1974	59	79	68	28	3	237
1975	54	55	59	23	6	197
1976	54	69	58	10	1	192
1977	59	54	55	20	1	189
1978	61	58	58	28	102	307
1979	63	48	54	12	90	267
1980	110	125	100	34	157	526
1981	80	85	74	27	123	389
1982	105	109	110	51	213	588
1983	119	135	129	58	232	673
1984	123	143	132	78	264	740
1985	149	229	187	111	365	1,041
1986	134	203	188	111	324	960
1987	130	217	154	82	320	903
1988	142	200	179	98	338	957
1989	78	137	114	63	247	639
1990	107	142	141	55	258	703
1991	140	174	167	74	421	976
1992	183	344	199	101	693	1,520
1993	175	318	177	95	711	1,476

(Continued)

Table 2.12 (Continued)

Year	*UK*	*USA*	*Germany*	*Japan*	*Others*	*Total*
1994	199	360	216	134	945	1,854
1995	202	491	256	147	1,241	2,337
1996	205	434	256	160	1,248	2,303
1997	191	451	257	156	1,270	2,325
1998	164	390	198	143	891	1,786
1999	194	488	218	158	1,166	2,224
2000	166	509	198	111	1,160	2,144

Source: The author has compiled these figures from Centre for Industrial Economic Research (1986 and 2001), *Industrial Data Book* (1986), *Industrial Data Book* (2000–2001), (1991–2000), Indian Investment Centre Monthly News Letters 1967–90, and India Investment Centre FDI Data, 1991–2000. The figures for the period 1991–2002 are numbers approved by the Government of India and not the actual number of collaborations.

objectives of the government pursued informally in the previous period. Nearly 80 foreign companies ceased their operations in India and the number of joint ventures from all foreign countries decreased dramatically. However, some new companies from USA, Europe and Japan ventured into India and the major British companies that had prior commitment in India consolidated their businesses with further investments.

In 1978–90 the government made a series of policy changes in export and import policies. Although the number of joint ventures and the amount of FDI in India fluctuated, the amount of FDI increased nearly 13 times. The number of foreign companies registered in India also doubled.

In 1991–2000 the poor balance of payments position and pressure of the IMF and World Bank to liberalize the Indian economy forced the government to accelerate the pace of liberalization. While the share of FDI from traditionally dominant countries like UK and USA fell, the share of FDI from other countries, including countries from Asia and the European Union increased from 53 per cent in 1991 to 86 per cent in 2000.

3
Analytical Framework

This chapter discusses the key hypotheses around which the book has been organized. It explains in detail the conceptual framework and the methodologies adopted in its investigation and analyses of firm-level business strategies. It provides a detailed explanation on how the sample cases were selected and how each case was studied. It discusses how each case was analysed using a variety of primary and secondary documents. Finally, it discusses the basis of adopting various statistical tools and the techniques adopted for analysis of various data on investments and performance indicators.

To find the determinants of success by foreign firms in a host country at least two issues need to be looked into. First, whether the FDI strategy of a firm is different in the host country from its business strategy in the home country. Secondly, whether the success of foreign firms depended on their FDI strategy itself or on the FDI policy of the host country.

With respect to home-country strategy, Porter (1980, 1985) among others, suggests that corporations need to invest in the value chain and build their competitive strategies at the business unit level. Ghemawat (1991) argues on how a firm's commitment could be a strategic option for success. Campbell *et al.* (1995) advocate that seeking parenting advantage can give a firm control on the performance of its business. Prahalad and Hamel (1990) recommend that firms should focus on their core competency to remain competitive. With respect to host-country situation, the strategy of foreign firms has been to seek resources, markets, and efficiency. More often than not these strategies are short-term in perspective. In the host country, foreign firms have sought to start their business from where they left off in their home market. This becomes a mismatch since the two situations generally differ.

If a foreign firm's success in the host country is internal to itself it is important to find out:

- whether successful FDI strategy involved holistic investments across a variety of value-adding activities or investment in sales and marketing alone, as has been generally observed;
- given the nature of Indian industries, whether investment in complementary businesses significantly contributed to its success;
- whether the determinants of success have been different for different industries and for different points of time or have been similar across industries and across time.

In trying to find the determinants of foreign firms' success[1] in India during the period 1900s–2004 this book has postulated the following hypothesis about successful firms.

1. They made *holistic investment*[2] across the various market functions of their respective industries.
2. Direct investment in *complementary businesses*[3] contributed significantly to their success.
3. Determinants of success have been similar across companies.

The analysis of successful FDI strategy in this book has been based on firm level strategy of multinational enterprises in India. Three cases, i.e. British American Tobacco (BAT), Unilever, and Suzuki Motor Corporation (SMC) have been studied in detail. The cases were selected scientifically using a five-step sampling method and were later triangulated by adopting hierarchical clustering method.

Hypothesis 1 has been verified by evaluating how a company invested in various areas of its business, i.e. (a) main business, (b) complementary businesses, (c) local management, (d) priority areas of India, and (e) local equity. Figure 3.1 lays out a framework for analysing how each of the three firms operated on all the five levels and how it moved from the inner circle to the outermost circle during their operations in India. Firms that invested in all the five layers have been considered to have adopted a holistic investment strategy.

Hypothesis 2 has been verified through multiple regression analysis by separately taking sales and PAT as dependent variables and investment in main business, complementary businesses and other areas[4] as independent variables.

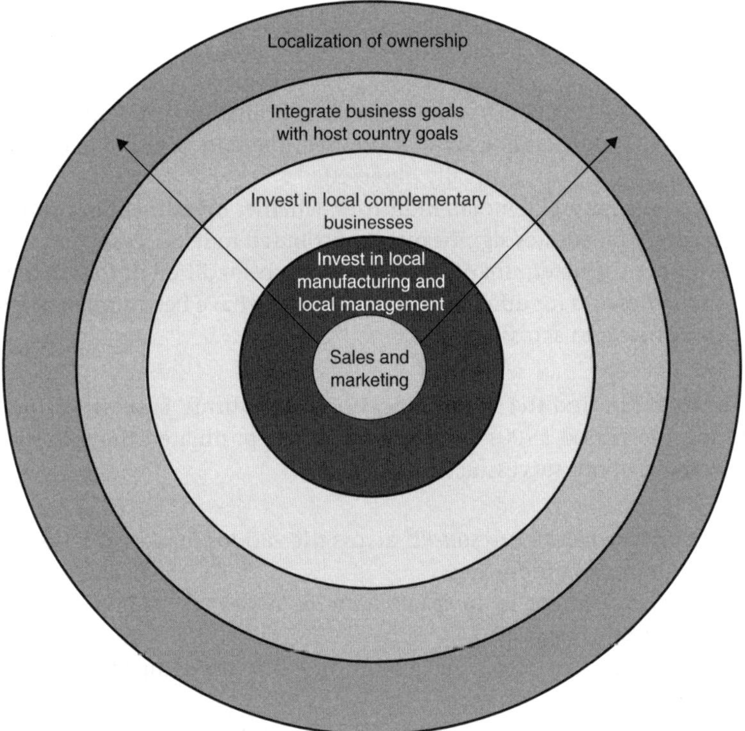

Figure 3.1 Direct investment pattern of successful foreign firms in India, 1906–2004

Hypothesis 3 has been verified by comparing the three cases to see whether their FDI strategies have been similar or different. By comparing the coefficients of independent variables, i.e. investment in main business, investment in complementary business, and investment in others against sales and PAT separately, hypothesis 3 has been explained.

Finally, the aggregate data (independent variables and dependent variables) of all the three cases from different industries have been subjected to both model-based multiple regression analysis and data based Artificial Neural Network analysis. Triangulating the findings through these two methods confirmed the findings suggested in the book. The findings from these analyses were compared with individual cases to verify and corroborate hypothesis 3.

Research methodology

Over the last hundred years, patterns of direct investment of the foreign companies in India have changed from the colonial period (1900s–1947), to the development period (1947–1990), and to the period of economic liberalization (1991 onwards). FDI strategies of companies have differed from country to country and industry to industry. Foreign companies following the same strategy have succeeded in some periods and failed in others. Also, there have been continuities and discontinuities in the regulatory policies in India during the last hundred years. In the above context the book discusses the determinants of successful FDI strategy in India during 1900s–2000.

Many researchers consider the case study method or Case-Based Research (CBR) as inductive and hence not suitable for theory building. In their view, this method, lacking rigour and unable to replicate business and management phenomena, is at best used for exploratory research. Paradoxically, CBR has produced some of the most powerful theories in management, the best management practices. Today, case-based teaching is the predominant pedagogy of teaching in business schools around the world. Chandler (1969) used the case method to develop a valuable management theory on strategy and structure. The network theory in international business by Axelsson and Johanson (1994) is yet another contribution of management theory through CBR method. CBR has produced some of best management practices like the Toyota Manufacturing System and Target Costing of Toyota Motor Corporation. CBR has gained importance especially in the last decade. It has been accepted and applied to understand and explain business as in William and Hatt (1981), Eisenhardt (1989), Yin (1994), Mintzberg (1994), Mason (1995), Dooley (1997), and Cooper and Schindler (1999). CBR has also gained importance in functional areas of management like strategy, finance as in Tufano (2001), marketing as explained in Johnston *et al.* (1999) and international business as in Yeung (1995).

Yin (1994) and Hamel *et al.* (1993) provide a detailed process of conducting a good case study. However, there is not much explanation on how CBR can be used as an effective tool for discovering new theories in management. There is no systematic approach to selecting cases from a population before the cases can be studied in-depth. It is rather suggested by Hamel *et al.* (1993) that cases should not be sampled. This is arguable. If a sample of cases were not selected in a systematic and scientific manner but handpicked depending on the convenience of the researcher, the research results will remain inductive.

Given the variety of factors that have affected FDI strategies in India, this study adopted the CBR method. In selecting the cases, a five-step sampling method was adopted. To substantiate the findings, the hierarchical clustering method was adopted to cluster the cases. Details of sampling methods have been discussed in the next section.

Methodology in selecting cases

Five-step sampling method

A five-step sampling method was designed such that the cases selected must represent the population of foreign companies that made direct investments in the host country, India. A representative sample of cases for this study meant that the sample cases should cut across time of operation (encompassing the colonial period, the development period, and the period of economic liberalization), origin, industry, size and performance of foreign companies in India. The sampling process included the following five steps.

(a) study the historical trends of FDI in India, 1900s–2000;
(b) select the population (manufacturing or non-manufacturing) where foreign firms have largely invested in;
(c) spot individual companies from the set of foreign manufacturing companies;
(d) sort the individual companies in the population of manufacturing companies on a three-dimensional (time, origin, and industry) matrix;
(e) select the cases that satisfy three key parameters, i.e. (a) entry to India prior to 1991, (b) size of company (annual sales; market share), and (c) consistency in performance (profit generating and profit sharing ability).

Study historical trends of FDI

A historical trend of FDI in India during the 1900s–2000 was undertaken. This helps to take stock of the amount of investments, the number of investing companies, and the nature and scope of investments during different periods. Given that data were at best sketchy and were not properly recorded in India or elsewhere, as many as 80 reports, books, articles, and data bases from different parts of the world were referred.

Select the population of investing companies

The manufacturing sector was chosen for the study because it formed a major chunk of foreign investments (see Figure 2.1). On the other hand, investment in non-manufacturing sector has steadily declined over the years, and companies in the non-manufacturing sector have been subject to a wide variation in their trends and policies in the Indian context. Companies in manufacturing also showed better consistency and commitment in their policies of investments. Consequently, these companies are more likely to have a steady pattern in their strategies.

Spot individual companies

The number of foreign companies registered in India had increased from four during 1901–10 to about 145 during 1991–2000 (CMIE: Centre for Monitoring Indian Economy 1989–2002). This study was able to identify the specific companies that operated at different time periods. A wide range of over 20 sources was used to gather information of the names, their operations in India and their performances

Sort the companies on a three-dimensional matrix

The three key parameters, i.e. year of entry, size, and financial performance of the companies were used as criteria for selecting a sample of cases from the previous population matrix of foreign manufacturing companies in India.

1. *Year of entry*: Outcomes of investment strategies in the manufacturing sector, which is the focus of the study, take some time to prove themselves. Therefore, this study focuses on companies that had at least a history of ten years of operation in India.
2. *Size of the company*: In studying the strategic behaviour of firms, large companies are better suited because they are likely to exhibit their behaviour explicitly. Smaller firms cannot take many of the strategic decisions because of resource constraints. In other words, even if small and medium firms inherently want to grow in size and performance like the large firms (Penrose 1995, Rugman and Verbeke 2002), they cannot grow because of their limited resource base. Moreover, large companies are resource-rich and they are in turn capable of influencing the environment. They attract attention and further, they have organized data. Knowing the FDI strategy of large companies will help us to infer the FDI strategy of firms in general, including small and medium firms. For this study, companies with annual sales

of INR10,000 million or more in 2000, the terminal year of the study period, have been considered.

Table 3.1 presents the history of the entry of foreign companies in 20-year slabs. It reveals the dominance of British firms until 1940. Many European firms joined the league during the next twenty years. In the subsequent years, the American firms and later the Japanese firms have also entered India in large numbers. Table 3.2 presents their country of origin. It shows the variety of manufacturing firms that have been in India. Table 3.3 presents their operational niche. Table 3.4 summarizes the time–origin–industry matrix of foreign companies that have been in India during the twentieth century.

3. *Financial performance*: Consistency in financial performance over a long period would confirm the robustness of the investment strategy employed. Two financial performance measures were used as qualifying criteria:

   (a) Profit-generating ability measured through PBDIT. This is also a good measure for comparing the efficiency of companies across industry. The industry effect on performance of companies from different industry is removed through this variable.
   (b) Profit sharing ability, measured through (PAT) is a good measure to compare companies within a specific industry.

   Companies that showed steady improvement in both PBDIT and PAT during 1991–2000 were chosen for the sample (see Figures 3.2–3.8). Industries like automobile, personal care and food, tobacco, electronics and machinery, pharmaceuticals, lube oils, paints and chemicals and others were taken for analysis and sample selection. The figures largely reveal the consistency in performance of firms within their respective industries.

In summary, the following three criteria were used to select the cases for detailed analysis:

1. Operations in India prior to 1991;
2. Annual sales of INR10,000 million or more in year 2000; and
3. Consistency in PBDIT and PAT during 1991–2000.

The qualifying criteria of entry–size–performance measures and how each company fares on these criteria are shown in Table 3.5.

Table 3.1 History of establishment of foreign companies

Period	*Companies*
Until 1920	Forbes Gokak, Parry & Company, Binny & Company, Unilever, Denso, Goodlass Nerolac, British American Tobacco, Glaxo, Ludlow Jute, etc.
1921–40	ICI, Philips, Swedish Match, Colgate Palmolive, General Motors, Ford Motors, Alfa Laval, BOC, Dunlop, VST Industries, Metal Box, Godfrey Philips, etc.
1941–60	Horlicks Limited, Cadbury Industries, Bayer, Siemens, Nestle, Electrolux, Vicks Product, IBM, Caltex, Standard Oil Co, Asahi Glass, Shimada, British Leyland, Grindwell Norton, BASF, Knoll, Novartis, Parke Davis, Pfizer, Abbot Universal, Otis Elevators, Monsanto, Sandvik, Pharamcia, etc.
1961–80	BPL, Continental-AG, Castrol, Cummins, Gulf Oil, E Merck, Procter & Gamble, Widia (India), Precision Gears, Frick Company, etc.
1981–2000	Bayer ABS Ltd, Castrol, ITW Signode, J&P Coats, Saint Gobain, Singer Machine, Yuken, Akzo Nobel, Daewoo Motors, Gillette India, Henkel, Honda Motors, Suzuki Motor Corporation, Hewlett Packard, Toyota Motors, Nissan Motors, ABB, Wartsila Oy, etc.

Four companies – BAT, Unilever, Nestlé and Suzuki Motor Corporation – satisfied all the selection criteria (see Table 3.6).

As only companies were going to be studied, and, since there were two companies i.e. Unilever and Nestle from the Personal Care and Food industry, only one of these two, namely Unilever, was chosen for detailed study. Its larger size in sale, PBDIT and PAT made Unilever a better case than Nestle. The subsequent hierarchical clustering method also confirmed the soundness of Unilever as a case for study.

Hierarchical clustering method

Following the five-step sampling method, the hierarchical clustering method was adopted to triangulate and confirm the sample chosen in the previous method. Cluster analysis groups persons or objects into unknown number of groups such that the members of each group have similar characteristics or attributes, clustered for maximum similarity.

In the Euclidean distance measure for clustering, if the coordinates of point -1 and point -2 are (X_{11}, X_{12}) and $(X_{21}$ and $X_{22})$, respectively, the

Table 3.2 Country of origin of foreign companies

Country of origin	*Company*
UK	Forbes Gokak, Parry & Co., Binny & Co., Glaxo, ICI, BOC, Metal Box, Dunlop, Godfrey Philips, British Leyland, Cadbury, VST Industries, Goodlass Nerolac, Unilever, British American Tobacco, BPL, J&P Coats, Horlicks, etc.
USA	Ludlow Jute, Colgate Palmolive, General Motors, Ford Motors, Vicks Product, IBM, Caltex, Standard Oil Co, Parke Davis, Pfizer, Otis Elevators, Monsanto, Castrol, Cummins, Gulf Oil, E Merck, Procter & Gamble, Singer Machine, Gillette India, Hewlett Packard, Cummins, Frick Company, ITW Signode, etc.
Japan	Asahi Glass, Shimada, Denso, Yuken, Honda Motors, Suzuki Motor Corporation, Toyota Motors, Nissan Motors, etc.
EU	Philips, Swedish Match, Alfa Laval, Electrolux, Bayer, Siemens, Nestle, BASF, Grindwell Norton, Pharmacia, Wartsila Oy, Continental-AG, Knoll, Novartis, Sandvik, Precision Gears, Saint Gobain, Akzo Nobel, Henkel, etc.

Table 3.3 Sectoral distribution of foreign companies

Sector	*Companies*
Automobile	General Motors, Ford Motors, British Leyland, Toyota Motors, Nissan Motors, Honda Motors, Suzuki Motors, Daewoo Motors, Asahi Glass, Denso, etc.
Health Care & Food	Unilever, Colgate Palmolive, Procter & Gamble, Nestle, Cadbury India, Parry & Co., Vicks Product, etc.
Tobacco	British American Tobacco, Godfrey Philips, VST Industries, etc
Pharmaceuticals	Glaxo, BASF, Bayer, Knoll, Abbot Universal, Parke Davis, Pfizer, E Merck, Novartis, Pharmacia, etc.
Electronics and machinery	Forbes Gokak, Philips, Swedish Match, Electrolux, Alfa Laval, IBM, Hewlett Packard, BPL, ABB, Wartsila Oy, Singer Machine, Cummins, Precision Gears, Sandvik Asia, Frick Company, Siemens, etc.
Paints & chemicals	ICI, Goodlass Nerolac, BOC, Caltex, Standard Oil, Castrol, Gulf Oil, Monsanto, Akzo Nobel, Henkel, etc.
Others	Ludlow Jute, Dunlop India, Metal Box, Continental-AG, Otis Elevators, Yuken, Gillette India, Grindwell Norton, ITW Signode, Binny & Co., Saint Gobain, etc.

Table 3.4 Time–origin–industry matrix of foreign companies

Time/origin		Industry						
		Automobile	*Healthcare and food*	*Tobacco*	*Pharmaceuticals*	*Electronics*	*Paints*	*Others*
Until 1920	UK USA		Unilever Parry & Co.	BAT, Imperial Tobacco Co. Peninsular Tobacco (ATC)	Glaxo	Forbes	Goodlass Nerolac	Binny & Co. Ludlow Jute
	Japan	Denso						
	EU		Margarine					
1921–40	UK			Godfrey Phillips VST Indus			ICI BOC	Dunlop Metal Box
	USA	General Motors Ford Motors	Colgate–Palmolive	ILTD				
	EU					Philips Swedish Match Alfa Laval		
1941–60	UK	British Leyland	Horlicks Cadbury					
	USA		Vicks Product		Parke Davis Abbot Labs Pfizer	IBM	Caltex Monsanto Standard Oil	Otis Elevators
	Japan	Asahi Glass Shimada						

	EU		Nestle	Pharmacia Bayer BASF Knoll Novartis	Siemens Electrolux Sandvik		Grindwell Norton
1961–80	UK				BPL		
	USA		Procter & Gamble	E Merck	Cummins, Frick Co.	Gulf Oil	
	EU				Widia (India) Precision Gears		Continental A.G
1981–2000	UK					Castrol	J & P Coats
	USA	General Motors Ford Motors			Singer Gillette HP, IBM		ITW Signode
	Japan	Suzuki Nissan Honda Toyota					Yuken
	EU				ABB, Wartsila Punjab Anand	Akzo Henkel	Saint Gobain

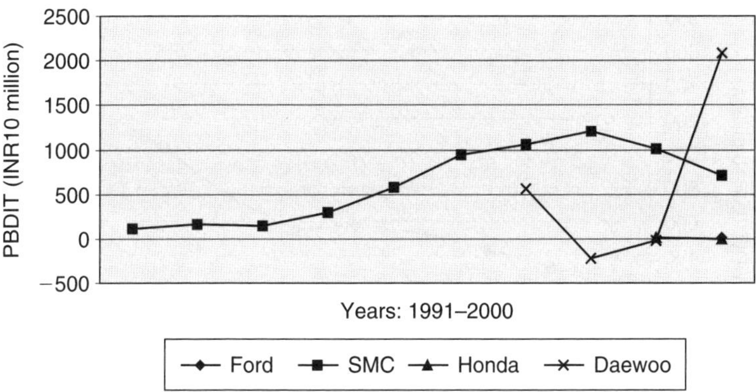

Source: Centre for Monitoring Indian Economy.

Figure 3.2 Performance of companies in car industry

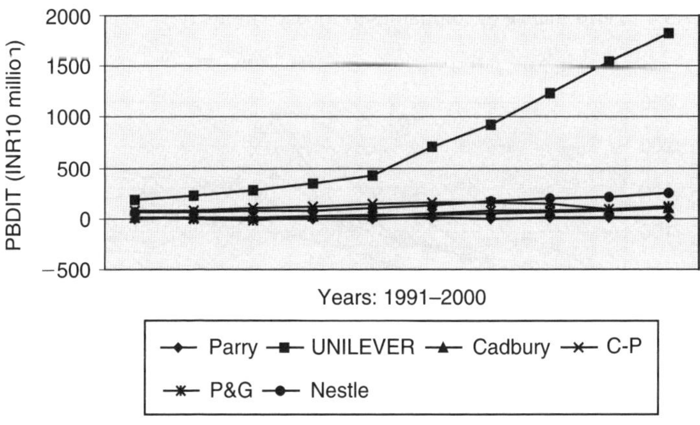

Source: Centre for Monitoring Indian Economy.

Figure 3.3 Performance of companies in personal care and food industries

distance between point −1 and point −2 is:

$$D_{12} = [(X_{11} - X_{21})^2 + (X_{12} - X_{22})^2]^{1/2}$$

The generalized formula for n variables is:

$$d_{ij} = \left[\sum_{k=1}^{n} (X_{ik} - X_{jk})^2 \right]^{1/2}$$

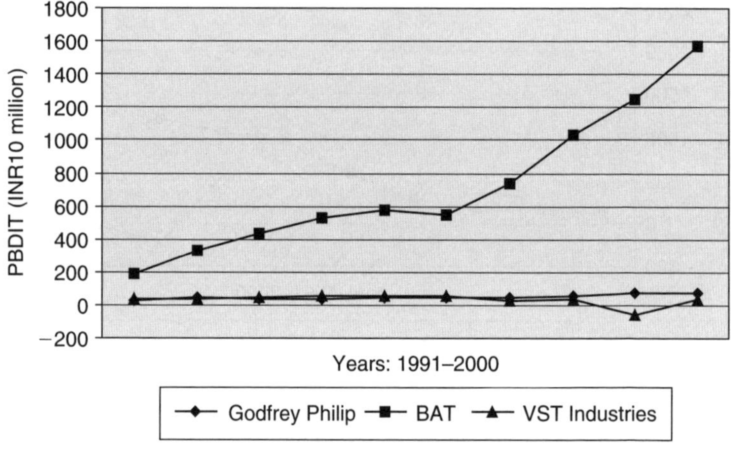

Source: Centre for Monitoring Indian Economy.

Figure 3.4 Performance of companies in tobacco industry

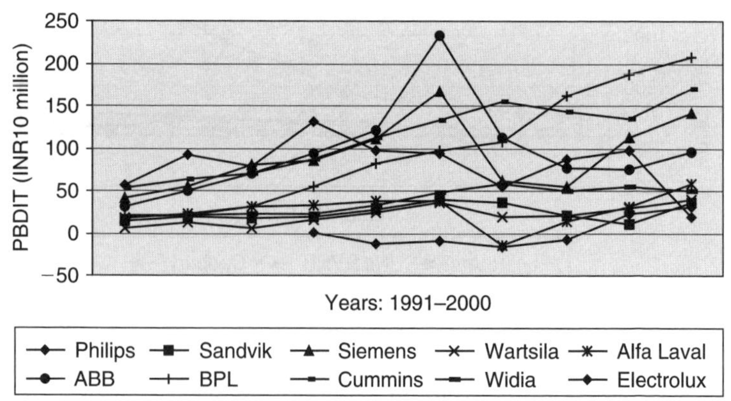

Source: Centre for Monitoring Indian Economy.

Figure 3.5 Performance of companies in electronics and machinery industries

where d_{ij} is the distance between the points i and j;
X_{ik} the coordinate of the point i along the axis k;
X_{jk} the coordinate of the point j along the axis k; and
n is the total number of variables (axes).

Clustering can also be done using correlation coefficients or association coefficients. In correlation coefficient, objects are grouped based on

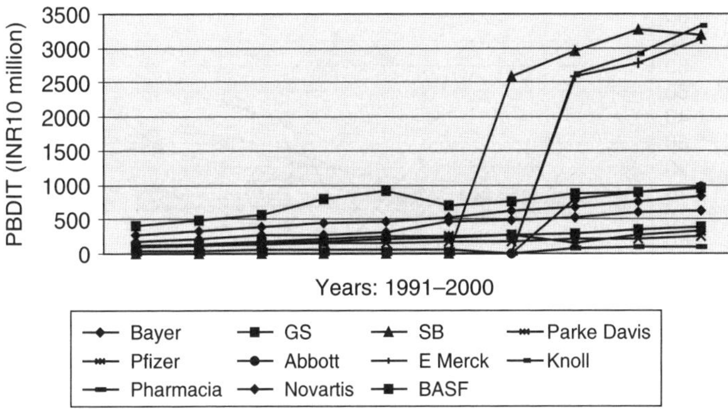

Source: Centre for Monitoring Indian Economy.

Figure 3.6 Performance of companies in pharmaceutical industry

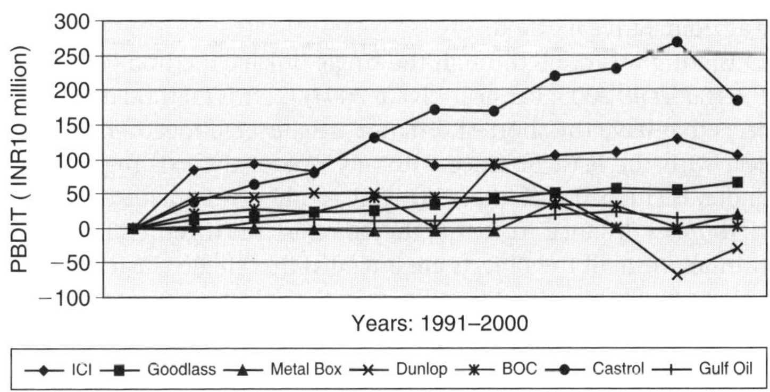

Source: Centre for Monitoring Indian Economy.

Figure 3.7 Performance of companies in lube oils, paints and chemical industries

the maximum value of similarity coefficient. In association coefficient, if a particular attribute is present in an object, the respective association coefficient is assumed as 1; otherwise, 0.

Hierarchical clustering method may be agglomerative or divisive. The agglomerative method is a bottom-up approach. Each object is assumed as a separate cluster. Objects are clustered in succession until a single cluster is formed. Divisive method is a top-down approach. Initially, all the objects are included in a single cluster, which is then divided into

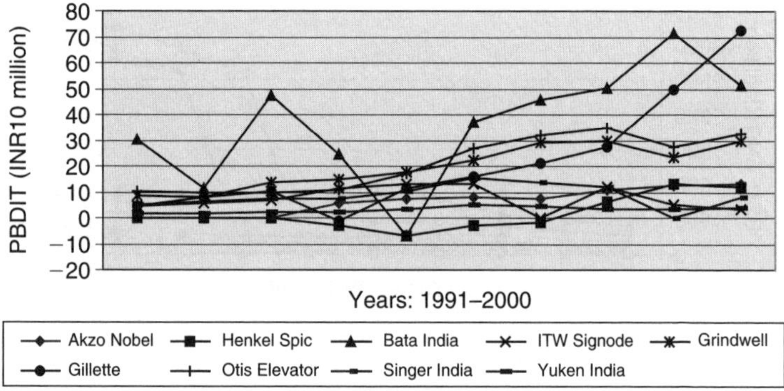

Source: Centre for Monitoring Indian Economy.
Figure 3.8 Performance of companies in other industries

sub-clusters until each object constitutes a cluster. The present study uses the agglomerative method.

Clustering was done through the single linkage method (Green *et al.* 1999; Hair *et al.* 2003; Panneerselvam 2004). In this method initially two objects that have the shortest distance are clustered together. If another object with the least distance with any one of the existing clusters is found, it is clubbed with that cluster; if another two unclustered objects with the least distance are found, they are clustered together. This process continues until all the objects are included in a single cluster. The final set of clusters is identified based on a certain clustering criterion, like a sudden jump in the distance while merging clusters.

All foreign companies were clustered on three financial parameters, i.e. sales, PBDIT and PAT. The clustering was done in 1990, 1995 and 2000. These years covered the last ten years of the study and a year prior to 1991, when major economic reforms were undertaken in India. Financial figures of all 51 foreign manufacturing companies registered in India were drawn from CMIE database (see Tables 3.7–3.9). Statistical Package for Social Sciences (SPSS 11) was used for clustering. As mentioned earlier, the single linkage method of the hierarchical clustering method was used for the test.

Hierarchical cluster analyses showed that in all the three years 1990, 1995 and 2000, the three companies – BAT, Unilever, and SMC – formed a distinctive cluster and the rest formed another distinct cluster. Figures 3.9–3.11 present the dendograms with the rescaled distance cluster combine for all the three years.

Table 3.5 Entry–size–performance measures – qualifying criteria

Industry	*Company*	*Entry before 1991*	*Sales Annual >= INR 10,000 million in year 2000*	*Consistent Performance (PBDIT & PAT)*
Tobacco	Godfrey Philips	√	×	×
	BAT	√	√	√
	VST Industries	√	×	×
Personal care & food	Vicks Product	√	×	×
	Proctor & Gamble	√	×	×
	Colgate–Palmolive	√	√	×
	Pepsi	√	×	×
	Coke	√	×	×
	Parry & Co.	√	×	×
	Unilever	√	√	√
	Cadbury	√	×	×
	Nestle	√	√	√
Automobile	General Motors	√	×	×
	Ford Motors	√	×	×
	British Leyland	√	√	×
	Daewoo Motors	√	√	×
	Toyota Motors	×	×	×
	Nissan Motors	×	×	×
	Honda Motors	×	×	×
	SMC	√	√	√
Pharmaceuticals	Parke Davis	√	×	×
	Pfizer	√	×	×
	Abbot Universals	√	×	×
	E Merck	√	√	×
	Glaxo	√	×	×
	Bayer	√	×	×
	Knoll	√	×	×
	BASF	√	×	×
	Novartis	√	×	×
	Pharmacia	√	×	×
Electronics & machinery	IBM	√	×	×
	Hewlett Packard	√	×	×
	Singer Machine	√	×	×
	Cummins	√	×	×
	Frick Co.	√	×	×
	ABB	√	×	×
	Siemens	√	×	×
	Philips	√	×	×
	Swedish Match	√	×	×
	Electrolux	√	×	×
	Alfa Laval	√	×	×

(Continued)

Table 3.5 (Continued)

Industry	*Company*	*Entry before 1991*	*Sales Annual >= INR 10,000 million in year 2000*	*Consistent Performance (PBDIT & PAT)*
	Sandvik Asia	√	×	×
	Precision Gears	√	×	×
	Wartsila Oy	√	×	×
	Forbes Gokak	√	×	×
	BPL	√	√	×
Lube oils, chemicals & paints	Caltex	√	×	×
	Standard Oil	√	×	×
	Castrol	√	√	×
	Gulf Oil	√	×	×
	Monsanto	√	×	×
	ICI	√	×	×
	Goodlass Nerolac	√	×	×
	BOC	√	×	×
	Akzo Nobel	√	×	×
	Henkel	√	×	×
Others	Ludlow Jute	√	×	×
	Otis Elevators	√	×	×
	Gillette India	√	×	×
	ITW Signode	√	×	×
	Binny & Co.	√	×	×
	Dunlop India	√	×	×
	Metal Box	√	×	×
	Continental AG	√	×	×
	Grindwell Norton	√	×	×
	Saint Gobain	√	×	×
	Yuken	√	×	×
	Bata	√	×	×

Table 3.6 Cases that satisfy selection parameters

Parameters/ company	Origin	Industry	Entry prior to 1991	Annual sales in year, 2000 >= 10,000 (million INR)	Consistent performance (1991–2000)
BAT[5]	UK/USA	Tobacco	√	√	√
SMC	Japan	Automobile	√	√	√
Unilever	UK/The Netherlands	Personal care and packaged food	√	√	√
Nestle	Switzerland	Personal care and packaged food	√	√	√

Table 3.7 Financials of foreign companies in India, 1990 (INR million)

Company	*Sales (manufacturing)*	*PBDIT*	*PAT*
ABB Ltd	91.7	14.3	4.13
Abbott India Ltd	80.95	10.71	4.73
Akzo Nobel Chemicals (India) Ltd	n.a.	n.a.	n.a.
Alfa Laval (India) Ltd	88.81	14.42	8.56
Asahi India Glass Ltd	24.41	6.51	2.04
BASF India Ltd	80.94	15.43	5.42
BOC India Ltd	163.27	20.95	0.25
BPL Ltd	184.36	14.75	4.35
Binny Ltd	108.84	6.91	–0.34
Cadbury India Ltd	108.35	15	5.55
Caltex Lubricants India Ltd	n.a.	n.a.	n.a.
Castrol India Ltd	112.97	12.04	4.64
Colgate–Palmolive (India) Ltd	272.61	53.03	25.05
Continental (chemicals & valves)	n.a.	n.a.	n.a.
Cummins India Ltd	227.16	35.72	10.91
Denso India Ltd	21.7	2.32	–0.78
Dunlop India Ltd	551.86	42.04	8.15
Electrolux Kelvinator Ltd	n.a.	n.a.	n.a.
Forbes Gokak Ltd	95.86	19.15	8.93
Frick India Ltd	9.16	0.65	0.23
Gillette India Ltd	17.06	3.03	1.07
Glaxosmithkline Pharmaceuticals	479.04	71.03	32.88
Godfrey Philips India Ltd	458.26	11.72	3.97
Grindwell Norton Ltd	54.05	5.94	1.73
Gulf Oil India Ltd	n.a.	n.a.	n.a.
Hindustan Lever Ltd/Unilever	1,175.69	123.75	54.97
Honda Siel Cars India Ltd	n.a.	n.a.	n.a.
ICI India Ltd	523.82	53.71	–12.18
ITC Ltd/BAT	1659.85	137.21	52.62
ITW Signode India Ltd	22.65	3.71	0.68
Kennametal Widia India Ltd	54.6	11.73	3.1
Maruti Udyog Ltd/SMC	1,180.86	107.12	41.99
Merck Ltd	65.12	7.45	3.38
Metal Box India Ltd	52.87	0.71	–13.78
Nestle India Ltd	252.09	34.46	14.63
Novartis India Ltd	246.31	32.14	13.75
Otis Elevator Co. (India) Ltd	42.83	8.48	3.57
Parke–Davis (India) Ltd [Merged]	88.5	8.99	5.15
Parry & Co. Ltd [Merged]	0	2.75	1.37
Pfizer Ltd	121.7	11.41	3.69
Pharmacia Healthcare Ltd	29.75	1.97	0.07
Phillips India Ltd	363.65	37.39	3.23

(*Continued*)

Table 3.7 (Continued)

Company	*Sales (manufacturing)*	*PBDIT*	*PAT*
Precision Gears Ltd	n.a.	n.a.	n.a.
Procter & Gamble	63.98	10.16	6.25
Punjab Anand Lamp Inds. Ltd	10.77	1.96	−0.78
Sandvik Asia Ltd	49.76	9.44	3.06
Siemens Ltd	381.46	56.01	13.58
Singer India Ltd	8.44	5.2	1.85
VST Industries Ltd	374.59	16.16	5.94
Wartsila India Ltd	6.2	1.44	0.16
Yuken India Ltd	7.4	1.17	0.33

Note: n.a. = not available.
Source: Centre for Monitoring Indian Economy.

Dissimilarities within the similarity

Some of the key differences in the three selected cases are shown in Table 3.10. They faced different sets of problems during their operations in India but emerged to be a single cluster of successful cases. The diversity in their characteristics makes the sample of cases representative of the population and makes the sample of cases robust and reliable for the analysis.

Methodology for studying individual cases

Each of the three cases was studied using the holistic framework of investments, as discussed in Chapter Three. Each case was analysed using Company Annual Reports (ITC Ltd, BAT's subsidiary, from 1955 to 2004; HLL, Unilever's subsidiary, from 1955 to 2004;[6] Maruti Udyog Ltd, SMC's subsidiary, from 1983 to 2004), Case Histories, Memorandum of Understanding, Company Prospectus (MUL's Prospectus submitted to Stock Exchange Board of India), Chairman's Annual Speeches (ITC Ltd and HLL) and other publications.

Interviews with senior executives of the companies (many of them retired) – selected on the basis of their involvement in strategic investment decisions – helped to get an insight into the decision-making process. See Tables 3.11–3.13 for the list of senior and top executives interviewed. The insights from the interviews enriched the investment data collected from various company sources. The author also attended the Annual General Meeting, 2004, of BAT to get a feel for the company in general.

Table 3.8 Financials of foreign companies in India, 1995 (INR million)

Company	*Sales (manufacturing)*	*PBDIT*	*PAT*
A B B Ltd	341.07	94.84	50.77
Abbott India Ltd	229.3	11.43	7.21
Akzo Nobel Chemicals (India)	13.93	7.26	3.6
Alfa Laval (India) Ltd	230.17	38.38	20.2
Asahi India Glass Ltd	58.67	11.86	4.18
BASF India Ltd	201.83	34.9	13.02
BOC India Ltd	244.39	44.07	20.81
BPL Ltd	837.59	82.8	48.39
Binny Ltd	182.17	30.8	20.26
Cadbury India Ltd	144.02	22.74	9.59
Caltex Lubricants India Ltd	n.a.	n.a.	n.a.
Castrol India Ltd	537.12	130.65	73.54
Colgate–Palmolive (India) Ltd	681.46	140.79	71.78
Continental (chemicals & valves)	1.21	0.31	0.07
Cummins India Ltd	544.39	111.87	49.92
Denso India Ltd	96.13	9.81	5.59
Dunlop India Ltd	725.12	50.28	12.56
Electrolux Kelvinator Ltd	9.74	−12.33	−14.53
Forbes Gokak Ltd	235.29	64.2	25.97
Frick India Ltd	22.4	1.03	0.7
Gillette India Ltd	69.33	11.67	5.09
Glaxosmithkline Pharmaceuticals	1,085.48	136.87	47.95
Godfrey Philips India Ltd	698.92	50.02	25.87
Grindwell Norton Ltd	119.24	17.69	6.13
Gulf Oil India Ltd	0	0.12	0.11
Hindustan Lever Ltd/Unilever	2,910.25	348.02	182.17
Honda Siel Cars India Ltd	n.a.	n.a.	n.a.
ICI India Ltd	563.72	90.63	33.15
ITC Ltd/BAT	3,696.37	573.47	261.64
ITW Signode India Ltd	108.8	25.87	9.77
Kennametal Widia India Ltd	101.06	22.72	7.65
Maruti Udyog Ltd/SMC	4,179.37	569.49	247.6
Merck Ltd	136.68	25.23	8
Metal Box India Ltd	19.13	−4.03	−5.24
Nestle India Ltd	697.88	80.39	40.47
Novartis India Ltd	282.2	157.71	121.7
Otis Elevator Co. (India) Ltd	81.95	17.04	8.63
Parke-Davis (India) Ltd	161.26	20.58	9.71
Parry & Co. Ltd [Merged]	6.26	3.47	0.43
Pfizer Ltd	225.27	23.48	8.1
Pharmacia Healthcare Ltd	55.27	5.96	2.88
Phillips India Ltd	365.87	130.86	44.23

(Continued)

Table 3.8 (Continued)

Company	*Sales (manufacturing)*	*PBDIT*	*PAT*
Precision Gears Ltd	n.a.	n.a.	n.a.
Procter & Gamble	219.03	24.43	15.52
Punjab Anand Lamp Inds. Ltd	38.73	8.05	3.26
Sandvik Asia Ltd	83.81	28.79	11.57
Siemens Ltd	716.07	110.24	35.12
Singer India Ltd	23.85	10.03	3.92
V S T Industries Ltd	599.63	58.07	26.15
Wartsila India Ltd	73.11	16.39	7.27
Yuken India Ltd	19.44	3.3	0.37

Note: n.a. = not available.
Source: Centre for Monitoring Indian Economy.

Multiple regression analyses were carried out to confirm the hypotheses for success of FDI in each of the three cases, to estimate how the investments in the following areas affected the annual sales and profit after tax.

(a) main business,
(b) complementary businesses, and
(c) other areas.

The Software Package for Social Sciences (SPSS) 11 was used for multiple regression analysis. Next, an aggregate multiple regression analysis was carried out taking the data of all the three cases from different industries. The objective was to determine the nature of impact of different investments on sales and PAT across the three cases. Subsequently, Artificial Neural Networking (ANN) analysis, a data-based model for analysis was carried out on the aggregate data to verify and triangulate the findings of regression, a model based analysis.

The econometric model for multiple regression analysis used was:

$$Y = C + \alpha X_1 + \beta X_2 + \gamma X_3$$

Where C is a constant, α, β, and γ are the coefficients of independent variables, i.e. X_1, X_2, and X_3.

In the next three chapters, each of the three cases, i.e. BAT, Unilever and SMC have been discussed in detail.

Table 3.9 Financials of foreign companies in India, 2000 (INR million)

Company	*Sales (manufacturing)*	*PBDIT*	*PAT*
ABB Ltd	508.32	74.62	37.2
Abbott India Ltd	322.72	85.23	68.51
Akzo Nobel Chemicals (India)	29.39	13.19	7.95
Alfa Laval (India) Ltd	191.4	31.14	21.34
Asahi India Glass Ltd	220.03	38.97	9.33
BASF India Ltd	366.07	67.5	19.98
BOC India Ltd	397.82	0.79	−79.44
BPL Ltd	2,014.67	207.31	107.13
Binny Ltd	17.97	−1.72	−16.38
Cadbury India Ltd	511.08	80.9	36.7
Caltex Lubricants India Ltd	n.a.	n.a.	n.a.
Castrol India Ltd	1,175.45	268.78	204.38
Colgate–Palmolive (India) Ltd	988.66	110.18	51.79
Continental (chemicals & valves)	0	0.01	−0.1
Cummins India Ltd	823.11	170.17	102.13
Denso India Ltd	197.22	13.51	1.43
Dunlop India Ltd	1.32	−30.58	−61.03
Electrolux Kelvinator Ltd	441.62	23.03	−5.15
Forbes Gokak Ltd	322.91	68.93	31.11
Frick India Ltd	29.66	6.35	4.07
Gillette India Ltd	121.45	49.74	19.42
Glaxo smithkline	1,608.16	286.62	174.67
Godfrey Phillips India Ltd	999.86	78.48	42.1
Grindwell Norton Ltd	184.8	29.62	13.86
Gulf Oil India Ltd	277.5	24.57	12.65
Hindustan Lever Ltd/Unilever	8,967.89	1,542.88	1,073.73
Honda Siel Cars India Ltd	628.78	0.97	−56.28
ICI India Ltd	767.48	104.6	64.15
ITC Ltd/BAT	7,279.61	1,575.19	792.44
ITW Signode India Ltd	149.51	24.49	14.55
Kennametal Widia India Ltd	217.44	55.67	27.88
Maruti Udyog Ltd/SMC	9,398.8	708.4	330.1
Merck Ltd	187.69	40.08	18.13
Metal Box India Ltd	n.a.	n.a.	n.a.
Nestle India Ltd	1,508.48	216.64	98.47
Novartis India Ltd	305.39	181.75	103.42
Otis Elevator Co. (India) Ltd	201.96	32.44	20.1
Parke-Davis (India) Ltd	228.78	87.42	62.45
Parry & Co. Ltd [Merged]	7.98	5.07	1.44
Pfizer Ltd	260.07	64.11	30.93
Pharmacia Healthcare Ltd	61	4.01	1.76
Phillips India Ltd	246.37	97.58	28.13

(Continued)

Table 3.9 (Continued)

Company	*Sales (manufacturing)*	*PBDIT*	*PAT*
Precision Gears Ltd	21.16	3.92	2.24
Procter & Gamble	468.26	92.43	56.86
Punjab Anand Lamp Inds. Ltd	103.39	20.09	11.83
Sandvik Asia Ltd	163.68	36.57	12.96
Siemens Ltd	819.96	112.44	35.12
Singer India Ltd	37.84	8.18	0.51
V S T Industries Ltd	662.16	40	15.7
Wartsila India Ltd	155.79	29.93	14.47
Yuken India Ltd	27.79	3.93	0.57

Note: n.a = not available.
Source: Centre for Monitoring Indian Economy.

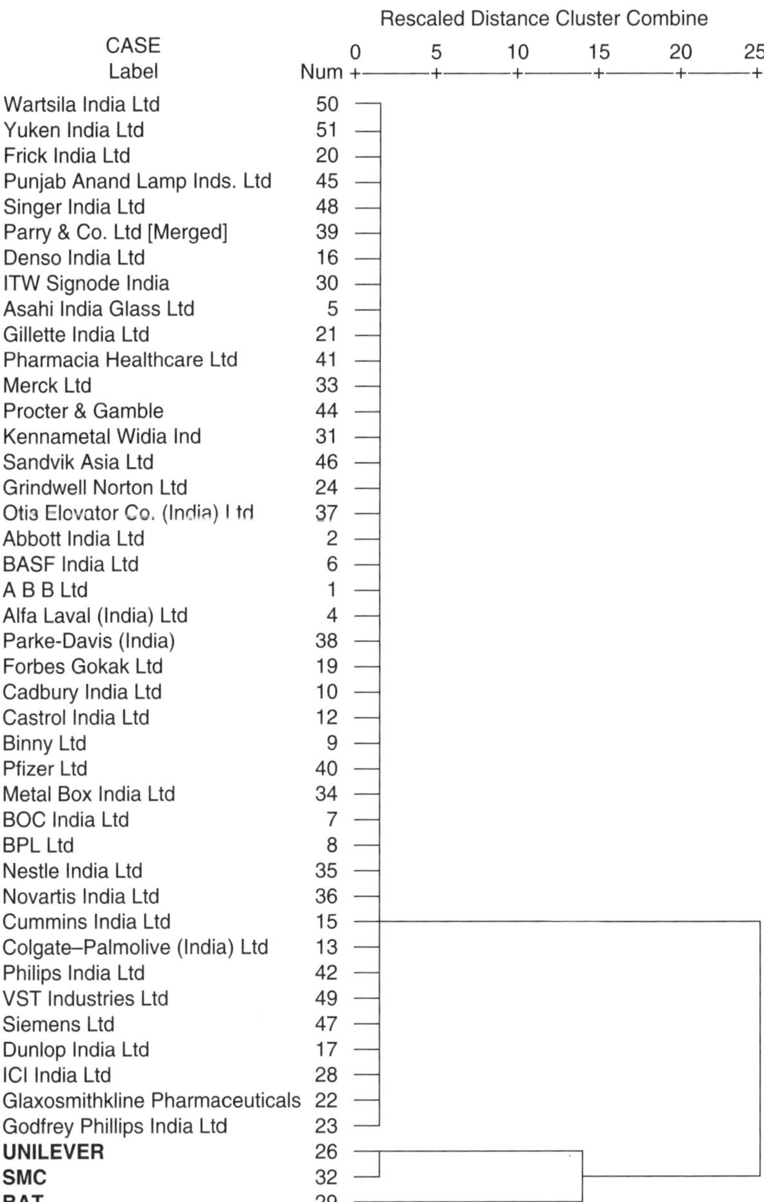

Figure 3.9 Hierarchical Cluster Analysis, 1990

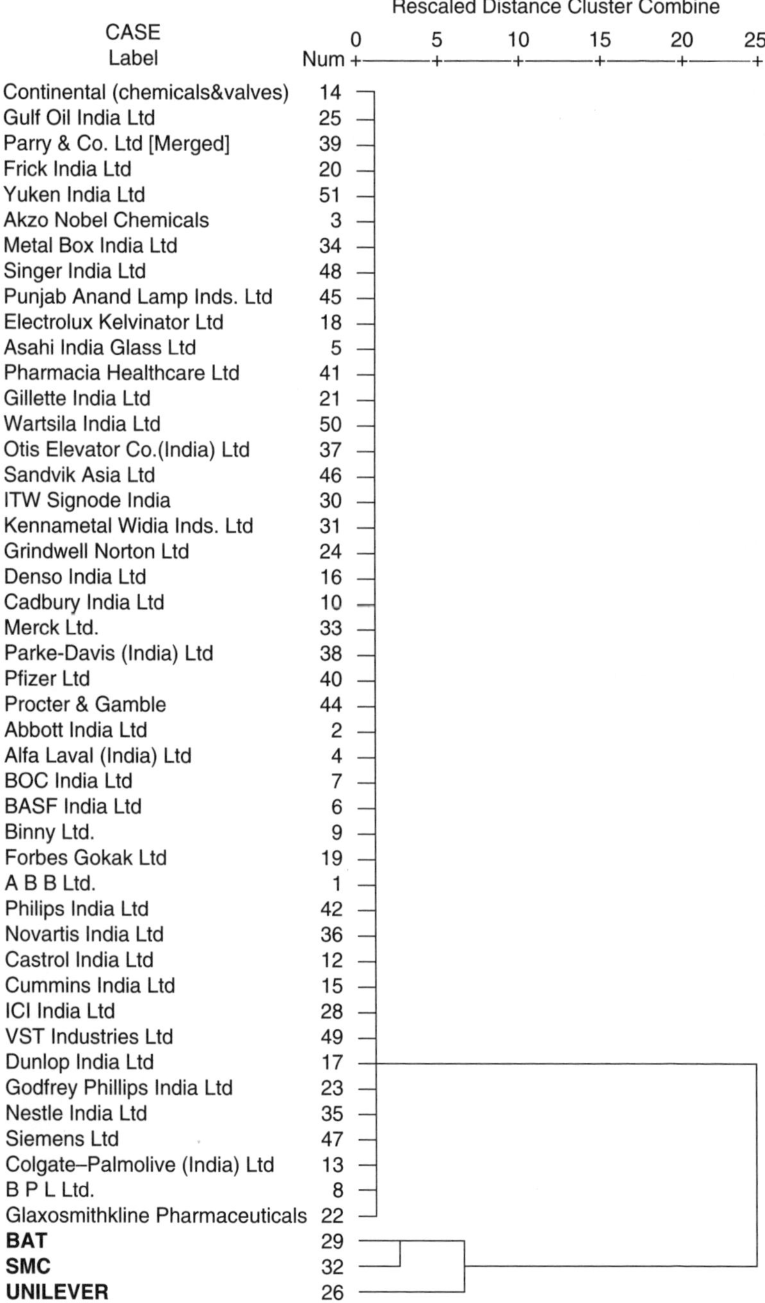

Figure 3.10 Hierarchical Cluster Analysis, 1995

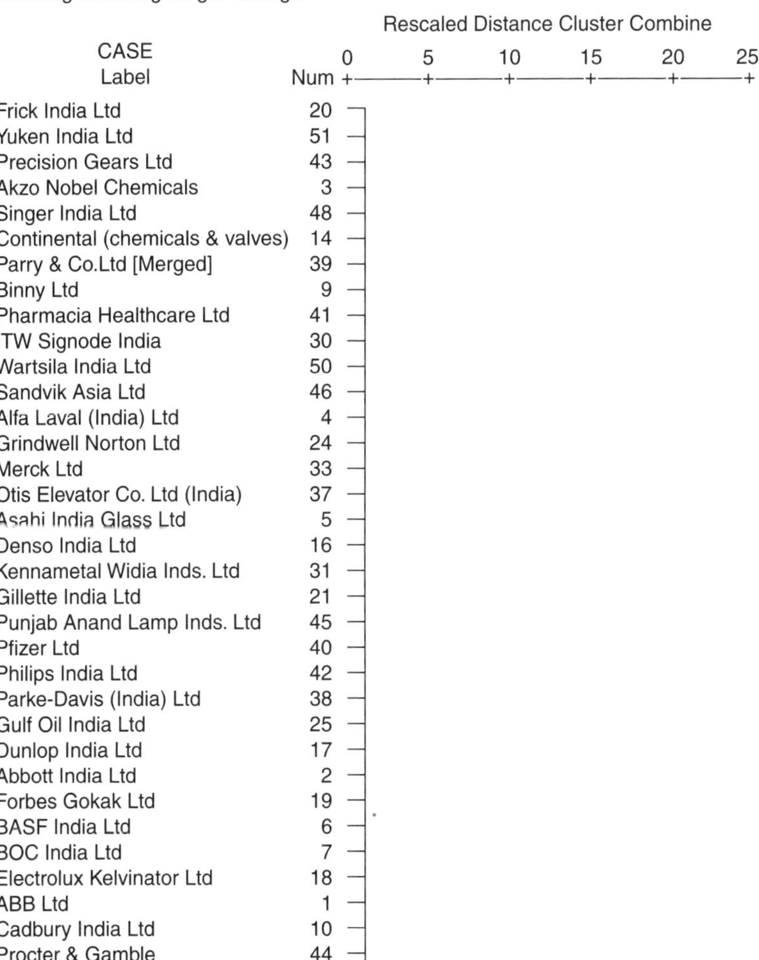

Figure 3.11 Hierarchical Cluster Analysis, 2000

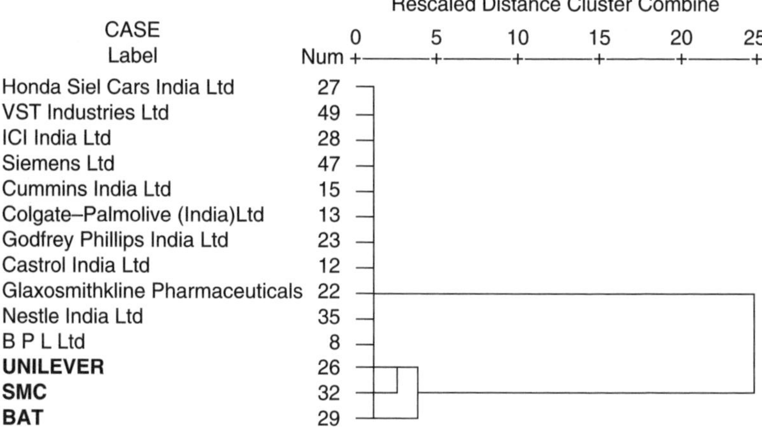

Figure 3.11 (*Continued*)

Table 3.10 Diversities of cases selected

Characteristic	*BAT*	*Unilever*	*SMC*
Country of origin	UK/USA	UK/The Netherlands	Japan
Industry	Tobacco	Personal care & packaged food	Automobile car
Year of operation in India	From 1906	From 1888	From 1983
Mode of entry	Wholly owned subsidiary/branch offices	Wholly owned subsidiary	Joint venture with GOI
Changes in ownership	Decreasing ownership from 100% to 32.5%	Ownership came down from 100% to 51% and remained steady at this level	Increasing ownership from 26% to 54.2%

Table 3.11 BAT/ITC senior and top executives interviewed*

Name	*Designation*	*Place and date of Interview*
Ajit N. Haksar	First Indian Chairman of ITC	New Delhi, 4 Mar. 2004
Samir Ghosh	Former Chairman	Kolkata, 9 July 2004
Champaka Basu	Historian of ITC	Kolkata, 9 July 2004
Abhijit Basu	Former Director	Kolkata, 9 July 2004
J. N. Sapru	Former Chairman	Kolkata, 9 July 2004
Anand Nayak	Executive Vice President, Corporate Human Resources	Kolkata, Mar. 2004
H. M. Jha	Vice President,Human Resources	New Delhi, 2 Mar. 2004
Rajendra Singhi	Deputy Company Secretary	Kolkata, 2 May 2003
L. N. Balaji	Head - Strategic Planning	Kolkata, 28 June 2004
Anjali Prasad	Assistant Company Secretary	Kolkata, 2 May 2003
Rajesh Poddar	Assistant Company Secretary	Bhubaneswar, Sept. 2003

Note: *The list of senior and top executives listed have served Unilerver/HLL in different capacities during 1949–2004.

Table 3.12 Unilever/HLL senior and top executives interviewed*

Name	*Designation*	*Date of Interview*
T. Thomas	Former Chairman of HLL, and Board Member, Unilever	Mumbai, 30 Oct. 2004
M.K. Sharma	Vice Chairman	Mumbai, 30 Oct. 2004
Dr S. Varadharajan	Former Head – R&D	New Delhi, 1 Aug. 2004
Dr A.S. Ganguly	Former Chairman	Mumbai, 29 Oct. 2004
S.M. Dutta	Former Chairman	Mumbai, June 2004
Dr NCB Nath	Scientist, R&D	Bangalore, July 2004
Irfan Khan	Former GM, Corporate Communication	Mumbai, 29 Oct. 2004
Debasis Ray	Manager, Corporate Communication	Mumbai, 30 Oct. 2004
Pramod Kabra	Group Controller	Mumbai, 28 Mar. 2003
John Mathew	General Manager, Control Assurance	Mumbai, 28 Mar. 2003

Note: *The list of senior and top executives listed have served BAT/ITC in different capacities during 1954–2004.

Table 3.13 SMC/MUL senior and top executives interviewed*

Name	*Designation*	*Place and date of interview*
Junzo Sugimori	Joint Managing Director, MUL and Director, SMC	Gurgaon (New Delhi) 22 Sept. 2003
R.C. Bhargava	Former Managing Director	Noida (New Delhi) 22 Sept. 2003
Keiji Nakajina	General Manager – Sumitomo	Tokyo, 9 Dec. 2001
Akino	Manager, Daihatsu Corporation	Kobe, April 2001
S. Ravi Aiyer	General Manager (Legal) & Company Secretary	New Delhi, July 2003
Prof. Amino Takahasi	Former General Manager, Honda Motors	Osaka, Jan. 2002

Note: *The list of senior and top executives listed have served SMC/MUL in different capacities during 1982–2004.

4
British American Tobacco, 1906–2004

BAT is a case of FDI in the tobacco and cigarette industry. This case is the oldest multinational enterprises among the three in terms of undertaking direct investment in India as early as 1907. This chapter discusses the process by which BAT developed a market for cigarettes in India from nothing. The analysis involves the study of nature and timing of investments of the company in its main business and complementary market functions, the manner in which it aligned itself to the requirements of the Government of India (GOI), the issues of localization of management and ownership and its financial performance in India. Most importantly, this case reveals how a foreign company invested across the value chain of its business and took full control of the cigarette industry in India even before 1970. Its strategy to localization of equity was so far sighted that today people in India perceive it to be an Indian company. The detailed confirmatory statistical analysis of the case, however, is provided in Chapter 7.

BAT owes its origin to James Buchanan Duke ('Buck Duke') who was in charge of a granulated tobacco factory in the USA in 1881. Buck Duke was the first to invest in cigarette machine in a big way when the other tobacco manufacturers were not interested in new technology. With this introduction of new technology, the sales of cigarettes increased to 837 million packets per year by 1889. At this time, Buck Duke's Educe Sons & Company produced 38 per cent of the total annual production in the US. Buck Duke also engineered the amalgamation of the other four companies with his company to form American Tobacco Company (ATC) with a capital stock of US$ 25 million. In due course, ATC under the leadership of Buck Duke absorbed nearly 200 small companies.

By the 1890s there were 13 main family businesses in the British market dealing in tobacco. Buck Duke offered £800,000 to Ogdens of Liverpool, a major cigarette manufacturer in Britain. With this move ATC had started a tobacco war in Britain. Taking into account this threat from ATC, W.D & H.O. Wills gathered the other players in Britain to form the Imperial Tobacco Company (ITC) (of Great Britain & Ireland) with Sir William Henry Wills as chairman. Once ITC was formed, the British tobacco companies shifted the price war to the US market by cutting the price of their cigarettes in the American market. ATC tried to match the price cutting and the price war continued for a while both in the American and British markets. The dwindling profits of the American and British tobacc companies as a result of the price war brought these two companies to the negotiating table.

In September 1902 the two companies agreed to stop this self-damaging exercise, and agreed to pull out from each other's domestic market. Also, to trade in their products outside their home territory they formed BAT, with ATC owning 67 per cent stock of the company. BAT was registered in the United Kingdom and Buck Duke became its first chairman (Basu 1988). With the formation of the new company Jellicoe and Page of BAT came to India in 1906 with two major cigarette brands, W.D. & H.O. Wills and Scissors.

Nature and timing of investments

Investments in local manufacturing and complementary businesses

From just trading in cigarettes BAT quickly graduated to the manufacture of cigarettes, setting up a cigarette factory in Monghyr, Bihar in 1907 through Peninsular Tobacco. In another five years it invested in local leaf processing and leaf growing. Subsequently, it steadily invested in several related areas of the cigarette business such as printing and packaging, duplex board, tissue paper, aluminium foil, cigarette-rolling machine, fibreboard container and filter rods. By 1970 BAT had invested in all the complementary businesses associated with cigarettes in India.

In retrospect, BAT chose to commit very early in India. Its investments in different market functions enabled it to manufacture cigarettes at a price affordable to local customers. Investing in building awareness of its products also promoted its success. Investments in building a distribution network was yet another area of importance.

In post-independence India ITC, BAT's subsidiary and the associate company, has been investing consistently in its main and complementary businesses. The annual Gross Block as reported in the company balance sheet has been taken as investment in main business. Investments

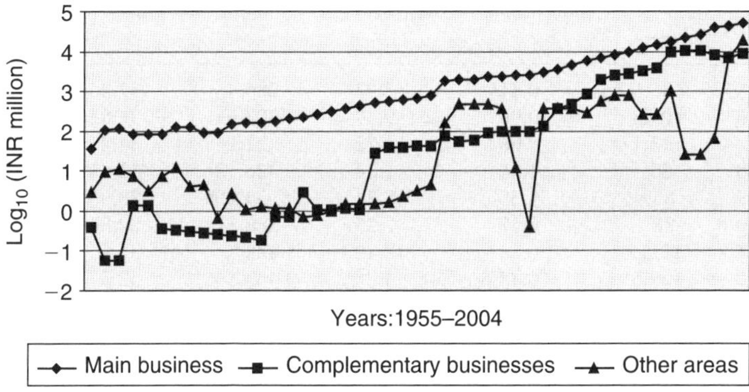

Source: ITC Ltd, Annual Reports, 1955–2004.

Figure 4.1 BAT/ITC business investments, 1955–2004

in subsidiary companies and other related businesses have been taken as investments in complementary businesses. Investments in government securities and other trade investments have been considered to be investment in others. During 1955–2004, while investing steadily in its main business, it had gradually begun to invest in its complementary businesses with a greater emphasis during the 1960s–1970s. Investments in other areas have fluctuated highly (see Figure 4.1). The multiple regression analyses of these investments with the sales and profit after tax, will be discussed in Chapter 7. For detailed data of actual investments and financial indicators see Table 4.1.

The ownership pattern and organizational structure of BAT in India has undergone several changes from the inception of BAT in 1902 upto the present stage. The consolidation process of BAT in India began upon the arrival of Jellicoe and Page of BAT in 1906. ITC from Britain and American Tobacco Company from USA had individual interests in the selling of cigarettes, tobacco leaf purchase and local manufacturing of cigarettes by around 1906. By 1910s, the partners of BAT had several investments in manufacturing, selling and leaf purchase of cigarette and tobacco business in India.

ATC had invested through Peninsular Tobacco (registered in London, 1905) in a cigarette manufacturing facility in Monghyr, India. ITC sold branded cigarettes in India through Dominion Tobacco (registered in London), Imperial Tobacco (registered in Calcutta, 1910) and Arcadian Tobacco (registered in London, 1913). Investment in Tobacco Leaf had begun through Indian Leaf Tobacco in 1912 with its registered office in Calcutta. Through these various business units, BAT manufactured and

Table 4.1 BAT/ITC investments and performance indicators, 1955–2004 (in million INR)

Year	*Main business*	*Complementary*	*Others*	*Sales*	*PBDIT*	*PAT*
1955	35.5	0.41	2.97	284.4	37.36	16.89
1956	109.3	0.06	9.49	303.64	36.82	18.67
1957	113.1	0.06	11.22	321.16	34.4	13.79
1958	83	1.36	7.34	326.12	31.45	13.2
1959	83.9	1.33	3.24	34.204	28.93	11.5
1960	86	0.37	7.25	368.81	29.84	14.16
1961	127	0.34	12.18	428	35.9	18.8
1962	129.5	0.32	4.25	463.3	32.3	14.6
1963	87.7	0.29	4.31	504.1	44.6	18
1964	91.4	0.27	0.63	558.1	28.9	9.9
1965	149.1	0.24	2.7	598	43.2	16.2
1966	156.7	0.22	1.08	696.3	48.7	20.6
1967	166.7	0.19	1.23	822	40.9	20.6
1968	180.7	0.73	1.13	1,078.8	66.3	26.6
1969	202.2	0.71	1.19	1,262.6	80.4	35.9
1970	219.8	2.98	0.68	1,451	91.2	32.3
1971	n.a.	n.a.	n.a.	1,677.8	89.4	35.7
1972	n.a.	n.a.	n.a.	2,000.7	96.9	40.3
1973	n.a.	n.a.	n.a.	2,171.9	91.9	23.3
1974	257.4	1.08	0.79	2,744.2	119.5	39.2
1975	310.1	1.11	0.99	3,251.1	66.3	26.6
1976	363.1	1.126	1.526	3,611.6	80.4	35.9
1977	445.3	1.061	1.518	3,668.8	91.2	32.3
1978	533.3	28.086	1.517	3,846.7	89.4	35.7
1979	575.1	39.005	1.607	4,228.7	96.9	40.3
1980	598.8	38.97	2.336	4,588	91.9	23.3
1981	656.9	42.17	3.263	4,366.1	119.5	39.2
1982	759.1	42.3	4.4	5,886.2	298.9	77.7
1983	1,891.5	74.7	162.5	7,659.3	426.7	244.7
1984	1,930.2	56.6	466.7	6,981.8	312	145.8
1985	1,980.8	57.8	482.1	8,119.8	333.3	151.4
1986	2,289.3	88.9	482.5	9,423.9	365.3	431.2
1987	2,362.2	94.21	378	10,651.6	493.1	439.4
1988	2,524.3	101.21	12.5	12,004.4	518.6	247.9
1989	2,638	101.3	0.4	10,676.4	530	292
1990	2,988	131.3	371	18,273	989.3	526.2
1991	3,509.9	366.51	371.3	23,163.8	1,322	775.2
1992	4,535.8	472.2	371.7	30,170.8	2,216.6	2,216.6
1993	5,622.8	840	280	38,096.7	2,828.8	1,553.1
1994	7,119	1,995.1	565.8	42,801.5	3,763.6	2,063.2
1995	8,297.9	2,536.6	779.2	47,093	4,395.1	2,616.4
1996	9,436.4	2,660.9	779.1	51,878.6	5,838.7	2,610.8
1997	12,741.5	32,60.6	275.2	59,906	7,697.7	3,469
1998	14,386.3	3,895.8	273.1	69,237.5	9,583.5	5,262
1999	17,183.1	9,845.7	1,019.6	77,009.6	11,944.1	6,234.2
2000	21,454.9	10,113.6	26.7	80,693.7	14,600.3	7,924.4
2001	26,680.8	10,310.8	26.3	88,271.1	18,361.5	10,062.6
2002	40,818.5	8,308.4	62.6	99,824.6	20,456.4	11,897.2
2003	44,156.1	7,071.8	6,738.1	111,944.7	23,233.7	13,713.5
2004	50,546.8	9,178.2	19,257.9	120,399.2	25,854.7	15,928.5

Note: n.a. = not available
Source: ITC Ltd, Annual Reports, 1955–2004.

sold various brands of cigarettes in India. Knowing the importance of a steady supply of tobacco leaf, BAT was also involved in distribution and trade of leaf tobacco.

The ownership pattern and organizational structure had undergone changes by 1953. BAT, through a series of acquisitions of businesses in the industry, had emerged as the biggest player in the Indian tobacco and cigarette business. BAT controlled virtually the entire tobacco and cigarette business in India by wholly owning firms such as Raleigh, Printers (India), Exchange Investment and Tobacco (India). These firms, in turn, controlled the various tobacco and cigarette companies in India.

Through Raleigh, BAT controlled 96.2 per cent of ITC, which, in turn, controlled the cigarette factories in Monghyr, Bangalore, Saharanpur, Kidderpore and Parel. ITC also controlled the printing factories in Monghyr and Tiruvottiyur. It was also responsible for the various brands it manufactured and marketed in India. The balance of 3.8 per cent of ITC was owned by the Carreras Tobacco Company of London. BAT wholly owned Indian Leaf Tobacco Development (ILTD) through Exchange Investment. BAT also held shares of its competitors such as All India Tobacco and Vazir Sultan Tobacco through Tobacco (India) and Printers (India).

By 1975, BAT held all its business interests through ITC and ILTD. BAT held 60 per cent of the shares in ITC Ltd but had 100 per cent equity in ILTD, the unit that was in tobacco leaf development in India. All the other business functions, including cigarette factories, printing factories, brands, selling and distribution were all bought under ITC. The hotels and export business, the new business ventures in the seventies were also under ITC.

Finally, by 2004, BAT brought all its businesses in India under a single entity, Tobacco (Manufacturer) India. Through Tobacco (Manufacturers) India, BAT held only 26.73 per cent equity of ITC. All the business functions and subsidiaries including ILTD, manufacturing, printing, brands, selling and distribution came under ITC Ltd. The company by now had also expanded to new business such as hotels, exports, and retailing. Indian financial institutions held 38.38 per cent, private Indian investors held 14.9 per cent, foreign financial Institutions held 9.6 per cent, Rothmans held 1.39 per cent equity and Myddleton Investments held 4.36 per cent equity – the balance of equity in ITC Ltd was held by others (see Chart 4.1, Tables 4.10 and 4.11 for the shareholding pattern in ITC).

The investment pattern of BAT in India clearly shows that the company had invested consistently along the value chain of the tobacco and cigarette business by 1970. It adopted various means for merging the

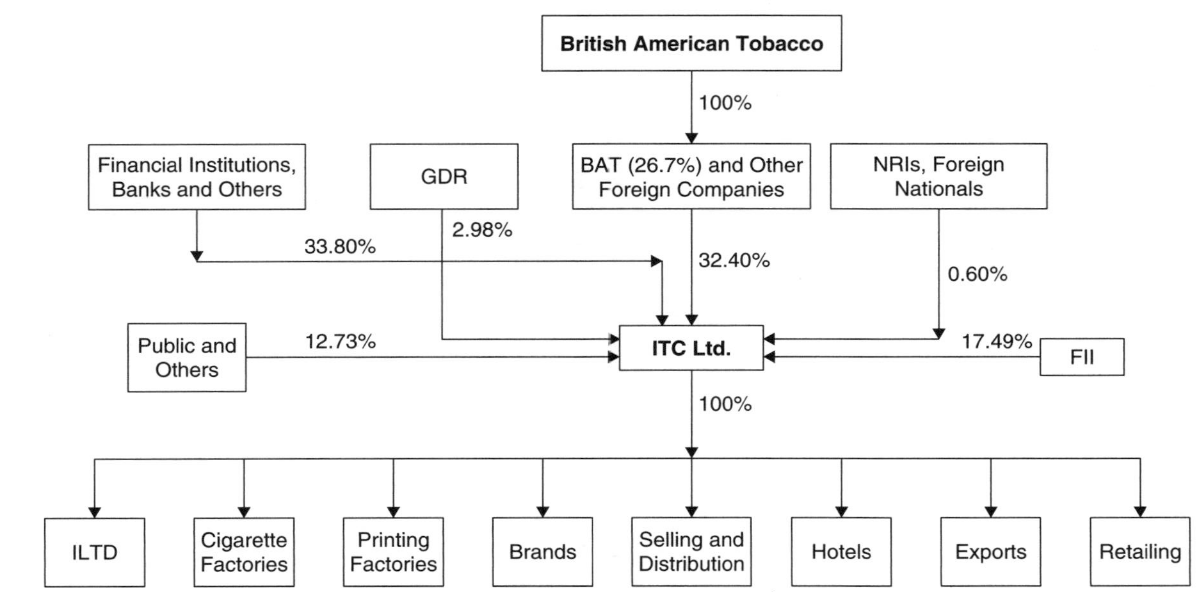

Chart 4.1 BAT investment and shareholding pattern, 2004–2005

business units of ATC and ITC, green field investments and also through acquisitions of local competitors. BAT further invested in its business value chain by developing and promoting subsidiary, associate and joint venture partners (see Table 4.2). As many as twenty wholly to partly

Table 4.2 BAT/ITC investments in complementary businesses

Wholly partly owned subsidiaries	
1.	ITC Hotels Ltd
2.	Srinivasa Resorts Ltd
3.	Fortune Park Hotels Ltd
4.	Bay Islands Hotels Ltd
5.	ITC Infortech India Ltd
6.	ITC Infotech Ltd, UK
7.	ITC Infotech (USA), Inc
8.	Russel Credit Ltd
9.	Greenacre Holdings Ltd
10.	Wills Corporation Ltd
11.	Gold Flake Corporation Ltd
12.	Landbase India Ltd
13.	BFIL Finance Ltd
14.	MRR Trading & investment Company Ltd
15.	Surya Nepal Private Ltd, Nepal
16.	ITC Global Holding Pvt Ltd
17.	BFIL Securities Ltd
18.	ITC Sangeet Research Academy
19.	ITC Education Trust
20.	ITC Rural Development Trust
Associates	
1.	Ansal Hotels Ltd
2.	Gujurat Hotels Ltd
3.	Megatop Financial Services and Leasing Ltd
4.	Newdeal Finance and Investment Ltd
5.	Peninsular Investments Ltd
6.	Russell Investments Ltd
7.	Asia Tobacco Company Ltd
8.	Classic Tobacco Company Ltd
9.	International Travel House Ltd
10.	Tobacco Manufacturers (India) Ltd, UK
Joint venture	
1.	King Maker Marketing Inc., USA
2.	ITC Filtrona Ltd
3.	Maharaja Heritage Resorts Ltd
4.	CL13 e-services Ltd

Source: ITC Ltd, Annual Reports, 1955–2004.

owned subsidiaries, ten associate firms and four joint ventures were part of the company. The network spread into industries such as cigarettes, tobacco, hotel, information technology, finances and services and social development sector. The development of its supply and intermediary network contributed to a smooth business operation and market linkage that were critical for growth and performance of the company.

Investment in local management

Most of ITC's serving executives consider that ITC has been an Indian company.[1] BAT gradually reduced the number of expatriates in its Indian operation: it was expensive to find British managers especially after the Second World War. The increase in Indian staffing in management also served to satisfy the GOI. Indian managers in ITC subsequently lobbied for the cigarette and tobacco business in India.

Abdul Rub Sardar Hussain was the first to be inducted as covenanted Indian Assistant on 1 September 1934. By 1947, there were 121 Indian managers comprising 44 per cent of the management. Indian managers were treated on equal terms with the expatriates by the middle of the 1960s. The expatriates received only the additional amount on overseas allowance. In 1964 the company instituted a pension for every worker. There were only seven expatriates in the company by 1972. The last Englishman, Tonny Drayton left in September 1979. Today, there are two British personnel, C.R. Green and J.B. Stevens as BAT's representatives on the Board of ITC.

Further, moving in the direction of indianization the company changed its name from Imperial Tobacco Co. of India Ltd to India Tobacco Limited in 1970, to ITC Limited in 1974, and ITC Ltd in 2001. Given the nature of its business and the worldwide opposition to tobacco, the company has successfully managed to create a system by which the local managers and stakeholders guard the business in the Indian context.

Investments in sourcing, marketing and distribution

The leaf tobacco business existed in India long before BAT arrived on the scene, but much of the production and selling was local. Only a few people used granulated tobacco. British and American companies such as ITC, Dominion, Arcadian, and Peninsular Tobacco traded only some of their brands in India.

BAT worked on creating its supply systems for procuring leaf tobacco, building awareness of granulated tobacco among the masses and developing the distribution systems. For procurement of raw materials it set up tobacco re-drying machines in Shahpur and Khajauli in 1908 and another in Dal Singsuai in 1912. A new business unit, Indian Leaf Tobacco, was set up in 1912 to purchase, distribute and trade tobacco leaf. This subsidiary became ILTD and subsequently part of ITC. This unit has been BAT's supply arm of leaf tobacco. ILTD invested a great deal to develop a good variety of leaf tobacco in India.

Initially, BAT sold its brands through Dominion Tobacco, registered in London. On 24 August 1910 it set up its selling unit in India, Imperial Tobacco Co. of India Ltd. To promote smoking ITC gave away free samples in the range of 50,000–100,000 cigarettes per district salesman per month. Lucky dips and cigarette shies were organized in regular stalls, weekly markets and occasional large gatherings of people in small towns during various religious festivals and the harvest season to popularize cigarette smoking. After cigarette advertising was banned, the company continued its promotional campaigns by sponsoring several arts, music and sport activities.

The company has also steadily invested in sales and distribution activities. Its products are now available in more than a million outlets in India. From selling through other companies' retail outlets it has moved to setting up its own lifestyle retail outlets and stores. Sales branches, production centres, cigarette factories, and other business units are located across the country (see Table 4.3). Considering the cigarette business alone, there have been as many as six factories, two printing and packing units and eight sales branches. For tobacco, there have been five production centres, thirteen marketing offices and a research centre. It has developed several brands in cigarettes, tobacco and other businesses. The company has acquired or developed a large number of brands over the years (see Table 4.4).

Timing of investment

The timing of investment adopted by the company has been particularly strategic and many foreign firms in a developing context could learn a lot from the way BAT has behaved in India. It began with sales and manufacturing and very soon invested in leaf procurement and leaf growing within India. Subsequently, it internalized printing, packaging, and production of items such as paper, aluminium foil, duplex and fibre boards and filter rods. Criticality of the market function determined the timing of investment by the company. Through this process, it could achieve better efficiency and control of its business operation with a smaller quantum of investment from time to time. By 1963, the company had invested across the value chain of its cigarette and tobacco business

Table 4.3 Branch location of different ITC businesses

Business function	*Locations*
	Cigarette
Sales Branches	Jullundur, Delhi, Kanpur, Patna, Jalpaiguri, Gauhati, Ahmedabad, Jabalpur, Calcutta, Bombay, Visakhapatnam, Madras, Coimbatore
Cigarette Factories	Saharanpur, Monghyr, Kidderpore, Parel, Bangalore, Bangalore(N), Munger, Kolkata
Printing & Packaging Factories	Monghyr, Tiruvottiyur *Production:* Monghyr, Tiruvottiyur *Marketing:* Bangalore, Bombay, Calcutta, Delhi, Madras, Hyderabad
	Tobacco
Production	Kidderpore, Parel, Saharanpur, Monghyr, Bangalore
Marketing	Calcutta,Bombay,Delhi, Madras, Patna, Gauhati, Ahmedabad, Jabalpur, Jullundur, Kanpur, Visakhapatnam, Coimbatore, Bangalore, Hyderabad, Nagpur, Saharanpur
District Offices-Marketing	Bombay(W), Calcutta(E), Delhi(N), Kanpur(C) , Madras (S)
Research	Bangalore
	Tobacco Leaf
Main Offices	Calcutta, Guntur, Mysore
L. P. Plants	Anaparti, Chirala
Research	Hunsur, Rajahmundry
Leaf Buying & Handling Dept.	Andhra, Gujarat, Karnataka
	Life Style Retail Outlet & Stores
Retail Outlet	New Delhi
Stores	*Club Stores:* New Delhi, Kolkata, Gurgaon, Bangalore, Coimbatore, Mumbai, Jamshedpur, *W.L Stores:* Agra, Ahmedabad, Ambala, Amritsar, Aurangabad, Bangalore, Baroda, Bareilly, Belgaum, Bhopal, Bhubaneswar, Chandigarh, Chennai(2), Coimbatore, Dehradun, Ernakulam, Goa, Hyderabad, Indore, Jaipur, Jallandhar, Jammu, Kanpur, Kolkata, Kozhikode, Ludhiana, Lucknow, Mangalore, Mumbai(4), N Delhi(4),Nagpur, Noida, Pune, Pondicherry, Ranchi, Surat, Secundarabad, Vishakhapatnam, Thiruvananthapuram, Trichy
Design & Technology	Haryana

Source: ITC Ltd, Annual Reports, 1955–2004.

Table 4.4 BAT/ITC manufactured brands

Year	*Brand Name*
	Smoking tobacco
As on 1965	Capstan Navy Cut Medium Flake, Capstan Navy Cut Fine Cut, Wills Flake, Ogden's Coolie Cut Plug, Bears' Virginia Bird's Eye, Wills Black Prince
As on 1969	Wills Capstan Navy Cut Medium, Wills Capstan Navy cut Medium Fine cut, Ogden's Coolie Cut Plug, Wills Navy Cut, Wills Navy Cut, Wills Navy Cut Fine Cut, Bears' Virgina Bird's Eye, Wills Black Prince
As on 1975	Capstan Navy Cut Medium, Capstan Navy Cut Medium Fine Cut, Wills navy Cut, Wills Navy Cut Fine Cut.
	Cigarettes
As on 1965	India Plain, India Plain Filter Tipped, Player's No.3, The Three Castles, Player's Gold Leaf Filter Tipped, Player's Medium, Wills Gold Flake, Capstan Medium, Wills Navy Cut Plain, Wills Navy Cut Filter Tipped, Berkeley, Scissors, Woodbine, Simla Filter Tipped, Savoy Filter Tipped, Embassy, Player's Navy Blue, Lex, Vanraj Tipped, Imperial Gold Flake, Honeydew, Mitchell's Sovereign Gold Flake, Akbar Shah, Bears' Specials, Elephant, Passing show plain, Passing show plain tipped, Star, King Stork, Red Lamp, Bat, Motor, Pedro, Red Bird Plain, Red Bird Tipped, Telegraph, Tiger, Battle Ax, Golden Tree
Addition by 1969	India Kings Filter Tipped, Player's Gold Leaf Filter Tipped, Wills Gold Leaf Filter Tipped, Player's Navy Cut Medium, Wills Capstan Medium, Wills Filter Kings, Wills Filter Tipped, Wills Navy Cut, Wills Capstan magnum, Wills Bristol Filter, Windsor Filter Tipped, Wills Berkeley, Wills Scissors, Wills 99, Wills Embassy, Bears' Honeydew, Bears' Elephant, Passing Show Tipped, Passing Show, Wills Star, Red Bird Tipped, Red Bird
Addition by 1975	Three Castles Filter Kings, Wills Flake Filter Kings, Wills Flake Filter Tipped, Wills Bristol Filter Tipped, Wills Virginia Filter Tipped, Chinar Filter Tipped, Plaza Filter Tipped, Wild Woodbine, Hunter Filter Tipped, Plaza Special, Star, Red Lamp, Sovereign Gold Flake, Pedro, Passing Show Plain, Metro, Guinea Gold
Addition by 2000	Three Castles Mild Filter Kings, Gold Crest Filter Tipped, Chinar Filter Kings, Scissors Standard, Flight, India Kings, Classic, Insignia, Berkeley, Checkers, Hi Val

Source: ITC Ltd, Annual Reports, 1955–2004.

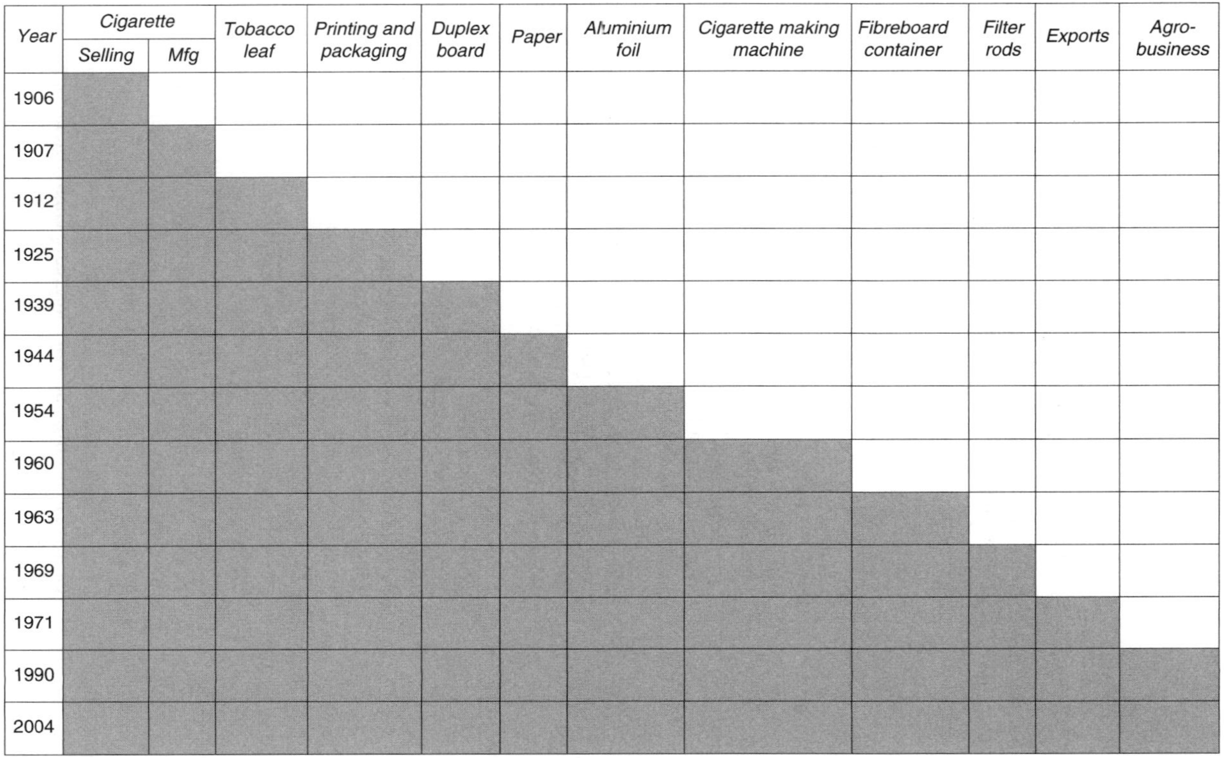

Year	Cigarette		Tobacco leaf	Printing and packaging	Duplex board	Paper	Aluminium foil	Cigarette making machine	Fibreboard container	Filter rods	Exports	Agro-business
	Selling	Mfg										
1906												
1907												
1912												
1925												
1939												
1944												
1954												
1960												
1963												
1969												
1971												
1990												
2004												

Chart 4.2 BAT/ITC timing of investment in various complementary businesses

in India (see Chart 4.2). The shaded portions in Chart 4.2 show the period of investment in each respective product or business function.

As a multinational enterprise BAT has uniquely preferred its local interest; to its global interests. From its main concern in tobacco, it has allowed the Indian subsidiary/associate ITC to diversify into areas such as hotels, marine products, exports, agri-business, and retailing (see Table 4.5). As the company had full control over the value chain of tobacco and cigarette business, it started to invest in other green field areas. While it may appear that ITC has de-emphasized the tobacco business in the recent years, tobacco and cigarette continue to be the core of its business accounting for about 80 per cent to its total revenue.

Integration of business goals to host country's national goals

Independent India's concern has been on generating employment, substituting imports by local production, increasing foreign exchange reserve through increasing exports, and adding private investment in some of the core industries and sectors such as handloom, handicraft, paper, vegetable oils, vanaspati, cement, fertilizers, heavy chemicals machine tools, research for development of new processes, and investment in backward areas. The Five Year Plan documents beginning in 1951 reflect these developmental goals (see Table 4.5). Many foreign companies decided to wind up operations in India when the government imposed certain conditions such as local production, investment in core sectors and export earnings in the 1960s and the 1970s. BAT swam against this current and invested heavily in India, ingeniously integrating its objectives with India's national objectives.

Growing and processing tobacco leaf generated direct employment among thousands of farmers and traders in the rural sector. ITC set up Triveni Handloom Ltd as a subsidiary unit in 1977, with a head office at Kanpur. The production centre at Saharanpur had 35 looms, which was increased to 300 within a year. ITC also built two showrooms at Badohi and Varanasi. The sales turnover increased from INR 0.27 million to INR 1.8 million. Almost 1800 local people were employed in this process, earning the company additional goodwill of both the government and the local people.

BAT also invested in areas of import substitution and in core sectors such as paper, paperboard, and hotels. Haksar (1993), reflecting on his 34 years of experience in ITC, indicated that BAT/ITC had a clear plan to align its business with the goals of the country. Table 4.6 presents a glimpse of this strategy and how the company developed its corporate

Table 4.5 Extracts from India's five-year plans, 1951–90

First plan (*1951–55*)

1. Fuller utilization of existing capacity in producer goods–industries such as jute and plywood and consumer goods–industries such as cotton textiles, sugar, *soap, vanaspati,* paints and varnishes
2. Expansion of capacity in capital and producer goods–industries such as iron and steel, aluminium *cement, fertilizers, heavy chemicals, machine tools,* etc.
3. Completion of industrial units on which a part of the capital expenditure has already been incurred, and establishment of new plants, which would lend strength to the industrial structure by rectifying as far as resources permit the existing lacunae and drawbacks, e.g. manufacture of sulphur from gypsum, chemical pulp for rayon, etc.
4. *Research into development of new processes*
5. *Investment in backward areas*
6. *Export promotion*

Second plan (*1956–61*)

1. Increased production of iron and steel and of *heavy chemicals, including nitrogenous fertilizers,* and development of heavy engineering and machine building industries
2. Expansion of capacity in respect of other developmental commodities and producer goods such as aluminium, *cement,* chemical pulp, dyestuffs and phosphatic *fertilizers,* and of essential drugs
3. Village industries: *handicraft, coir industry* & sericulture
4. *Stepping up Indian content of cars to 80%*
5. Disposal of industries
6. Modernization of *Rural industries*
7. Modernization and re-equipment of important national industries that had already come into existence, such as jute and cotton textiles and sugar
8. Fuller utilization of existing installed capacity in industries where there were wide gaps between capacity and production
9. Expansion of capacity for consumer goods keeping in view the requirements of common production programmes and the *production targets for the decentralized sector of industry*
10. *Export promotion*

Third Plan (*1961–66*)

1. Completion of projects envised under the second five year plan which are under implementation or were deferred during 1957–58 owing to foreign exchange difficulties
2. Expansion and diversification of capacity of the heavy engineering and machine building industries, castings and forgings, alloy tool and special steels, iron and steel and ferroalloys and step-up of output of *fertilizers* & petroleum products
3. Increased production of major basic raw materials and producer goods such as aluminium, mineral oils, dissolving pulp, basic organic and inorganic chemicals and intermediates inclusive of products of petrochemical origin
4. Khadi & Village Industries: *handloom, handicrafts,* sericulture & *coir*

(*Continued*)

Table 4.5 (Continued)

5. Increased production from domestic industries of commodities required to meet essential needs such as essential drugs, paper, cloth, sugar, *vegetable oils* and housing materials and
6. *Export promotion*

Fourth plan (*1969–74*)
1. Completing investment in relation to which commitments had already been made
2. Increasing existing capacities to levels required for present or future developments, in particular, providing more adequate internal supplies of essentials in increasing demand or needed by *import substitution or for export promotion*
3. Taking advantage of internal developments or availabilities to build new industries or new bases for industries
4. *Village industries*; and
5. *Export promotion*

Fifth plan (*1974–79*)
1. 20 point economic programme. In addition to the other key focus areas of the country, some polices relevant to the three cases studies
2. *Paper & newsprint, cement, vegetable oil & vanaspati*
3. Khadi & Village Industries: *coir, handicraft, handloom*
4. *Research & education*
5. *Export promotion*

Sixth plan (*1980–85*)
In addition to the other key focus areas of the country, some polices relevant to the three cases studies:
1. *Paper & newsprint, cement, vegetable oil & vanaspati*
2. *Development of backward regions*
3. *Development of ancillaries*: appropriate technology, research, development & training
4. Khadi & village Industries*: handloom, handicraft & coir*; and
5. *Export Promotion*

Seventh Plan (*1986–90*)
In addition to the other key focus areas of the country, some polices relevant to the three cases studies
1. To maximize the utilization of wage goods and *consumer articles* of mass consumption at reasonable prices and of acceptable quality
2. To maximize the utilization of existing facilities through *restructuring*, improved productivity and *up-gradation of technology*
3. *Paper & newsprint*
4. *Development of backward regions*
5. *Chemicals and up-gradation of process technology*
6. Khadi & village Industries*: handloom, handicraft & coir*
7. *Export Promotion*

Note: Underlined words are my emphasis indicating areas in which the company invested.
Source: Five year plans, Planning Commission, GOI, <http://planningcommission.nic.in/plans/planrel/fiveyr/welcome.html>

Table 4.6 ITC Ltd, mission, scope and contents of activities and accomplishment, 1969–82

National economic policies	*Activities*	*Industries' products*
1. *Employment-livelihood*	1. *ITC Ltd – division*	1. *Tobacco*
– Educated – uneducated	– ITC-HO-HQ as Investor – Central Services	– Cigarettes
– Urban – rural	– ITC – India Tobacco Division	– Leaf
– Direct – indirect	– ILTD – Indian Leaf Tobacco Div. PPD–Packaging printing	– Exports
	– Real estate & ITC centre	– Machinery
2. *Investment & development*	– Information services – electronic data processing – computers	
– Core	– Marketing, exports & imports	2. *Packaging*
– Priority areas	– GLT	– Printing
– Overcome shortages	– Machine construction	– Flexibles
– Backward area development	– Technical training centre	– Systems
	– R&D – integrated research centre – Bangalore	– Inks (Invest)
3. *External resources–conservation*	– Rajamundry agronomic research auto analysis – experimental farms	
– Earning foreign exchange		3. *Paper*
– Bilateral trade	– Hissar-Agronomic – Experimental Farms	– Board
– Self-reliance	– Welcome Group Hotels	– Papers
– Self-sufficiency	– Garments (Entrepreneurial Dev.)	– Pulp (Ashoka)
4. *Economic activity – competition*	– Mehfil (Pan Masala – Dry Pan etc.)	4. *Tourism*
– Promoting small–medium scale	2. *Wholly partly owned subsidiaries*	– Hotels
– Promoting ancillaries	– Delhi & Orient Tobacco Ltd	– Travel trade
– Promoting self-employment	– All India Tobacco Ltd	– Specialty
– Employment	– Finance Investments Ltd	– Restaurants
	– Sage Investments Ltd	– Overseas hotels
5. *Natural resource utilization*	– Summit Investments Ltd	
– Rural	– ITC US Ltd	5. *Marine PS*
– Sea – 2000 Mile Coastline	– HIMEC Ltd – Mktg–Import–Investment–Export Consultancy	– Fish exports
	– CS-Calcutta Cold Storages	– Prawn exports

6. *Public – Consumer Service* 7. *Domestic Resources – Exchequer* – Direct tax revenue – Indirect tax revenue	3. *Companies promoted* – Bhadrachalam Paper Boards Ltd – Tribeni Handlooms Ltd – Tufftools Ltd (Later sold) – CPA Consultants share registrars – Travel House Ltd – Coronet Hotels & Supplies Ltd (not activated) 4. Companies–acquired-invested-in – Roll print – India cements (2) – Ashoka paper (4) – Coates of India (inks) – Alfit Corp. (sold out later to partners) – Surya-Tobacco – Negotiated 1980 5. Ancillaries – 144 units – Shopping arcades	6. *Real estate* – ITC centre – Housing 7. *Construction materials* – Cement 8. *Services* – Information (export) – Share registrars – Marketing – T&D – R&D – Cold storage 9. *Entrepreneurial* – Carpets – exports – Garments – export – Tools export 10. *Marketing* – Tea – Tobacco 11. *Agro-based* 12. *Soya beans* 13. *Development*

strategy to link it to the development goals of India. It developed a list of activities that were linked to the national economic policies and then identified the industries' products it would focus upon. This type of strategy development is extremely rare among foreign firms in a host country situation. BAT identified different areas such as (a) import substitution, (b) export promotion, (c) investment in core industries, and (d) investment in the social sector to connect its corporate strategy with the development strategy of the host country. It is indeed interesting that a tobacco–cigarette company could associate itself and participate in the development process of a host country.

Import substitution and exports

BAT began early on to substitute its imports locally. By 1945 it was able to reduce its import component by 20 per cent, by 1949 by 70 per cent, and by 1957 by 95 per cent. It invested in local manufacturing from 1907 and concentrated on local sourcing of tobacco leaf as early as 1912. It substituted the imports of cigarette paper in the 1950s for investing in manufacturing paper. Subsequently, it invested in duplex board and aluminium foil. By 1963 BAT invested in filter rods. BAT internalized other market functions downstream of the value chain like the production of machinery for packing cigarette by 1960.

ITC started off with marine exports in 1971. It earned INR 7.3 million of foreign exchange by 1973 and qualified to be recognized as an Export House. In the ensuing years, however, the business incurred losses.[2] By 1980 the company's annual export earning was about INR 335 million and in the next ten years increased by about five times. In the 1990s the value of exports rose to about INR 10 billion (see Figure 4.2 and Table 4.7). The hotel business, targeted at foreign tourists in India, was successful in earning foreign exchange. ITC chose to invest in the high-end of the hotel market, building its own hotels or tying in with existing establishments. Table 4.8 lists hotels in the Welcomgroup chain of ITC hotels. The company internalized valuable real estate properties around the country at cheap prices by entering into the hotel business.

In 1990, ITC set up the International Business Division (IBD) to cater for the export of agricultural commodities. IBD has focused on exports of vegetable oils, grains, pulses, soyameal, rapeseed meal, rice, wheat products, sesame seeds, castor oil, coffee, spices, black pepper, frozen and cooked shrimps, and prawns. IBD contributes nearly 60 per cent of the ITC group's foreign exchange earnings.

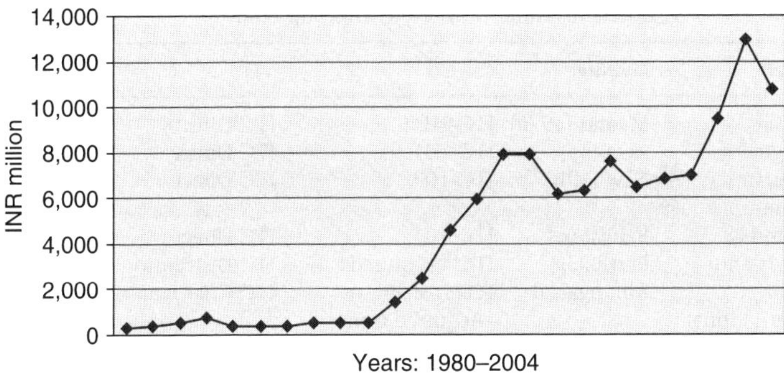

Sources: Centre for Monitoring Indian Economy (1955–2004).

Figure 4.2 BAT/ITC foreign exchange earnings, 1980–2004

Table 4.7 Foreign exchange earnings, 1980–2004 (million INR)

Year	*Foreign exchange earnings*
1980	334.7
1981	355.7
1982	532.0
1983	726.0
1984	352.6
1985	355.2
1986	407.1
1987	531.6
1988	524.1
1989	561.3
1990	1,459.7
1991	2,482.6
1992	4,620.5
1993	5,935.3
1994	7,912.6
1995	7,867.7
1996	6,192.4
1997	6,347.3
1998	7,590.8
1999	6,495.5
2000	6,877.0
2001	6,971.3
2002	9,475.7
2003	12,940.0
2004	10,775.1

Source: Annual Reports, ITC Ltd.

Table 4.8 ITC hotels division – the Welcomgroup chain

Hotel	*Location*	*Owners*	*Via*
Chola	Madras (1975)	ITC–HD	ITC Direct
Mughal	Agra	ITC–HD	ITC Direct
Maurya Sheraton	New Delhi	ITC–HD	ITC Direct
Wind	Bangalore	ITC–HD	ITC Direct
Bay Island	Port Blair	ITC – acquired	ITC Distributor
Rama International	Aurangabad	ITD Distributor Acquired from Gaylord Group	ITC Chairman
Banjara	Hyderabad	ITC Distributor	ITC Chairman & Surinder Gadhoke of HD (IDBI Request)
Umaid Bhawan Palace	Jodhpur	Maharaja Jodhpur	ITC Chairman
Usha Kiran Palace	Gwalior	Maharaja Gwalior presently on 15-year lease	ITC Chairman
Searock	Bombay	Luthrias	Dammi Sabharwal of HD Finalised by ITC Chairman
Mansingh	Jaipur	H.Hundhra taken over by Agarwals	ITC Chairman Ex IDBI S.Gadhoke arranged Agarwals take over
Royal Castle	Khimsar		ITC Chairman
Mumtaz	Agra	Agrawals	S. Gadhoke & R Sarin of HD
Cidade De Goa	Goa-Panjim		ITC Chairman
Highlands	Kargil Ladakh Bhutan	Independent Party	Chairman HD R.Lakshman & ITC Chairman
Maurya Patna	Patna	Sinha Family	Chairman HD R.Lakshman & ITC Chairman
Hotel Druk	Phuntsholing Bhutan	Independent party	Chairman HD R. Lakshman
The Dolphin	Waikkal Sri Lanka	Sri Lankan	Chairman HD R. Lakshman
Gurkha Houseboats	Srinagar	Wangnoo Family	Anil Channa of HD
Nilambag Palace	Bhavanagar	Maharaja Bhavnagar	GM Searock
Vadodra	Baroda	Jt. Venture Gujarat IDFC	A Bhatia of HD & writer as First Mfg. Director of Jt. Venture
Manjura	Mangalore	Independent Party	Ravi Rao of HD
Adyar Park	Madras	Independent Party	Ravi Suri of HD
Asia	Jammu Tawi	Independent party	
Siddharth	Delhi	Garg Group	
Kathmandu	Kathmandu Nepal	Rana Family	Chairman HD R. Lakshman & Chairman ITC

Source: Centre for Monitoring Indian Economy.

Investments in core industries: paper, paperboard and hotels

The government had been urging private business to invest in paper and paperboard manufacture. In 1944 BAT worked with Bengal Paper to develop and manufacture cartridge paper. In 1946 it promoted Tribeni Tissue to manufacture cigarette paper. In 1981, when ITC wanted to enter the cement business, the Industrial Development Bank of India (IDBI)[3] suggested it should invest in a loss-making paper company, Ashok Paper, with units in Assam and Bihar. ITC invested Rs 95 million in Ashok Paper, 25 per cent of the paper mill's equity. However, ITC's cement and paper projects did not take off due to delays in government machinery. In 1979, ITC promoted Bhadrachalam Paperboards Ltd, which soon became the market leader both in the quality and volume of the paperboard business. In 1990, ITC acquired Tribeni Tissue Ltd, which was managed by the Tribeni Tissue Division. In November 2002, Bhadrachalam Paperboards Ltd division was merged with the Tribeni Tissue Division to form the Paperboards and Specialty Papers Division. In 2004, ITC acquired the paperboard manufacturing facility of BILT Industrial Packaging Co. Limited (BIPCO), Kovai, near Coimbatore, Tamil Nadu. For this project the company benefited from governmental incentives for investing in a backward area.

While some of the investments in hotels, exports, agri-business, were in line with the host country priorities, these businesses were also carefully chosen so that the company leveraged its existing resources and local tax incentives to develop these businesses. It clearly shows the business ingenuity of the company.

Investments in social sector

BAT has encouraged and supported the arts, culture, sports, weaving, farming, and other social developments from the beginning. BAT business ventures in tobacco leaf, paper, paperboard, handloom and marine-based products touch the lives of many people and are compatible with socio-economic development. BAT/ITC has also been involved in several other social and community-based development projects.

Its willing support of investments in several priority sectors of the government was a conscious decision of the company to align itself to the needs of the country.[4] Its support of a variety of social causes has helped the company to earn the goodwill of the government. By creating jobs in rural areas and among farmers it has created a strong lobby for itself with the government. By sponsoring sports and music and other social functions, it is able to campaign for its cigarette brands extremely well.

Investments in such social activities has increased its business profile favourably.

ITC's recent effort to align its business goals with social goals has been the innovation of e-Choupal.[5] Each e-Choupal costs about US$3,000–6,000 to set up and about US$100 to maintain. One e-Choupal can serve up to 600 farmers from nearly 10 villages within a radius of 5 km. Today, e-Choupal service has reached to over 1 million farmers in nearly 11,000 villages. Under the e-Choupal business model, the company provides computers and Internet access in rural areas. The system enables farmers to get closing prices on local mandis,[6] track global price trends and also to learn new farming techniques. The company also offers to buy the crop directly from the farmers at the previous day's closing price on local mandi through its processing centres. The supply is weighed electronically and prompt payment is given for both the crop and the cost of transport.

The e-Choupal movement has benefited the farmers in terms of more accurate weighing, quick processing and prompt payment, and access to a wide range of information, including market price knowledge and market trends. The company has also benefited immensely from this business model. It is able to simplify its procurement of agricultural produce that it exports ultimately through its International Business Division. ITC is able to control the quality of the produce by educating and training farmers in good agricultural practices. The company also uses e-Choupal as its distribution network to sell agricultural inputs such as seeds and fertilizer and other consumer goods to farmers. BAT/ITC's miscellaneous contributions in the social sector are listed in Table 4.9.

Localization of ownership

BAT's ownership in various businesses in India

By 1907 BAT had already invested in manufacturing and the selling of cigarettes and the local trading of leaf tobacco through its various subsidiaries in India. Subsequently, it invested in various downstream and upstream cigarette and tobacco businesses in India. BAT created several companies for its various business functions. The pattern of shareholding and investments during 1905 to 2002 presented in Charts 4.1 and 4.2 shows how BAT controlled several businesses in India. BAT controlled Peninsular Tobacco in its manufacturing activity, Dominion Tobacco, Imperial Tobacco and Arcadian Tobacco in selling and Indian Leaf Tobacco in its the tobacco leaf business. Later it added Printers (India), Exchange Tobacco and Vazir Sultan to its list of companies.

Table 4.9 Miscellaneous BAT/ITC investments in the social sector

- Contribution towards the promotion of the Army Scriptures Readers' Association
- Contribution to Girl Guides
- Rehabilitation assistance to cyclone victims, 1977
- Assistance in forming the Indian Tobacco Curers' and Growers Association (1971–72) when the prices of tobacco fell; lobbying with the government to buy the excess tobacco produced through the State Trading Corporation.
- Investing in Tribeni Handloom Limited to revive the traditional craft of carpet weaving (1971–72). This helped improve the quality of life of nearly 1,800 people with increased income.
- Distribution of condoms (brand name Nirodh) in a huge territory covering Madhya Pradesh, Karnataka, Andhra Pradesh, Tamil Nadu, Kerala, Pondicherry and part of Maharashtra. Using its extensive distribution network, ITC was able to increase the sale of Nirodh from 6 million in the 1960s to 57 million in the 1980s.
- Provision of Annual Grant of Rs 1,000 to the Imperial Council of Agricultural Research in Delhi for two postgraduate studentships in tobacco and its cultivation
- Donation to the Delhi School of Economics
- Development of nearly 16,000 hectares under social and farm forestry, 1998
- Donation of books and uniform to nearly 7,500 children
- Micro-credit policies benefiting about 9,000 women
- Environmental initiatives for preserving the environment and rainwater harvesting for self-sufficiency, 2002–2003. ITC–Welcomgroup has created a teaching module that enables school teachers to effectively communicate environmental concerns and implemented in 366 schools across Karnataka, Delhi, Rajasthan, and Chandigarh. ITC constructed two collecting ponds with a storage capacity of 8700 kilolitres at the new Bangalore factory to meet the needs of air handling unit, cooling towers, machine and gum wash, canteen utilities and toilets.
- Wide-ranging sponsorship in sports. In the 1940s, BAT promoted cricket by donating INR 60,000. Subsequently, it sponsored sports like kite flying, khokho, kabadi, archery, wrestling, tonga, cricket, hockey, football, five-a-side soccer, tennis, polo, and golf; sponsored several major tournaments like Wills Trophy Limited Overs Cricket, Wills Trophy Cricket, and Wills Trophy Golf; active role in publications on different sports (Wills Book of Excellence: Olympics, Wills Book on Tennis, Wills Book on Football, and Wills Book on One-Day-Cricket); sponsoring the Wills Award for Excellence in Sports Journalism.
- Sponsorship of classical music: sponsored the Annual Sangeet Sammelan in Delhi, 1971; helped set up the Sangeet Research Academy in Aldeen, Calcutta, 1977
- Participated in the Festival of India in the United States, 1985
- Started ITC WelcomArt, a forum to promote the cause of art and artists, showcasing the works of both well known and unknown but talented artists, 2002–2003

Until 1953, BAT wholly owned these companies through various organizational arrangements. By 1975, it reorganized all these and subsidiary units under the control of ITC. ILTD remained a separate entity of BAT until 2001, when it was finally merged with ITC. BAT reduced its shareholding to 60 per cent in its subsidiary ITC by 1975 but maintained 100 per cent equity until it was merged with ITC in 2001.

BAT had been heavily investing in cigarette and cigarette-related businesses until around 1975. Although cigarettes constitutes still about 80 per cent of its revenue, in the last three decades, ITC has entered into other sunrise industries such as hotel, exports, marine and agro-based products.

Indian equity in ITC Ltd

Diluting foreign equity with Indian equity has been the most difficult experience of foreign firms in India. However, BAT was quick to adapt to the proposal of the Indian Government in 1953. While other large foreign companies like Unilever resisted the dilution of equity, the managers of BAT were in favour of it.[7] BAT agreed to the proposal of the management to dilute because of its experience in other countries.[8]

Until 1919 BAT was in total control of its businesses in India. In 1921 Thomas Bears and Sons, Bears, and Exchange Tobacco held nearly 25 per cent of its equity in various businesses. However, all these companies were wholly owned by BAT. By 1953 BAT controlled all its businesses in India through its subsidiaries Raleigh Investment, Tobacco Manufacturers (India) and Printers India.

The dilution of BAT's equity with Indian equity started in 1954, falling to 75 per cent in 1969, 60 per cent in 1974, and 40 per cent in 1976. Currently, BAT holds only about 32 per cent of the equity in its Indian operation (see Figure 4.3 for trends in ownership pattern). The ownership share of BAT and Indian public and financial institutions are shown in Tables 14.10 and 4.11. This trend of localization of local equity is different from the traditional ownership seeking foreign multinational enterprises. While most foreign firms sought to increase their ownership in the host economy, BAT let allowed local participation to rise in its equity. This is contradictory to the general practice of MNEs. Companies like General Motors, Ford Motors, and IBM divested from India when they were directed by the host country to include local equity in their respective businesses.

In recent years, there has been some controversy on the issue of ownership of BAT in ITC. In 1994, J. N. Sapru, former chairman of ITC, stated that ITC does not need BAT. In 1995 there were several allegations and

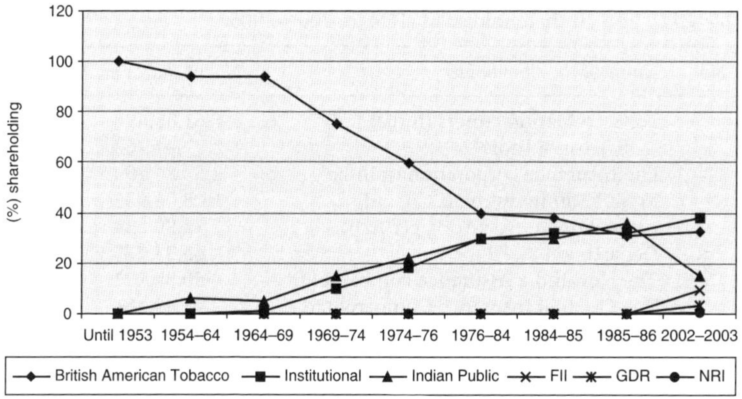

Notes: Institutional: Indian Institutions; FII: Foreign Institutional Investor; GDR: Global Depository Receipt; NRI: Non-Resident Indians.
Sources: ITC Ltd, (1955–2004), *Annual Reports*.
Figure 4.3 Change of BAT/ITC ownership, 1953–2004

Table 4.10 ITC equity holding, 1953–2004

Year	*BAT & other foreign companies (%)*	*Institutional (%)*	*Indian private investors (%)*	*FII (%)*	*GDR (%)*	*NRI (%)*
Until 1953	100	–	–	–	–	–
1954–64	94	–	6	–	–	–
1964–69	94	1	5	–	–	–
1969–74	75	10	15	–	–	–
1974–76	60	18	22	–	–	–
1976–84	40	30	30	–	–	–
1984–85	38	32	30	–	–	–
1985–86	31	32	36	–	–	–
2002–2003	32.5	38.38	14.9	9.62	3.09	0.7
2004–2005	32.40	33.80	12.73	17.49	2.98	0.60

Source: ITC Ltd, Annual Reports, 1955–2004.

counter allegations between K. L. Chugh, the then chairman of ITC and BAT. This public drama on ownership issue followed a spate of raids by officials of the Enforcement Directorate (ED)[9] on grounds of ITC violating the Foreign Exchange Regulation Act, 1973. The enquiries by the ED led to the arrest of several top executives of ITC, including Chugh. By June 1997 BAT and ITC resolved their differences as BAT licensed ITC

Table 4.11 Top 10 shareholders of ITC Ltd, 2004–2005

Sl. No	*Name of the shareholder*	*No. of shares held*	*%*
1	Tobacco Manufacturers (India) Ltd	6,61,85,496	26.66
2	Unit Trust of India*	2,77,44,763	11.18
3	Life Insurance corporation of India*	2,63,26,794	10.61
4	Myddleton Investment Co. Ltd	1,08,06,932	4.35
5	Citibank N.A. New York, NY ADR	73,90,034	2.98
6	Department**	65,83,777	2.65
7	The New India Assurance company Ltd	50,88,091	2.05
8	The Oriental Insurance Company Ltd	48,99,186	1.97
9	General Insurance Corporation of India	46,63,674	1.88
10	National Insurance Company Ltd	34,43,442	1.39
	Rothmans International Enterprises Ltd		

Notes: * Excludes mutual fund holdings; ** shares underlying global depository receipts.

to manufacture and sell some of its prestigious global brands, including 555, State Express and Benson and Hedges.

This public drama adversely affected ITC's subsidiary, ITC Classic Finance. ITC Classic, the flagship financial services company with 49 per cent equity from ITC Ltd was formed in 1986. With the stock market crash in 1992, ITC Classic made huge losses and also lost its customer base because of the legal tangle of ITC with the government. In 1998, ITC Ltd disposed of ITC Classic by amalgamating it with ICICI, a financial institution in India. These incidents in the relationship between ITC and BAT were aberrations in almost a hundred-year history of BAT in India.

Performance indicators

Sales, PBDIT, and PAT

BAT has consistently performed well in India during its operations there. Sales have grown steadily over the years. Available sales data of the years 1955–2004 show a consistent growth during the period. The PBDIT and PAT figures for 1955–2004 also show increasing trends (see Figure 4.4 and Table 4.1). PBDIT indicates the company's operational efficiency and can be used to compare BAT with companies from other industries. PAT indicates the company's profit generating ability and can be used to compare BAT with other companies in the cigarette industry. The company has been a dominant player in the cigarette business and has actually made competition irrelevant. In all its businesses including hotel, food, tobacco and cigarettes, the company has maintained a high market share

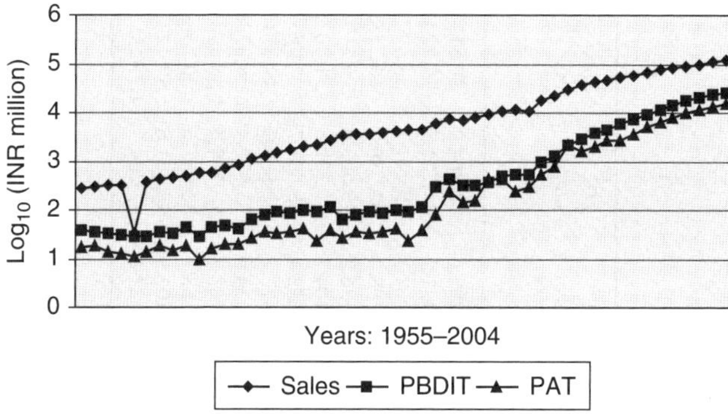

Source: ITC Ltd, (1955–2004), Annual Reports.
Figure 4.4 BAT/ITC sales, PBDIT and PAT, 1955–2004

of over 60 per cent thoughout the 1990s, the period that has seen most competition in India (see Table 4.12).

Market share

A pioneer in the cigarette business in India, BAT has continued to be a strong market player in the Indian tobacco industry. Despite the increased competition since the Industrial Licensing Policy, 1991, ITC has increased its market share in cigarettes from 63 per cent in 1990 to over 80 per cent in 2003–2004. ITC's various businesses, i.e. cigarettes, tobacco, hotels and packaged food business, account for over 55 per cent of the market share in terms of sales turnover throughout the last 14 years. ITC's market share is way ahead of the rest of its competitors (see Table 4.12).

Summary: FDI strategy of BAT

BAT has had a holistic investment pattern in India over the last hundred years. BAT's strategy in India appears to have been to start its business at the level of the host country and not from the level the company was in its business in the UK and USA. Besides investing in manufacturing cigarettes in India in 1906, it also invested in several complementary businesses such as extensive distribution and marketing networks, the growing of tobacco leaf, the production of paper for cigarette wrapping, packaging, machinery for tobacco making, etc.

Statistical confirmatory tests in Chapter 7 establishes the strong positive association of BAT's investment in its main business functions

Table 4.12 Annual sales of ITC and its competitors, 1991–2003 (INR million)

Year	*Asian Hotels Ltd**	*Bharat Hotels Ltd**	*Hotel Leelaventure Ltd**	*Indian Hotels Co. Ltd**	*EIH Ltd**	*GTC Industries Ltd**	*RDB Industries Ltd**	*Ruchi Soya Inds Ltd***	*Sun Paper Mill Ltd***	*Godfrey Phillips India Ltd****	*VST Industries Ltd****	*ITC Ltd****	*Total Market*	*ITC's Share*
Dec. 91	310.9	255.4	213.3	1,562.8	901.6	2,525.7		353.5		5,325.2	4,298.6	22,864.9	38,611.9	59.22
Dec. 92	330.5	348.4	329.9	2,032.2	1,267.5	2,480.1		987.0		7,005.9	5,421.1	29,721.7	49,924.3	59.53
Dec. 93	411.6	416.0	512.4	2,381.4	1,616.1	2,667.3		1,245.4		6,943.2	6,063.3	37,441.1	59,697.8	62.72
Dec. 94	570.1	467.4	726.0	2,937.2	2,098.7	2,952.4	15.9	2,391.9		6,712.3	5,708.4	42,138.2	66,718.5	63.16
Dec. 95	893.2	631.6	835.1	3,725.0	2,745.3	4,001.1	275.9	3,385.5	394.0	7,523.4	6,396.3	45,603.6	76,410.0	59.68
Dec. 96	1,350.2	814.9	1,246.1	5,243.0	3,988.3	6,394.9		6,962.8	507.6	7,843.0	6,104.7	51,351.6	91,807.1	55.93
Dec. 97	1,660.4	937.6	1,309.0	5,768.2	4,447.2		204.4	9,616.3		8,772.3	5,682.4	58,687.7	97,085.5	60.45
Dec. 98	1,500.6	910.5	1,143.0	5,956.5	4,372.7	5,108.2	179.6	13,071.1		10,146.0	6,473.7	68,509.3	1,17,371	58.37
Dec. 99	1,355.6	671.0	1,216.8	6,032.8	4,422.3	3,797.6	149.5	17,251.3	458.2	10,471.7	7,054.0	75,992.4	1,28,873	58.97
Dec. 00	1,158.8	665.3	1,220.3	6,186.8	4,229.4	4,148.7	192.0	19,212.3	467.1	10,826.3	7,463.8	79,719.4	1,35,490	58.84
Dec. 01	1,166.3	660.3	1,225.1	7,067.7	4,795.1	4,627.0	197.0	25,949.9	561.4	9,925.0	7,563.7	86,997.5	1,50,736	57.72
Dec. 02	926.6	557.5	866.4	6,001.5	3,759.9	3,626.6	231.8	28,404.5		9,447.4	6,807.8	98,491.6	1,59,122	61.9
Dec. 03	1,066.6	745.9	1,344.2	5,852.4	3,840.9	3,342.6	166.0	34,092.3		10,802.2	6,683.6	11,0284.1	1,78221	61.88

Notes: * refers to hotel business; ** refers to packaged food business; *** refers to cigarette and tobacco business.
Source: Centre for Monitoring Indian Economy.

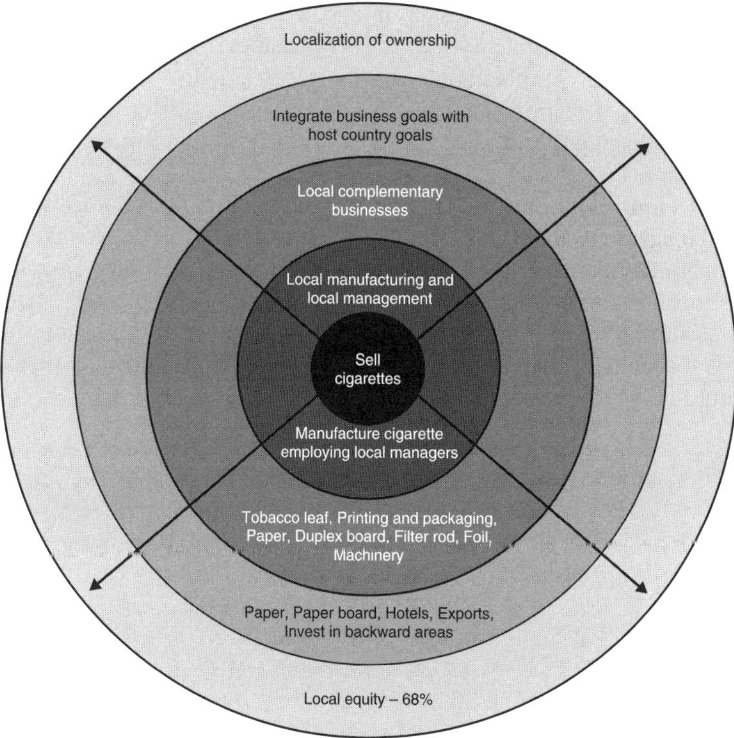

Figure 4.5 Holistic FDI Pattern of British American Tobacco in India, 1906–2004

complementary businesses with its financial performance. The causality of investments and performance can be analysed through the timing of investments in various complementary businesses. The company invested in critical complementary business functions such as leaf growing, packaging, printing, paper and duplex board, machinery for cigarette rolling and filter rods. In the early years of its operation, while the market was not large, the demands on investments were high. It appears that sales and profits followed investments.

BAT aligned itself very well with the policies of the host nation, investing in several priority areas of the host government. It invested in cement, paper, hotels, export and in backward areas in a way that its existing business could benefit from such seemingly unrelated businesses. The company adopted a holistic FDI pattern in India during

1906–2004. It not only invested in its core activity of cigarette production and sales but also in a wide variety of business functions. It invested in several of its complementary businesses, aligned well with some of the industry development objectives of the host country, and also let local management and local equity participate in its business in India (see Figure 4.5).

BAT's most important strategic shift was the policy of indianization of its management since the 1930s. By 1979 its subsidiary, ITC Ltd was completely managed by Indian managers. BAT agreed that Indian financial institutions and private investors own the majority of the equity shares of its subsidiary in India. If BAT were to continue with this ownership policy even with increasing liberalization policy of the host country, it would prove to be a unique model to watch.

5
Unilever PLC, 1932–2004

Unilever PLC is a case of FDI in the fast moving consumer product industry. It is also an example of oldest multinational enterprises in India and the world over. This chapter discusses the process by which Unilever developed a market from nothing – none of its products were in use and there was no support industry and basic infrastructure to conduct its business. The task of building awareness of its products with the potential consumers and a distribution network across the length and breadth of India, which had little road transport and communication, was the challenge for this company. This case also reveals how the company invested in all related businesses to complement its main business of manufacturing personal care products such as soaps, detergents, toiletries, and packaged food products. The analysis involves the study of nature and timing of investments of the company in its main business and complementary market functions, the manner in which it aligned itself to the requirements of the GOI, the issues of localization of management and ownership and its financial performance in India. The detailed confirmatory statistical analysis of the case, however, is provided in Chapter 7.

William Hesketh Lever founded Lever Brothers in 1885 in the United Kingdom. Lever Brothers began to export laundry soap (Sunlight brand) to India in 1888 and bathing soap (Lifebuoy brand) in 1895 and began selling packed tea in 1903. Lever Brothers established sales agents in Kolkata, Mumbai, Chennai and Karachi (now part of Pakistan) to sell its products in the Indian sub-continent. Its competitors at the time were the British firms: United Traders, Northwest Soap Company, and Premier Soap Company, and Margarine Unie (Dutch) selling hydrogenated fat/oil. Soap and packaged food were at the time unknown commodities in India. Low market demand and poor infrastructure of roads, transport services and communication facilities were challenges to marketing. During the first 40 years Lever Brothers, its competitors and Margarine Unie, sold different brands of soaps and hydrogenated oils that were produced in the UK, and the Netherlands.

In 1930, Lever Brothers and Margarine Unie merged to form Unilever PLC, leveraging their individual strengths in personal care products and food products. This led to the merger of Lever Brothers and Margarine Unie in India and they operated under the newly formed enterprise Unilever. However, the new entity also largely focused on selling products that were produced in the UK.

Around 1930, the British Government under pressure from the local legislators was considering introducing import duties in India, which triggered Unilever to directly invest in local production in India. Unilever had until then simply traded its products in India and developed awareness about them. Its local subsidiaries that undertook direct investment activities in India were Hindustan Vanaspati Manufacturing Company (HVMC, incorporated on 27 June 1931), Lever Brothers (India) Limited (LBIL, incorporated on 17 October 1933), and United Traders (incorporated on 14 May 1935).[1]

Nature and timing of investments

Investments in main business and complementary businesses

For many foreign companies, selling had remained the main business in India. However, Unilever went into manufacturing very early, systematically internalizing many of the market functions that were complementary to its core business. Many of the complementary businesses have now become part of its main business. The investment pattern has been holistic and appropriate for a host country that severely lacked industry infrastructure and support institutions. Today, Unilever has nearly a hundred factories and about 2,000 suppliers and associates. It has invested systematically in a number of related businesses such as soaps and personal products, chemicals, synthetic detergents, and packaged food items (see Table 5.1). It has set up manufacturing facilities of its various product categories across the country (see Table 5.2).

HVMC set up a plant at Sewri, Bombay in 1932 to manufacture vanaspati (hydrogenated cooking oil/fat). Within the next two years, Lever Brothers India Ltd (LBIL) began to manufacture soap at Sewri. Unilever, thereafter, steadily invested in the various complementary business functions. In 1943, it set up a unit in Garden Reach Factory to produce soap. Unilever also invested in its intermediary and core sectors

Table 5.1 Investments in various manufacturing units

Year	*Business area*
Soaps & personal products	
1933	Application made for setting up soap factory next to the Vanaspati factory at Sewri
1934	Soap manufacture begins at Sewri factory in October; North West Soap Company's Garden Reach Factory, Kolkata rented and expanded to produce Lever brands
1943	Personal Products manufacture begins in India with plant at the Garden Reach Factory
1958	Research Unit starts functioning at Mumbai Factory
1975	Ten-year modernization plan for soaps and detergent plants; Jammu project work begins
1986	Khamgaon Soaps Unit starts production Yavatmal Personal Products unit starts production
1989	Toilet soap plant in Orai in UP was commissioned
1992	Dabgram soaps unit commissioned
Chemicals	
1966	Nickel catalyst production begins in Taloja
1969	Fine Chemicals Unit starts production in Mumbai
1971	Mr V.G. Rajadhyaksha presents plan for diversification into chemicals to Unilever Special Committee – plan approved
1974	Pilot plant for industrial chemicals at Taloja
1976	Construction work of Haldia chemicals complex begins; Taloja chemicals unit begins functioning
1979	Sodium Tripolyphospate plant at Haldia commissioned
1988	Company in collaboration with National Starch Corporation, USA undertook to set a new facility at Pondicherry for the manufacture of fictionalized biopolymers
1993	Company set up Hot Melt Adhesive manufacturing facilities at Taloja
Synthetic detergents	
1977	Jammu synthetic Detergents plant inaugurated
1983	A new plant for synthetic detergents in Chindwara district of MP commissioned; company took on lease a detergent and toilet soap factory at the request of Punjab govt. owned by a joint sector company Stephans Chemicals Ltd
1984	Synthetic Detergent unit was set in Chhindwara (MP)
1988	The company took on lease cum purchase basis the detergents undertakings of Union Home Products Ltd, Mangalore
1989	Synthetic Detergent plant at Sumerpur in UP & Cracking catalyst plant at Haldia commissioned
1991	Company proposed to set up a 17,000 tpa Film sulphonation plant at Taloja to manufacture a range of detergent actives

(*Continued*)

Table 5.1 (Continued)

Year	*Business area*
Packaged food items	
1932	Vanaspati manufacture starts at Sewri
1959	Pilot project for growing peas; trial milk collection projects
1964	Etah dairy set up, Anik ghee launched; Animal feeds plant at Ghaziabad
1965	Ghaziabad plant for dehydration of peas, Hima dehydrated peas in market
1986	Agri-products unit at Hyderabad starts functioning – first range of hybrid seeds comes out
1989	Vegetable oil plant commissioned at Kandla free trade zone
1991	Seed & Tissue culture projects commissioned at Hyderabad

Sources: HLL Annual Reports, 1955–2004, and <http://www.hll.com>.

such as fine chemicals (1969), nickel catalyst (1969), industrial chemicals (1974), and synthetic detergents (1977) that were in the vertical value chain of its business (see Chart 5.1). In the packaged food segment, Unilever invested in growing peas and milk collection in 1959. It set up its dairy unit in Etah in 1964 and also invested in the dehydration of peas, the development of hybrid seeds, and tissue culture in the subsequent years. Extraction of oil from sal seed, a local plant resource, was through the company's research and development activity. A vegetable oil manufacturing unit was set up in Kandla in 1989 (see Chart 5.2).

From around the 1950s, the GOI suggested that large companies should invest in core sectors. While many foreign companies saw this as a major impediment for doing business in India, Unilever used it to its advantage. By investing in its complementary and intermediate industries, Unilever created a stable supply system of raw materials for its main business at a much lower cost. The several tax incentives for setting up factories in backward areas also reduced its cost of production.

Before 1956 Unilever had different business units in India. By 1930, Unilever had four wholly owned subsidiaries, namely, Lever Brothers (India) Ltd, United Traders, Margarine Unie, and North West Soap Company Private Ltd. By 1935, Lever Brothers took over North West Soap Company. Margarine Unie had 100 per cent equity in Hindustan Vanaspati Manufacturing Company (HVMC).

Major consolidation of Unilever companies in India took place in 1956. The various business units of Unilever were merged to form Hindustan Lever Ltd (HLL), in which Unilever had 51 per cent shareholding. Lever

Table 5.2 Manufacturing locations of HLL, 2003

Product	*Location*	*District*	*State/union territory*
Soap	Dabgram	Jalpaiguri	West Bengal
	Calcutta	Kolkata	West Bengal
	Khamgaon	Akola	Maharashtra
	Sewree	Mumbai	Maharashtra
	Pondicherry	Pondicherry	Pondicherry
Personal products	Sewree	Mumbai	Maharashtra
	Silvassa	Dadra & Nagar Haveli	Dadar & Nagar Haveli
	Pondicherry	Pondicherry	Pondicherry
Synthetic detergent	Jammu	Jammu	Jammu & Kashmir
	Sumerpur	Hamirpur	Uttar Pradesh
	Garden Reach	Kolkata	West Bengal
	Kandla	Kachch	Gujurat
	Sewree	Mumbai	Maharashtra
	Chhindwara	Chhindwara	Madhya Pradesh
	Medak	Medak	Andhra Pradesh
Chemicals	Andheri	Mumbai	Maharashtra
	Sewree	Mumbai	Maharashtra
	Taloja	Raigarh	Maharashtra
	Pondicherry	Pondicherry	Pondicherry
Food products	Zahura	Jalandhar	Punjab
	Bareilly	Bareilly	Uttar Pradesh
	Bangalore	Bangalore	Karnataka
	Sewree	Mumbai	Maharashtra
	Sewree	Mumbai	Maharashtra
	Ghaziabad	Ghaziabad	Uttar Pradesh
	Calcutta	Kolkata	West Bengal
	Pune	Pune	Maharashtra
	Sewree	Mumbai	Maharashtra

Source: Centre for Monitoring Indian Economy.

Brothers, HVMC, Joseph Crossfield, and Willam Gossage were wholly owned by HLL. Lever Brothers held United Traders, North West and Premier Soap (see Chart 5.3).

By 1991, the shareholding structure had been simplified. HLL held 51 per cent share in Brooke Bond India Ltd (Tea Estate India and Doom Dooma India) and Lipton India Ltd. By 1994, HLL was merged with Tata Oil Mills Company[2] (TOMCO), a Tata Group company. Meanwhile HLL

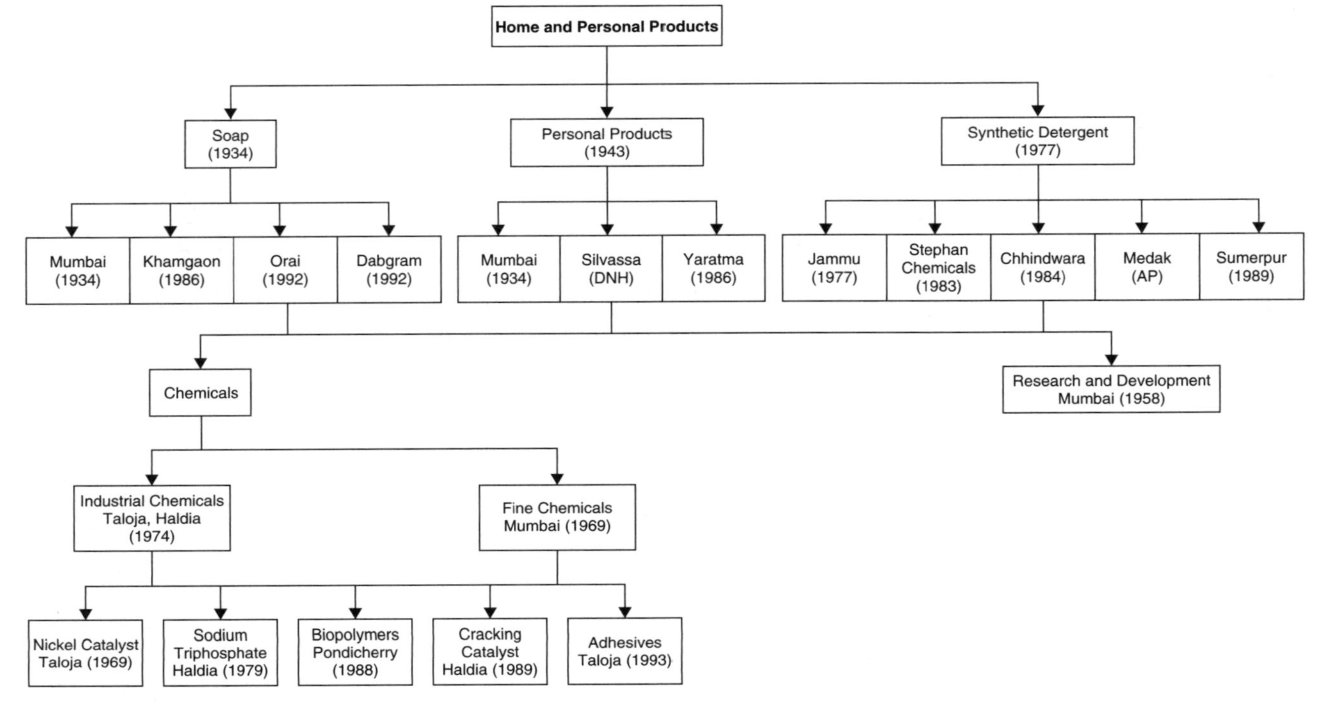

Chart 5.1 Investments in home and personal products, 1934–2004

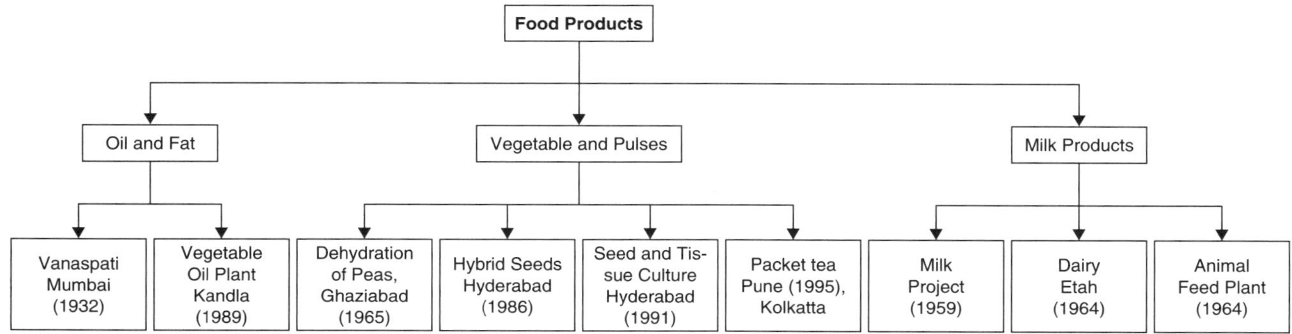

Chart 5.2 Investments in food products, 1932–2004

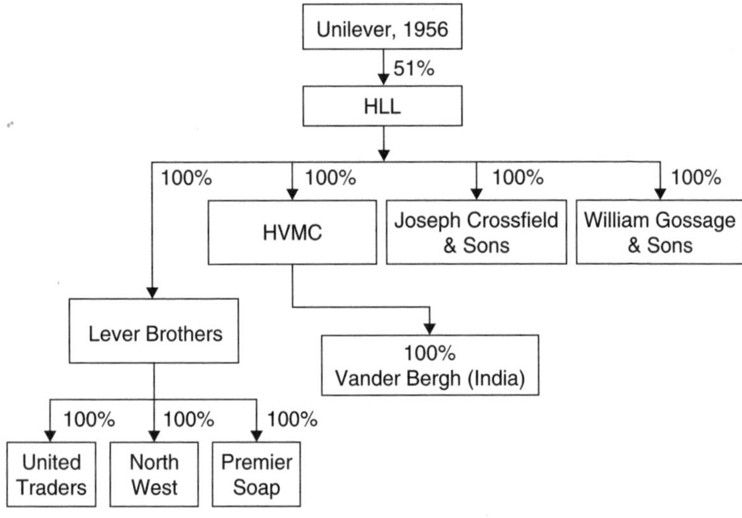

Chart 5.3 Investment and shareholding pattern of Unilever in India, 1956

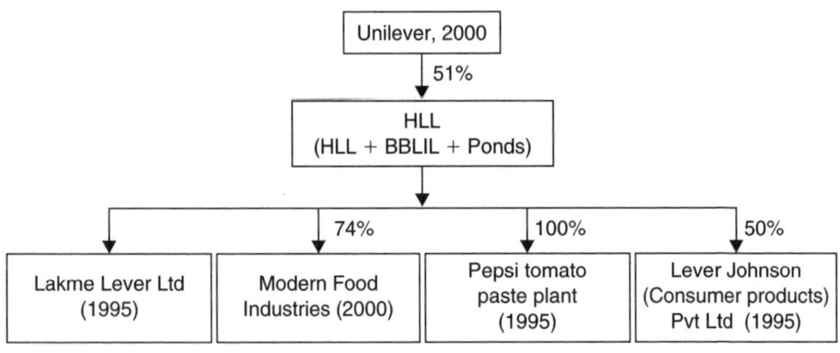

Chart 5.4 Investment and shareholding pattern of Unilever in India, 2000

acquired stakes in other companies. It had 80 per cent equity in Nepal Lever Ltd, 50 per cent in Kimberley-Clark Lever Ltd, 100 per cent in Kwality and 100 per cent in Milk Food.

Through various mergers and acquisitions, HLL had grown to be a huge conglomerate by 2000. HLL was a merger of Brooke Bond Lipton India[3] (BBIL) and Ponds.[4] It had stakes in Lakme Lever, Modern Food, Pepsi Tomoto, and Lever Johnson (see Chart 5.4).

While HLL has several changes in the shareholding structures since its formation in 1956, Unilever has skilfully maintained a 51 per cent share in equity of HLL from 1956 to the present day. It is also interesting to note that while most foreign firms preferred to increase their ownership,

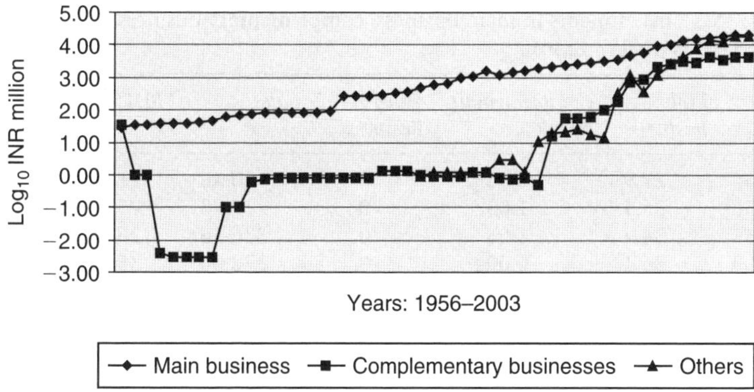

Source: Compiled from HLL Annual Reports, 1955–2003.
Figure 5.1 Investment[5] of Unilever in India, 1955–2003

whenever they had any opportunity, Unilever has craftily maintained its ownership level at 51 per cent in HLL/HUL.

Analysis of investments made by Unilever for 1956–2003 has been based on the Annual Reports of HLL. Gross Block in the balance sheet is taken as investments in the main business. Investments in subsidiaries and related businesses are taken as investments in complementary businesses. Investment in government securities and other unrelated activities is taken as investment in others. As Unilever internalized several business activities, some activities that were complementary at one stage have become gradually part of the main business.

The company's investments in its main business have grown phenomenally during the last 50 years, from INR28 million in 1955 to INR21,417 million by 2003. Similarly, investment in complementary businesses has grown from INR0.103 million in 1956 to INR4,273 million in 2003. Investments in complementary businesses after the merger of all Unilever subsidiaries in India fell for a few years, then stabilized, and subsequently have grown steadily (see Figure 5.1 and Table 5.3).

Investment in local management

The wartime shortage of trained European managers was a compelling factor in employing Indians at management level. In 1937, for the first time, Prakash Tandon, an Indian by origin was appointed at Junior Management level. In 1942, the company decided that Indians who proved their mettle and replaced Europeans should enjoy privileges equal to them. In 1944, 15 out of 57 employees at the management level were

Table 5.3 Investments in main business, complementary businesses and others: 1955–2003 (INR million)

Year	*Main business*	*Complementary business*	*Other business*	*Sales*	*PBDIT*	*PAT*
1955	27.9	3.32	0	40.36	21.03	8.97
1956	35.1	1.03	0	277.78	25.25	10.40
1957	34.4	1.03	0	336.16	26.76	10.02
1958	36.1	0.004	0	372.08	35.32	12.86
1959	37.3	0.003	0	422.97	46.92	20.84
1960	38.6	0.003	0	461.19	49.32	24.95
1961	43	0.003	0	499.18	45.79	22.55
1962	46.7	0.003	0	538.54	51.84	23.49
1963	60.6	0.103	0	595.47	47.78	14.75
1964	69.4	0.103	0	618.70	42.75	16.49
1965	77.7	0.58	0	714.80	51.90	17.15
1966	85.3	0.73	0	846.68	61.08	22.11
1967	84.6	0.81	0	932.82	64.42	20.01
1968	81.7	0.81	0	925.88	70.93	23.94
1969	84.5	0.81	0	1,087.91	72.84	27.50
1970	86.8	0.81	0	1,192.10	67.84	22.77
1971	89.7	0.81	0	1,341.03	94.28	30.06
1972	266.8	0.81	0	1,404.38	117.35	36.65
1973	267.3	0.81	0	1,326.81	112.23	32.46
1974	278.3	0.81	0	1,457.29	120.49	34.25
1975	304	1.28	0	2,059.88	182.35	47.72
1976	325.8	1.28	0	2,129.92	226.18	69.50
1977	364.9	1.29	0	2,616.83	247.43	78.22
1978	484.2	0.99	0.91	3,010.36	293.45	93.09
1979	574.9	0.94	1.22	3,226.33	364.85	175.96
1980	629	0.94	1.22	3,999.04	411.00	165.28
1981	978.8	0.94	1.22	4,807.84	521.50	207.24
1982	1,067.9	1.24	1.22	4,572.39	558.07	221.97
1983	1,667.6	1.24	1.22	5,011.73	537.51	185.64
1984	1,144.1	0.78	2.98	5,389.98	601.44	216.76
1985	1,471.5	0.76	2.98	6,179.49	759.93	325.58
1986	1,634.1	0.82	1.22	7,145.72	791.45	390.72
1987	1,971.9	0.51	10.09	7,953.70	985.12	464.95
1988	2,096.5	15.11	18.7	8,454.06	1,160.99	487.77
1989	2,265.6	58.76	20.36	1,0081.65	1,225.95	538.11
1990	2,673.5	58.76	26.42	12,011.48	1,463.06	658.51
1991	2,977.4	59.56	16.42	15,065.83	1,775.18	802.02
1992	3,304.7	104.97	13.64	17,570.28	2,177.68	984.76
1993	3,655.9	180.82	328.67	20,631.67	2,722.15	1,272.71
1994	4,917.9	691.83	1,222.63	28,264.83	3,558.14	1,899.63
1995	5,638.4	858.79	369.49	33,669.47	4,159.83	2,392.21

(Continued)

Table 5.3 (Continued)

Year	Main business	Complementary business	Other business	Sales	PBDIT	PAT
1996	9,542.3	2,131.19	1,156.57	66,001.08	7,159.44	4,142.62
1997	10,358.2	2,621.09	2,694.57	78,197.08	9,222.19	5,603.71
1998	13,841.3	3,118.76	4,176.32	94,818.49	12,290.37	8,057.11
1999	14,810.6	2,991.49	7,389.65	10,1424.88	15,390.86	10,699.40
2000	16,687.4	4,403.46	13,918.96	10,6037.90	18,091.79	13,100.93
2001	19,358.7	3,526.02	13,163.29	10,9719.00	20,957.70	15,409.50
2002	19,943.6	4,422.95	19,554.58	10,3394.00	23,404.00	17,697.40
2003	21,417.2	4,272.96	21,778.52	10,5982.00	35,595.50	17,717.90

Source: HLL Annual Reports, 1955–2003.

Indians. By 1955, Indians constituted about 65 per cent of managers. When the Unilever subsidiaries in India merged to form HLL in 1956, there were three Indians on the eight-member Board of Directors. In 1961, Tandon took over from S.H. Turner as Chairman. By then, of the 205 managers 191 were Indians. From then on Unilever subsidiaries in India have been led by Indian Chairmen, namely, T. Thomas, V.G. Rajadhyaksa, A.S. Ganguly, S.M. Dutta, K.B. Dadiseth and M.S. Banga. Employing competent local managers made economic sense. The parent company was able to execute its plans in India through carefully selected local managers.[6] Renaming the company with 'Hindustan' as part of its name clearly shows how the company attempted very early on to identify itself with India. Prakash Tandon, the first Indian covenanted manager was appointed to HVMC in 1937. Subsequently, he rose to be the Chairman of the company in 1961. V.G. Rajadhyaksha took over as Chairman from Tandon in 1968. Subsequently, T. Thomas took over the Chairman's position and Indian managers have continued to lead the company from the top (see Table 5.4). From as early as 1937, the company has attempted to localize management by recruiting local managers. It is interesting to note here that Unilever started to localize its management in India prior to the wish expressed by the Government – an idea that many other foreign companies objected to. Uniever did, however, see the economic rationale for doing so and wasn't just simply agreeing to local government wishes.

Investment in distribution network and marketing

Initially, in the 1900s, like all other foreign companies, Lever Brothers faced the huge hurdle of trying to overcome poor road transport and

Table 5.4 Localization of management

Year	*Localization of management*
1937	Prakash Tandon, one of the first Indian covenanted managers joins HVM
1942	Unilever takes firm decision to 'train Indian managers to take over junior and senior management positions instead of European managers'
1944	W.G.J. Shaw & C.S. Petit become joint Managing Directors of the three companies
1947	M.G.J. Shaw leaves, C.S. Petit takes charge
1951	Parkas Tandon becomes first Indian Director
1953	A.J.C. Hoskyns-Abrahall takes over as Chairman from C.S. Petit
1955	65% of managers were Indians
1957	S.H. Turner takes over as Chairman from A.J.C. Hoskyns-Abrahall
1961	P.L. Tandon takes over from S.H. Turner as the first Indian Chairman; 191 of the 205 managers were Indians.
1968	V.G. Rajadhyaksha takes over as Chairman from Prakash Tandon
1973	T. Thomas takes over as Chairman from V.G. Rajadhyaksha
1980	A.S. Ganguly takes over as Chairman from T. Thomas
1990	S.M. Datta takes over as Chairman from A.S. Ganguly
1996	K.B. Dadiseth takes over as Chairman from S.M. Datta
2000	M.S. Banga takes over as Chairman from K.B. Dadiseth, who joined the Unilever Board

Sources: The author has compiled this data from various Annual Reports and official reports of the company.

communications, infrastructure in order to conduct business in India. In 1895, Unilever appointed agents in Bombay, Madras, Calcutta and Karachi to sell Lifebuoy soap. At this stage the wholesalers received the products through company salesmen and consignee agents and sold the products to the retailers. In 1941, the company set up its own sales force at these places, appointing registered wholesalers in each market to whom the company sold its products. In the subsequent stages, the company introduced Redistribution Stockists and third party Carry and Forwarding Agents (see Chart 5.5).

Currently, the company's Redistribution Stockists in India number about 7,000 reaching nearly 1,000,000 retail outlets. The retail outlets in the rural areas number nearly 3,800, covering nearly 50,000 villages. The Redistribution Stockists finance stock, provide manpower, provide service to retailers, implement promotional activities, extend indirect coverage, reports sales and stock data, screen for transit damage, etc. In order to rationalize the logistics and planning task, Mother Depots and Just-in-Time Systems have been introduced. An internet-based network,

First Stage (Early Years)		Second Stage (1940s)		Third Stage		Fourth Stage
Company HQ ↓ Company Salesman, Consignee ↓ Wholesalers, Large retailers ↓ Retailers ↓ Consumers	⇨	Company HQ ↓ Registered Wholesalers (in each market) (through distribution units of the company) ↓ Retailers ↓ Consumers	⇨	Company HQ ↓ Company Depots ↓ Redistribution Stockist (RS) (through distribution units of RS) ↓ Retailers ↓ Consumers	⇨	Company ↓ Third Party Carry & Forwarding Agents (C & FA) ↓ Redistribution Stockist (RS) ↓ Retailers ↓ Consumers

Source: The chart has been constructed using the data from company history and Annual Reports of HLL/HUL.

Chart 5.5 Evolution of distribution network

Table 5.5 New product-market development

Year	*New product*
1888	Sunlight soap introduced in India
1902	Pears soap introduced in India
1903	Brooke Bond Red Label tea launched
1905	Lux flakes introduced
1913	Vim scouring powder, first range of Erasmic toilet preparations introduced
1914	Vinolia soap launched in India
1918	Vanaspati introduced by Dutch margarine
1922	Rinso soap powder introduced
1924	Gibbs dental preparations launched
1926	Hartogs registers Dalda Trademark
1939	Concentration on building up Dalda Vanaspati as a brand
1947	Pond's Cold Cream launched
1951	Lakme, India's first cosmetic brand
1959	Surf was launched in the market
1964	Anik ghee launched; Sunsilk shampoo launched
1965	Hima dehydrated peas in market; Signal toothpaste launched
1966	Lever's baby food, more new foods introduced, & Taj Mahal tea launched
1969	Rin bar launched; Bru coffee launched
1971	Clinic shampoo launched
1974	Liril was marketed
1975	Close Up toothpaste launched
1978	Fair & Lovely skin cream launched
1988	Lipton Taaza tea launched
1991	Lifebouy Plus, Breeze Sandalwood, Surf Ultra detergents launched
1993	Launch of Vim bar
1994	Huggies diapers and Kotex feminine care products marketed; HLL Wall's introduced
1995	HLL enters branded staples business with salt; Brooke Bond A1 launched
1996	HLL introduces branded atta (flour); International Surf Excel launched
2001	HLL decides to focus on powder brands; enters Confectioneries category; launches relevant services like Lakme Beauty Salons

Source: HLL Annual Reports, 1955–2004, and <http://www.hll.com>.

called RS Net, a network of Redistribution Stockists (RS) has been implemented to supply stocks to RS on a continuous replenishment basis. In 2003 the company set up the Direct Selling Channel with Aviance, a company with international range of customized beauty solutions.

HLL has been in the forefront of introducing new products. In recent years it has developed some innovative products such as 'Fair & Lovely' and 'Rin Bar' for the parent company's world market (see Table 5.5).

Timing of investment

As far as personal care products were concerned, the company initially sold in India, two types of soap bars – one for washing clothes and the other was bath soap. In the meantime it introduced other personal care products in to the country. Unilever began to invest in the local manufacturing of soap in 1934. In 1943, it began to invest in manufacturing personal care products. Thereafter, it went about systematically investing in its complementary or support activities such as raw materials and other value-added products. To strengthen its in-house research for new products, the company set up a Research and Development Unit in Bombay in 1958.

Steve Turner, the last British Chairman of Unilever operations in India believed that Indian scientists were capable of innovating new products and processes and hence pushed for setting up a Research & Development Unit in India. Scientists such as V.G. Rajadhyaksa and S. Varadharajan were invited to take charge of the research activity in India.[7]

The company invested in the local manufacturing of several critical raw materials for its soap and personal care product-making: nickel catalysts (1966), fine chemicals (1969), industrial chemicals (1974), synthetic detergents (1977), followed soon after by investment in sodium tripolyphosphate, and film sulphonation (1991) (see Chart 5.6). The beginning of the shaded area in each column indicates the year when the investment in the area indicated on the top of the respective column was begun.

In the packaged food products segment, Unilever made the first direct investment in India in 1931 to locally produce vanaspati. To support its production of milk-based products the company invested in a milk collection project in 1959, later internalizing the sourcing of milk. By 1964, the company invested in both a dairy and animal feed unit. The company initially incurred losses in its dairy project but turned it around after creatively investing in the supply chain.

When the company was incurring losses on its dairy project in Etah, the Chairman, T. Thomas visited the site to investigate why the supply of milk to the dairy fell short of the farmers' commitment. He discovered that the farmers were too poor to feed the cows supplied by the company. They also gave first priority to their family need for milk. Thomas introduced the micro credit system to the farmers to circumvent the problem. This arrangement helped the diary project to take off finally. Many people's view is that micro credit was a social project in the Etah region but Thomas says that it was taken up purely from a business perspective.

Year/ product	*Soap*	*Personal product*	*Nickel catalyst*	*Fine chemicals*	*Industrial chemicals*	*Synthetic detergent*	*Sodium tripoly phosphate*	*Film sulphonation*
1888	Trading							
1900s		Trading						
1934	Manufacturing							
1943		Manufacturing						
1966			Manufacturing					
1969				Manufacturing				
1974					Manufacturing			
1977						Manufacturing		
1979							Manufacturing	
1991								Manufacturing

Chart 5.6 Timing of investment in complementary businesses – personal care products

Investment in research and development of dehydration of peas started in 1959; in 1965, the company invested in commercial dehydration of peas. Further, moving up the value chain, the company invested in producing hybrid seeds in 1986; in 1988, it invested in functional biopolymers. In 1991, Unilever invested in tissue culture (see Chart 5.7). The beginning of the shade in each column indicates the year when the investment in the area indicated on the top of the respective column was begun.

Integration of business goals to host country's national goals

Unilever has continuously aligned itself with the host country demands in India, integrating the requirements of the host government with its own business objectives. For instance, when in the 1930s the British Government, under pressure from Indian representatives, introduced import duties on soap and packed food items, Unilever decided to invest in the local manufacture of vanaspati and soap in India. After India's independence, the Indian Soap Manufacturers' Association started a movement against the continuing presence of Levers in the Indian market (Fieldhouse, 1978). Further, in the 1950s the GOI classified personal care products and packaged food items as non-essential items and companies in such businesses were restricted to import raw materials required for making soap and hydrogenated oil or fat. The Government also introduced statutory price controls on vanaspati during 1966–75 and on soap during 1967–74. This section explains how Unilever aligned its business to meet the local government's requirement for import substitution, export promotion, and investments in social sector.

Import substitution and exports

The early investments in the Indian chemical industry by British companies helped Unilever procure some of its raw materials locally. However, as the edible oil and chemical industry was poorly developed in India, Unilever had to import the raw materials. In order to maintain the supplies of its raw materials, the company had to look for alternative supplies from within India. An R&D section was therefore set up in 1958 with Indian scientists with the objective of developing substitutes for imports. Gradually, the R&D efforts were directed to improve the functional delivery of products and boost the export business. The company estimates that it has saved foreign exchange of about US$1.2 billion every year during the 1970s and later through its R&D efforts. Some of the import substitutes discovered were (a) a recombinant strain of yeast, developed

Year/ product	*Vanaspati*	*Milk collection*	*Dairy*	*Animal feed*	*Dehydration of peas*	*Hybrid seeds*	*Functional bioploymers*	*Tissue culture*
1900s	Trading							
1931	Manufacturing							
1959		Manufacturing			R&D Activity			
1964			Manufacturing	Manufacturing				
1965					Manufacturing			
1986						Manufacturing		
1988							Manufacturing	
1991								Manufacturing

Chart 5.7 Timing of investment in complementary businesses – packaged food products

by protoplast fusion between sugar-tolerant fast growing *S. cerevisae* and fat accumulating *R. gracilis*, (b) tissue culture for crops such as coconut and cardamom, (c) potato microtuber, and (d) infant nutrients and shadow nutrients. The use of unconventional oils, such as neem, karanja, castor and rice bran for soap-making was pioneered by the company.

In the early 1950s, the GOI encouraged companies to export their products to earn foreign exchange for the country. In 1965–66, it imposed restrictions on imports of edible oils and associated products. In other words, the regulations required that a firm was required to earn foreign exchange in order to be eligible for receiving foreign exchange from the Reserve Bank of India for purposes of imports by that firm. In 1970, it enacted the Monopolies and Restrictive Trade Practices Act, which made export of a portion of their sales mandatory for large companies. In 1981, there was a new Export–Import Policy to similar effect.

Unilever undertook several measures to fulfil these export requirements. In 1962, it started an Export Department. The following year Indexport Ltd, a fully owned subsidiary of HLL, was set up in Bombay. In 1965, the company first exported to Russia. In 1967, it found markets for exporting items such as textiles, yarn, handloom fabric, and engineering goods manufactured by third parties in India. From outsourcing exportable items from India the company invested in setting up factories in Madras to manufacture leather garments and other leather products, including wool-on-leather and wool-on-garment (see Table 5.6).

Since its traditional products such as soap and toiletries have usually had low export value Unilever had to develop new products to meet the export requirements. One of the products it developed was cold-water soluble instant tea dust and the technology to isolate and process a powerful ultraviolet-ray-absorbing sunscreen from naturally occurring vegetable oil.

The company has steadily improved its export volume, from INR2.8 million in 1956 to INR14,370 million in 2003 (see Figure 5.2 and Table 5.7). The company has also earned several awards of recognition for its export performance, including the Solvent Extractors' Association Award in 1997 for being the highest exporter of rice bran extraction. The Government recognized HLL as a Star Trading House in Exports in 1992 and as a Super Star Trading House in 1995.

Investment in the social sector

Of its nearly hundred manufacturing units, the company has set up 28 factories in backward areas, in order to capitalize on the government's incentives for such a policy measure. Investments in areas classified as

Table 5.6 Export activities of HLL

Year	*Export activity undertaken*
1965	First time exports to Russia
1966	Restriction on edible oil & associated products
1967	Found overseas markets for articles like textiles, yarn, handloom fabrics & engineering goods manufactured by third parties in India
1968	Exports of non traditional items
1969	Exports of non traditional items like sal seed oil
1970	Exports of Hima food products and exports of synthetic detergent to Russia
1974	Exports increased to 52 countries
1975	Export earnings touched INR40.5 million
1976	Exports to 38 countries
1980	The Indian subsidiary, HLL was recognized as an Export House
1981	Recognized as an Export Trading House
1982	New investment in 100% export projects in Soap, Personal products, Marine Products, Readymade Garment & Plant Protection Chemicals
1992	A factory to manufacture Wool-on-Leather and Wool-on-Garments for exports was commissioned in Chennai

Source: HLL Annual Reports.

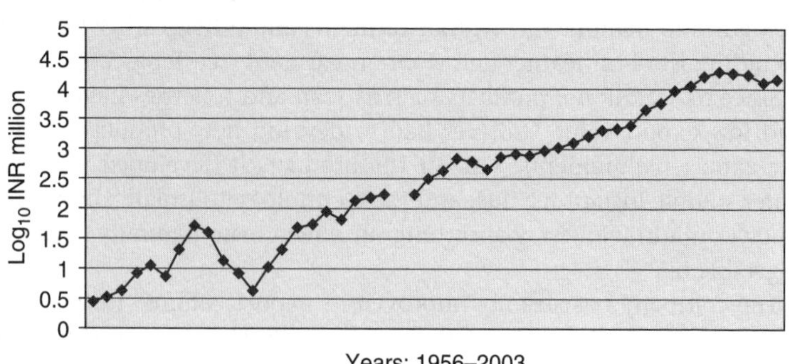

Source: Compiled from HLL Annual Reports (1956–2003).
Figure 5.2 Export earnings of HLL, 1956–2003

backward regions were exempted from taxes on profit for a period of 5–10 years. The company's social programmes include the Integrated Rural Development Programme, special education for mentally and physically challenged children, micro-financing, a rural education programme, and support for an earthquake-affected region in Gujurat.

Table 5.7 Export earnings of HLL (INR million)

Year	*Export amount*	*Year*	*Export amount*
1956	2.8	1980	420
1957	3.3	1981	700
1958	4.2	1982	620
1959	8.4	1983	465
1960	11.2	1984	740
1961	7.4	1985	840
1962	20.1	1986	790
1963	51.2	1987	920
1964	39.3	1988	1,040
1965	13.7	1989	1,300
1966	8.1	1990	1,620
1967	4.2	1991	2,020
1968	10.8	1992	2,240
1969	20.1	1993	2,550
1970	47.8	1994	4,560
1971	55.2	1995	5,820
1972	88.2	1996	9,210
1973	67.0	1997	11,520
1974	137.2	1998	16,640
1975	149.4	1999	19,968
1976	175.1	2000	17,992
1977	n.a.	2001	17,741
1978	176	2002	12,412
1979	320	2003	14,370

Source: HLL Annual Reports, 1955–2003.

It started Integrated Rural Development in Etah, Uttar Pradesh to provide training to farmers on health and to lend micro-finance to villagers. This scheme also helped in the sustenance of the company's dairy project in Etah. While A.S. Ganguly (former Chairman of HLL) mentioned in an interview that these projects were a measure of HLL's contribution to social causes, T. Thomas (another former Chairman) said business was the sole objective. Involvement in the social sector increased profits, by reducing the cost of manufacturing and transport, obtaining tax incentives, and earning goodwill from the large base of users of its products. Nevertheless, the projects have benefited the rural masses. For example, the project in the Etah region in Uttar Pradesh has expanded from 30 to about 500 villages.

The project to provide special education for mentally and physically challenged children in Ankur (Sikkim) and Kappagam (Tamilnadu) was started in 1993 and 1998, respectively. In 2001, it helped reconstruct the earthquake-affected Yashodadham village in Gujurat and in 2002, it helped the Government in Madhya Pradesh to set up fair-price shops in villages.

Executives from HLL were appointed on several government projects and rendered other support to the Government. For instance, managers from HLL were appointed to work on setting up public sector companies in the 1970s at the Government's request, the company compensating the managers on such deputation for the low salaries they received from the Government. V.G. Rajadhyaksa, former Chairman of HLL, was appointed Member Planning Commission. A.S. Ganguly (another former Chairman) was appointed Scientific Adviser to Prime Minister Rajiv Gandhi.

Localization of ownership

Unilever's ownership

By 1935, Unilever wholly owned three large companies in India, namely, Lever Brothers (India), Margarine Unie, and United Traders. Lever Brothers (India) also had 100 per cent shares of Northwest Soaps and Margarine had 100 per cent shares of Hindustan Vanaspati Manufacturing Company (HVMC). In 1956, Unilever merged all its businesses (HVMC, William Gossage and Sons (India) Pvt Ltd, and Joseph Crossfield and Sons Pvt Ltd) under the single new subsidiary, HLL. Subsequently, United Traders Pvt Ltd was taken over by HLL and Van der Bergh (India) Pvt Ltd, a wholly owned subsidiary of HVMC, became a wholly owned subsidiary of HLL.

Following the Industrial Licensing Policy, 1991, the company acquired a 51 per cent stake in Brooke Bond India Ltd and Lipton India Ltd, 100 per cent equity in Kwality and Milk Food by 1994, and 74 per cent of Modern Food Industries Ltd, the first public sector company to be divested by the GOI, in 2000.

In the personal care product segment, in 1993, Tata Oil Mills was merged with HLL. By virtue of Unilever's worldwide mergers and acquisitions in 1994, HLL acquired a 50 per cent stake in Kimberley-Clark Lever Ltd. In 1995, HLL hived off Stephan Chemicals and acquired Wheel Detergents. By 2000, it had 51 per cent control on Ponds and had extended its expansion to Nepal by acquiring 80 per cent stake in Nepal Lever (see Table 5.8).

Table 5.8 Ownership in HLL, 1955–2002

Year	*Unilever (%)*	*Indian private investors & others (%)*
1955	100	–
1956	90.0	10 557,000 ordinary shares @ INR10 per share were issued to the public
1965	86.0	14
1966	85.0	15
1977	81.43	18.57
1978	64.0	34.0
1980	51.0	49.0
1982	Government allowed Unilever to retain 51% shareholding in HLL	49.0
2002	51.55	Indian Public: 22.91% Financial Institution: 24.58%

Source: HLL, Annual Reports.

Indian equity in HLL

In early 1950s, Minister of Finance, T.T. Krishnamachari persuaded the Chairman of Lever Brothers to sell part of its shares and thereby set a good example as a progressive organization (Fieldhouse, 1978). Unilever accordingly reduced its equity holdings gradually from 100 per cent to 51 per cent. In 1956, Unilever sold 10 per cent of its shares to the Indian public in exchange for the promise of a free flow of profit remittances and of no increase in taxation. Indeed, Unilever could get its pound of flesh through the negotiations with the Government on the issue of including local equity in its business. Many other companies such as General Motors and Ford Motors were simply put off by this policy and closed their operations in India. The subsequent increase of local equity was as follows: 14 per cent (1965), 15 per cent (1966), 18.57 per cent (1977), 34 per cent (1978), and 49 per cent (1980) (see Figure 5.3 and Table 5.8). The issue of further dilution remained with the Government until 1982, when it allowed Unilever to retain 51 per cent control in HLL on the grounds that Unilever's operation in India involved production of high technology products and it exported[8] substantial amounts of its local production. HLL earned large amounts of foreign exchange, but it did meet the 60 per cent exports volume to qualify to retain 51 per cent control. Many have argued how HLL qualified to be engaged in high technology product research. It has also been observed that although

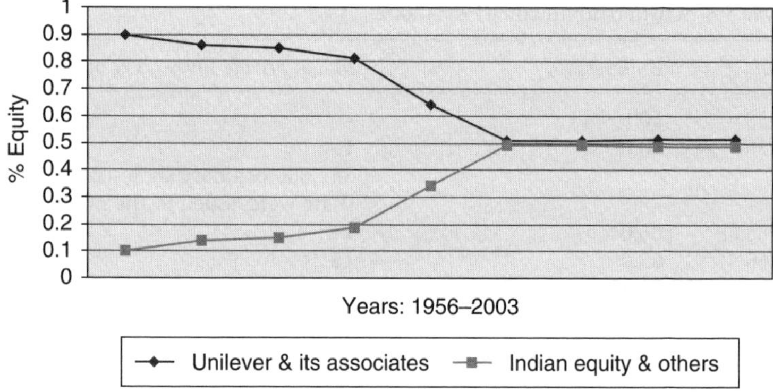

Source: HLL (1956–2003), Annual Reports.
Figure 5.3 Percentage shareholding of Unilever vs Indian equity

Unilever was willing to dilute its equity, the Indian management of HLL wanted Unilever to retain its majority stake in the company.[9]

Performance indicators

Financials: sales, PBDIT and PAT

Unilever began investing in local manufacturing of vanaspati in 1932. Between 1935 and 1941 the sale of its vanaspati increased by 400 per cent, from 11,222 tons to 43,065 tons. The company began investing in the local manufacture of soap in 1934. Between 1935 and 1941 the sale of its soap increased by over 100 per cent, from 9,897 tons to 20,040 tons (Fieldhouse, 1978). An analysis of the company's Annual Reports for 1955–2003 reveals that it has performed remarkably well in all areas, with consistent increase in sales, PBDIT and PAT (see Figure 5.4 and Table 5.9). Sales, PBDIT and PAT have steadily grown during 1955–2003. While the other companies have similar figures, the figures for HLL/HUL are a class apart (see Figure 3.3).

Market share

HLL/HUL holds about 55–60 per cent of the market share in the personal care and packaged food segment, considerably overshadowing major players such as Procter & Gamble, Nestlé, Cadbury, Nirma, and Dabur (see Figure 5.5 and Table 5.9). Although there has been a dip in its market share following the Industrial Licensing Policy, 1991, it maintains its strong lead.

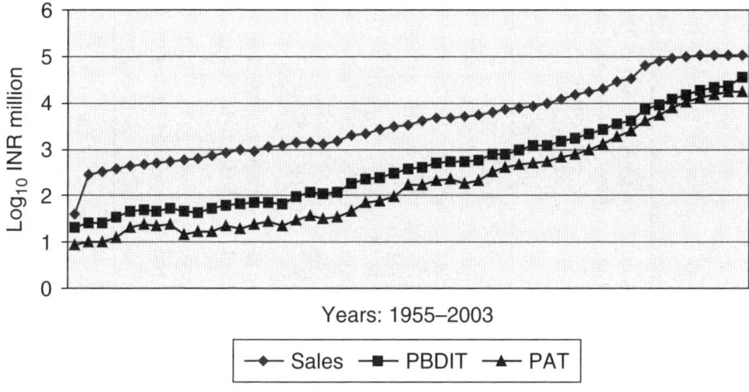

Source: HLL Annual Reports (1955–2003).

Figure 5.4 HLL sales, PBDIT and PAT, 1955–2003

Summary: FDI strategy of Unilever

Unilever's FDI strategy is similar to that of BAT. When it first made direct investments in India in 1932, it not only invested in its main business of either soap or packaged food but also in several complementary businesses that were required to support the investments in the main business. For personal care products the complementary businesses included local production of various raw materials, oil substitutes, nickel catalyst, fine chemicals, industrial chemicals, and sodium tripolyphosphate. In the packaged food product segment, the company invested in complementary business functions such as milk collection, microfinancing the farmers, developing animal feed, developing hybrid seeds, developing dehydration technology, and tissue culture, etc. Further, for these product segments, the company had to systematically develop the dealer and wholesaler networks in the whole India.

The company aligned its business objectives with the policies and programmes of the host government. It invested in chemicals, fertilizers and oil mills. It undertook research and development to develop substitutes of raw materials for soap making. Through its exports, it generated the much-needed foreign exchange for the country and for itself so that it could import essential raw materials for local production. It invested in several backward areas in line with the backward area development objectives of the host country, India, receiving several tax incentives that reduced its cost of production. It also internalized the various

Table 5.9 Annual sales of HLL and its major competitors (INR million)

Year	*Cadbury India Ltd*	*Colgate-Palmolive (India) Ltd*	*Dabur India Ltd*	*Godrej Consumer Products*	*Henkel Spic India Ltd*	*Marico Industries Ltd*	*Nestle India Ltd*	*Nirma Ltd*	*Parry & Co. Ltd (Merged)*	*P&G Hygiene & Health Care Ltd*	*Hindustan Lever Ltd*	*Total market*	*HLL's share*	*Total market including all players in all businesses of HLL*	*HLL's share under this context*
Dec. 88	738.5	2,294.5	1,046	–	–	–	2,080.1		444.5	518.1	10,017.8	17,139.5	*58.45*	20,614.2	*48.6*
Dec. 89	675.8	2,733.2	883.2	–	–	–	2,564.9		418.4	667.5	11,932.1	19,875.1	*60.04*	34,434.9	*34.7*
Dec. 90	1,083.5		1,491.6	–	–	–	3,121.9		254.5	755.9	14,634.4	21,341.8	*68.57*	36,928.6	*39.6*
Dec. 91	1,222.9	4,052.9	1,898.1	–	–	1,058.3	3,978.8	2,012	379.2	983.5	17,810.6	33,396.3	*53.33*	51,751.1	*34.4*
Dec. 92	1,424.6	4,216.9	2,447.7	–	–	1,594.4	4,901.6	2,434.8	68.5	1,464.7	20,868.7	39,421.9	*52.94*	62,653.3	*33.3*
Dec. 93	1,572	4,948.6	2,569.3	–	–	2,103.2	5,661.2	1,865.8	115	2,066.8	24,360.6	45,262.5	*53.82*	70,467.5	*34.6*
Dec. 94	1,449.8	6,020.7	3,171.3	–	62.1	2,364.4	7,121.6	3110.6	135.7	2,735.5	32,468.4	58,640.1	*55.37*	89,368.7	*36.3*
Dec. 95	2,530.8	6,815.9	4,055.8	–	125.3	2,833.4	9,974.6	4,157.3	129.8	2,730.1	37,829.6	71,182.6	*53.14*	108,711.6	*34.8*
Dec. 96	3,138.8	8,512.8	5,639.3	–	466.6	3,485.4	12,073.2	4,926.1	163.4	3,802.4	71,378.8	113,587	*62.84*	162,096.7	*44.0*
Dec. 97	3,541.4	9,656.6	7,075.2	–	557.8	4,096.9	14,293.3	9,116.6	170.4	4,063.9	83,633	136,205	*61.4*	189,249.2	*44.2*
Dec. 98	4,283.3	10,235.4	8,131.7	–	1,418.9	4,901.3	16,060.5	12,059	130.3	4,574.3	102,615.7	164,410	*62.41*	215,284.3	*47.7*
Dec. 99	5,110.8	9,993.1	9,182.7	–	2,720	5,523.3	15,464.3	14,731	168.4	4,836.3	109,783.1	177,513	*61.85*	234,607.5	*46.8*
Dec. 00	5,711.4	10,895.7	10,462.9	–	3,009.2	6,490.2	16,802.8	17,187	198.5	4,928.5	114,583	190,269	*60.22*	253,784.9	*45.1*
Dec. 01	7,295.7	11,768.8	11,726.1	0	3,404.6	6,592.4	19,272.8	24,292	211.5	4,643.8	118,617.9	207,826	*57.08*	276,612.5	*42.9*
Dec. 02	7,956.1	11,608.9	11,676	5,204.8	3,452.3	6,729	20,589.5	22,761	196.9	4,655.6	110,560.4	205,390	*53.83*	272,513.4	*40.6*
Dec. 03	8,428.5	10,568.9	12,363	5,330.3	–	7,395.7	22,855.1	24,164	195.6	4,896	105,982*	202,179	52.4	–	–

Notes: *Sales figure is in the Annual Report of HLL, 2003. The data of CMIE are normalized across the industry. Hence the data of the Annual Reports and data of CMIE may vary slightly.
Source: Centre for Monitoring Indian Economy.

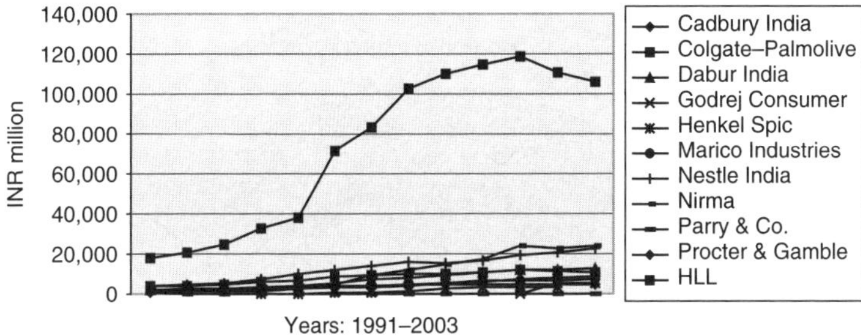

Source: Centre for Monitoring Indian Economy.

Figure 5.5 Sales of HLL and its major competitors, 1991–2003

market functions in the downstream of its main business of personal care and packaged food.

The policy of Indianization of its management since the 1930s was in line with the Indian Government's policy of creating local employment. The company treated the Indian managers on par with the British managers. Recruiting local managers also helped the company to reduce its overheads. By 1965, 65 per cent of the managers were Indians and by 1961 Indian managers constituted over 93 per cent of the managers. From having a 100 per cent ownership, Unilever diluted its equity to 51 per cent in 1980 and has maintained this level of ownership.

Contrary to the FDI pattern of most foreign companies in India during the last century Unilever's FDI pattern has been holistic. Holistic investment means investment in sales and marketing, local manufacture, complementary or support industry, and other social sectors. The company invested in selling soaps and vanaspati during its first 40 years. Since 1932, it has invested in local manufacturing of its various products. It has also invested in its related businesses such as fine chemicals, catalysts, industrial chemicals, dairy, animal feed, and tissue culture. Under the suggestion of the GOI, it also invested in oil milling, fertilizer, exports, and built factories in backward areas; which indeed helped the company. It also employed local managers as early as 1937 and included local equity in its business. It has gradually invested across the various layers of its business functions (see Figure 5.6). This strategy has not only generated rich dividends for the company but also given it a stronghold in the Indian market.

As with BAT, many of Unilever's major investment decisions have been made as a result of the current business situations at different periods in India's history and of the regulatory framework of the country. The

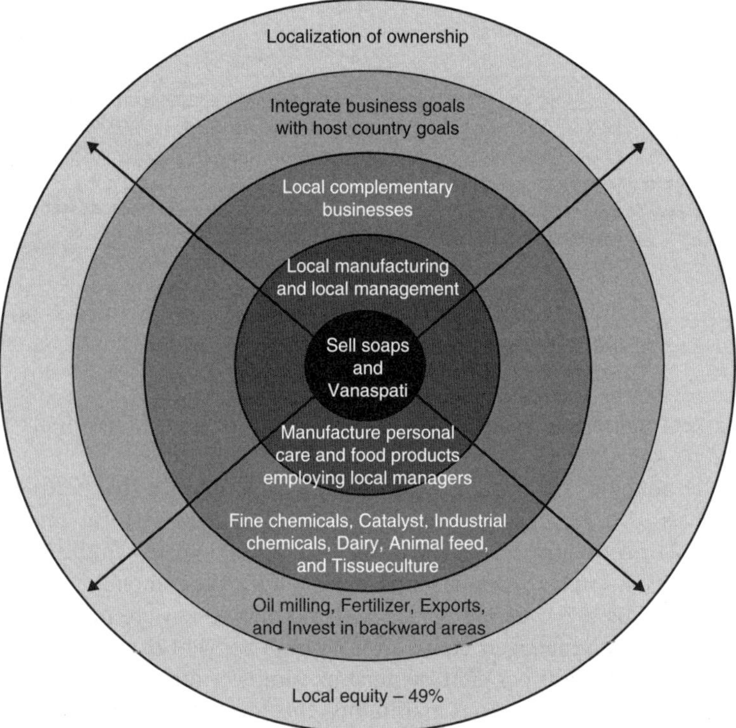

Figure 5.6 Holistic FDI pattern of Unilever in India, 1932–2004

strategy as we see it today may have been actually arrived at after trial and error by the managers in the company. However, the strategy in retrospect provides an insight into how a foreign firm can succeed in a host country like India. Unilever has been committed to staying in India since the 1930s, when it started to manufacture its products in India. It invested heavily across its industry value chain, astutely aligned its business objectives with the objectives of the host country, and shared the management and equity with the host country. Statistical confirmation of the positive impact of investment in main business activity and complementary businesses on the financials of the company is discussed in Chapter 7. Like BAT, Unilever's strategy in India appears to have been to carry out its business from a level where the host country, India, was placed and not from a level that Unilever was placed in its business in the United Kingdom and the Netherlands.

6
Suzuki Motor Corporation, 1982–2004

Suzuki Motor Corporation (SMC) is a case of FDI in the Indian automobile industry. This case is relatively new as compared to the previous two cases that have already been discussed. This chapter discusses the process by which SMC invested in various business functions in India during the period 1982–2004. The analysis involves the study of the nature and timing of investments of the company in its main business and complementary market functions, the manner in which it aligned itself to the requirements of the GOI, the issues of localization of management and ownership and its financial performance in India. The detailed confirmatory statistical analysis of the case, however, is provided in Chapter 7. This case brings out some of the perspectives of long term investment that we saw in the last two cases, throws up a new dimension, especially on the issue of ownership seeking behaviour of firms, and shows how holistic investment perspectives have been relevant in a developing country context even in recent times.

Indian car industry before 1982

The first motor car was brought to India in 1898 and import of fully assembled cars was sluggish until 1928. General Motors established an assembly plant in Bombay in 1928 to assemble cars and trucks using completed knocked down kits imported from USA. Soon after Ford Motor established assembly plants in Madras in 1930 and Calcutta in 1931. Subsequently, the Birla Group established Hindustan Motors Ltd in Calcutta in 1942 and the Walchand Group set up Premier Automobile Ltd in Bombay in 1944. Standard Motor Products Ltd, a British car company also tried to manufacture cars in Madras in 1948 but with little success.

In 1947, the Government of Britain in India appointed a 'Panel on Cars and Tractors' to examine the feasibility of manufacturing cars in India. The Panel's report strongly recommended the promotion of the transport vehicle industry for faster economic development in the country. However, the GOI considered passenger cars a luxury and hence it was not a priority. Neither did the government have a policy for private investment in the local manufacturing of passenger cars. In 1953, a legislation of the GOI required that foreign car companies that assembled cars in India must manufacture them in India within three years. The big automobile assemblers such as General Motors and Ford Motor ceased their operation in India the same year, 1953 (Venkataramani, 1990).

With the decision of automobile majors to wind up their operations in India, the passenger car industry was left to Hindustan Motors (HM) and Premier Automobile (PAL). HM produced Ambassador and PAL produced Premier Padmini. These cars were large and expensive to run and not many people could afford to buy cars for personal transport except for some government officials and rich people. Moreover, the car component industry was undeveloped and car service centres were not easily available. Only about 50,000 cars were sold annually during this period. Two local manufacturers met this demand with Hindustan Motors manufacturing 30,000 cars and Premier Automobile manufacturing the balance of 20,000 cars. The low volume of cars sold in the country and the lack of infrastructure and service centres provided little incentives for entrepreneurs to invest in the car industry for the next 30 years until SMC entered India.

MUL and SMC before 1982

Maruti Udyog Limited (MUL)

Maruti Ltd was started by Sanjay Gandhi in 1969 to produce small passenger cars. Sanjay Gandhi acquired 120 hectares of land and built 80,000 square meters of covered factory area but had little success in manufacturing cars. The company was subsequently liquidated in 1977. By an Act of the Parliament, GOI acquired Maruti Ltd in October 1980 and renamed it as Maruti Udyog Ltd (MUL). With this acquisition, the GOI established Maruti Udyog Ltd (MUL), a public sector company in February 1981. Then the Prime Minister of India, Indira Gandhi, took a personal interest to make this project a success and fulfil the dreams of her son, Sanjay Gandhi, who had struggled to make small passenger cars in India before he was killed in an accident.

The Government set a very large production target for MUL to produce 100,000 small passenger economy cars within the first five years. Indira Gandhi appointed some of the best managers in the country to meet this huge task. Suman Moolgaonkar, then the Chairman of Tata Engineering & Locomotive Works was made the Chairman of MUL. V. Krishnamurthy, former Chairman of Bharat Heavy Electricals Ltd (BHEL) was appointed Vice-Chairman and Managing Director, and R.C Bhargawa, Director, Commercial of BHEL was assigned the post of Director (Marketing and Sales) in MUL. Some changes in the Ministry of Industries were also sought to speed up the decisions related to implementation of MUL.

Early in 1981, the Government of India invited nearly 11 large established car companies from the UK, France, West Germany, Italy and Japan to provide low cost fuel-efficient car engine of below 1000cc. Despite several rounds of negotiations, many of these car majors were not keen to invest in India, as they probably did not think there would be much demand. Towards the final round of negotiations, Mitsubishi Motors of Japan seemed to be the sole contender to be the foreign partner. However, SMC entered the race late and was chosen because of its high speed of response to the Indian side. The joint venture agreement between MUL and SMC was finally signed on 2 October 1982.

Suzuki Motor Corporation (SMC)

Michio Suzuki founded the Suzuki Loom Works in Hamamatsu, Shizuoka prefecture in 1909. Michio Suzuki, the founder of Suzuki Motors had a great interest in cars. In 1936, he purchased a car for US $4000 from Britain and started his experiment until 1939 due to changes in the policy of Government of Japan during Second World War. Many technical personnel in the factory were diverted to manufacture war-related equipments as required by the government. Further, since 1951 Toshijo Suzuki, who became the President of Suzuki Motor after Michio Suzuki, had favoured the motorcycle business rather than the car business. However, Suzuki Motors had continued to supply important components such as crankshafts and pistons for the six-stroke engines of Isuzu Motors. From being a textile manufacturer, it went on to manufacture motorized bicycles in 1952. It changed its name to Suzuki Motors Company Ltd in 1954 as the company's business interest in personal transport grew stronger. In 1955, it came up with the Colleda brand of motorcycle and, subsequently, in 1961, Motors Works was separated from Loom Machine Division as the company's interest in automobile increased.

When SMC entered the automobile business in Japan, there were several established companies such as Toyota, Nissan, Isuzu and Mitsubishi, and others. Therefore, SMC carved out a niche for itself in small and fuel-efficient cars. 'Suzulight' a 360cc, 2-cycle car was first produced and marketed in Japan. However, it could hardly make much progress in the small car business. Unlike Toyota and Nissan, Suzuki Motors did not have the required finances to expand its business until the mid-1970s.

Many of the financial problems of Suzuki Motors were solved with Osamu Suzuki's entry into the company. Osamu Suzuki was a banker with a good banking network. He married the granddaughter of Michio Suzuki, the founder of SMC and, subsequently, was able to improve the financial status[1] of the company. Subsequently, Suzuki Motors introduced several models in the 1970s. Models such as SC 100 were introduced in 1978, followed by Alto/Fronte SS40 in 1979. In 1980, SS80 Alto/Fronte were launched, which became the Maruti 800 model in India.

The international expansion of Suzuki Motors in the car segment came about forcefully after Osamu Suzuki became the President of the company in 1978. The joint venture in India was the most ambitious project of Osamu Suzuki and it helped SMC to expand its operations in the overseas markets. Osamu's leadership was crucial to the success of Suzuki Motors' bid to enter India. His quick decision-making style gave Suzuki Motors an edge over Mitsubishi Motors in the final rounds of negotiations with MUL.

While many global automobile companies saw India as a small market and did not see much potential for growth, Osamu Suzuki visualized a huge potential[2] for cars in India. Contrary to the logic of most foreign car manufacturers SMC predicted that the demand for cars in India would rise to 200,000 cars per annum by 2000. In 1983, MUL set a target to manufacture 100,000 passenger cars (800cc) per year, a volume that was higher than its domestic production in Japan. Until 1959, it produced less than 500 cars per annum. During the period 1968–71, it produced over 100,000 per annum. However, after this rise in production, the production figures dwindled and by 1981, it produced only about 66,000 small cars. By this time, it had experimented with the production of cars with engines greater than 660cc and was still a very small producer of such cars in Japan with only about 21,000 cars per year. The total volume of cars produced by SMC in 1981 was only around 88,000 (see Table 6.1). The terms and conditions of the joint venture, especially the clause on

Table 6.1 SMC: annual production of passenger cars

Year	*Less than or equal to 660cc*	*Greater than 660cc*
1954	3	–
1955	28	–
1956	228	–
1957	399	–
1958	480	–
1959	480	–
1960	–	–
1961	–	–
1962	–	–
1963	1,551	–
1964	1,953	–
1965	1,437	660
1966	2,017	1,176
1967	43,495	545
1968	106,534	285
1969	124,550	670
1970	156,307	465
1971	125,582	342
1972	92,634	654
1973	79,429	657
1974	57,879	
1975	41,988	21
1976	50,346	
1977	56,988	
1978	63,533	125
1979	66,652	3,304
1980	78,315	16,176
1981	66,249	21,241
1982	93,445	29,521
1983	84,857	64,320
1984	63,154	116,157
1985	39,634	210,802
1986	43,163	262,960
1987	38,115	265,356
1988	42,706	265,941

Source: SMC (1990), 70 years of Suzuki Motors Corporation.

minority shareholding by the foreign company, were also not acceptable to the major car manufactures and hence many declined to be a partner to it. However, Suzuki Motors accepted to be a minority shareholder with a 26 per cent shareholding, and all other terms in the agreement that other foreign companies had declined (see Chart 6.1).

- Provide technical know-how, assistance and information for the manufacture, sale and after-sale service of products and parts of MUL
- Supply components for passenger cars
- Depute technical personnel to MUL facility
- Help MUL develop manufacturing processes and integrate certain Japanese management practices such as kaizen (continuous improvement)
- Train personnel
- Help develop and manage the supply chain for input products
- MUL will not manufacture in, or export products covered by agreements with SMC to, any territory except those permitted by SMC
- MUL will not enter into agreements with any other manufacturer to sell any product or part that competes with any product or part covered by license agreements of MUL with SMC, and
- MUL will not otherwise sell, distribute or promote the sale of any product that competes with products covered by our license agreement with SMC

Source: MUL Prospectus, 2003.

Chart 6.1 Excerpts from SMC's agreements with GOI, 1982

Nature and timings of investments

Local manufacturing and complementary businesses

In 1980s, the Indian car industry was in its infancy. When SMC began its operations in India, it faced a tough challenge to make the joint venture sustainable and profitable. Although, the joint venture encountered little bureaucratic hassles from Government bodies and agencies, its main challenge was the poor component manufacturing infrastructure.

SMC could not import car components as it faced two major problems at this time. First, it had to produce cars that were affordable to people in the middle-income segment. Importing components from Japan would have increased the cost of the cars it manufactured. Secondly, it was bound by the GOI's policy to include local components in its production and import substitution was a priority of the country since the Second Five year Plan of GOI (see Table 4.5).

SMC had to invest not only in design and assembling of cars through MUL but also in many other car-related businesses soon after its investment in MUL. It invested extensively both in MUL and other complementary market functions of the Indian car industry. In 1983, SMC invested INR17.3 million in MUL and added another INR71.28 million in 1984. It continued to invest steadily in MUL in the next seven years, with investments rising to INR208 million in 1989. It made the next

Table 6.2 SMC's Investments in MUL, 1983–2004

Date/year	*Amount (in INR)*
24 Jan. 1983	17,300,000
1 Mar. 1984	39,200,000
29 Mar. 1984	32,087,000
31 July 1985	5,198,700
18 Feb. 1986	50,300,000
19 May 1986	4,700,000
30 Sept. 1986	24,300,000
3 Mar. 1987	24,300,000
21 Dec. 1987	24,400,000
20 May 1988	10,620,000
10 Jan. 1989	208,566,400
20 June 1992	220,486,000
2002	120,000,000 + 3280,000,000 (as premium)
2002	10,000,000,000 (to buy GOI Shares)

Source: MUL Prospectus, 2003 and MUL Annual Reports.

Table 6.3 Capital stock of SMC in the Indian car component industry, 1983–90 (million Yen)

Indian Partner	*1983*	*1984*	*1985*	*1986*	*1987*	*1988*	*1989*	*1990*
Subros Ltd	–	–	60	60	60	n.a.	150	150
Bharat Seat Ltd	–	–	–	30	n.a.	n.a.	1200	1200
Machino Plastics Ltd.	–	–	–	–	1,080	1,080	1,080	1,080
Asahi Indo India	–	–	–	–	–	74	74	74

Note: n.a. = not applicable.
Source: SMC Annual Reports, 1983–2000.

direct investment of INR220.5 million in 1992. From 2002, SMC began to invest heavily in MUL as the competition in the car market increased (see Table 6.2).

While investing in MUL was core to the operation of SMC in India, MUL could not sustain itself if it did not procure good quality car components from the local car industry. With an undeveloped car ancillary industry in India during this period, SMC had to strengthen its supply lines by carefully investing its limited capital in car-components makers in India. In Subros, it invested 60 million Yen in 1985 and 90 million Yen in 1989. In Machino Plastics, it invested as much as 1080 million Yen in 1987. Similarly, it invested in Bharat Seats and Asahi India (see Table 6.3).

Table 6.4 List of car component vendors promoted by SMC/MUL

Sl No	*Component manufacturer*	*Components manufactured*
1.	Bharat Seats Ltd	Car seat
2.	Caparo Maruti Ltd	Sheet metal sub-assemblies
3.	Climate Systems India Ltd	Aluminum radiators
4.	Denso India Ltd	Parts and components
5.	J.J. Impex (Delhi) Private Ltd	Service & repair
6.	Jay Bharat Maruti Ltd	Sheet metal components
7.	Krishna Maruti Ltd	Car seats
8.	Machino Plastics Ltd	Injection plastic parts
9.	Mark Auto Industries Ltd	Automotive assemblies & components
10.	Mark Exhaust Systems Ltd	Exhaust systems & door sashes
11.	Nippon Thermostat (India) Ltd	Automotive components
12.	Sona Koyo Steering Systems Ltd	Steering gear systems
13.	Suzuki Metal India Ltd	Aluminum die casting, cylinder block, etc.
14.	Subros Ltd	Air conditioning, coolers, refrigerators
15.	Asahi India Glass Ltd	Tempered glass for cars

Source: MUL Prospectus, 2003 and MUL Annual Reports.

Besides investing directly in car components, SMC trained and developed several hundred component manufactures in India. By 2003, MUL had over 300 component vendors. Fourteen of these vendors were either joint venture companies or associate companies or Group companies of SMC (see Table 6.4). SMC was able to motivate many of the Japanese component makers such as Denso, Machino Plastics, Nippon Thermostat, Sona Koyo, and Suzuki Metal to invest in India.

In the overall analysis, the company invested steadily in the main business and the complementary business during its short period of operation in India. The investments in the main business, MUL and other complementary business, and components makers have grown in tandem. Its investment in other unrelated businesses appears to have been opportunistic and has highly fluctuated over the years (see Figure 6.1 and Table 6.5).

The investment characteristics of SMC are similar to the previous two cases that have been discussed earlier. By investing in local component makers, SMC was not only able to meet the requirement of local procurement of components as per agreement but was also able to reduce its cost of production. The impact of these investments on the financial performance of the MUL will be analysed in Chapter 7.

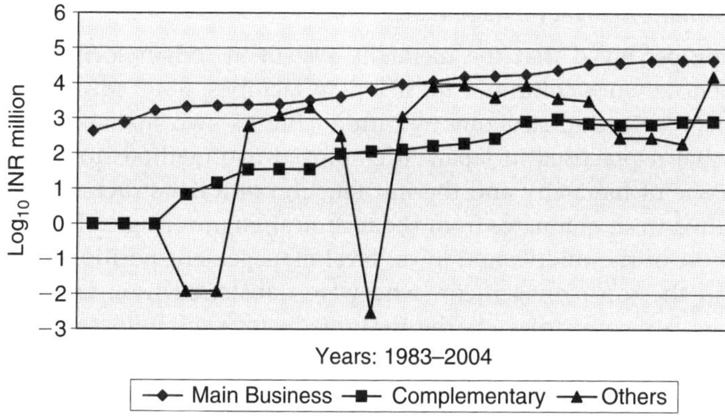

Source: MUL, (1983–2004), Annual Report.

Figure 6.1 SMC/MUL business investments, 1983–2004

Table 6.5 MUL investments and performance indicators (INR million)

Year	*Main business*	*Complementary*	*Others*	*Sales*	*PBDIT*	*PAT*
1983	194.9	–	–	–	–	–
1984	424.3	–	–	41.7	37.1	17
1985	749.6	–	–	1242.3	77	9
1986	1682	–	–	2863.6	202.1	30
1987	2188.1	6.82	0.012	6303.3	420.8	102.3
1988	2313.8	14.47	0.012	7665.5	669.6	222.8
1989	2460.7	35	606.5	9257.7	722.5	264.7
1990	2596.9	35.7	1255.5	11770.1	939.3	419.4
1991	3281.5	35.7	2092.4	14885.6	998.5	481.2
1992	4126.1	98.4	317.1	19137	1012.5	290.7
1993	6325.1	116.4	0.003	21500.5	1030.6	365.8
1994	9580.9	131.8	1140.8	27929	3030	861
1995	11638.3	166	8302.5	41494	5653	2476
1996	15757.8	196.8	9105.2	64130	9875	4276
1997	16470	270.8	4074.6	76803	10825	5101
1998	18172.2	838.7	8856.3	82066	12300	6519
1999	23637	986	3858	77814	10393	5230
2000	34999	732	3242	93151	7313	3301
2001	38657	671	284	89287	1474	−2696
2002	43847	684	284	90809	5700	1045
2003	45138	835	197	90636	6986	1464
2004	45667	853	15920	112840	12647	5421

Source: MUL, (1984–2004), Annual Reports.

Investment in local management

Having perceived that the hierarchy system in Indian society greatly influenced work culture in most Indian factories, SMC tried to set up a flat organization structure by introducing its own management system that it practised in Japan. It employed two methods to overcome the issue of hierarchy and the introduction of a flat structure. First, it recruited fresh graduates from the technical/engineering colleges to fill up most of the middle and lower level management positions. Only a few in the top management, who were transferred from large public and private companies. As the fresh graduates were unbiased as far as management styles were concerned, they could easily be trained in the various Japanese management styles. Top Indian managers in Maruti Udyog Ltd also supported the introduction of Japanese management[3] in the factory. Many of the Japanese management systems such as Quality Circles, employee participation in the production decision-making, production incentives, company union, and in-house training have been successfully transferred to the work culture of MUL.

Secondly, it undertook an extensive training programme for fresh recruits. Suzuki Motors sent several Japanese workers and executives to the Indian factory at Gurgoan, New Delhi. Every year nearly seven employees of SMC were sent to work in MUL and another three to four employees of SMC were sent to its component-making subsidiaries such as Asahi India Safety Glass and Subros Limited.

Not only all employees from SMC, Japan were sent to companies of Indian partners but also many employees from MUL were sent to factories of SMC in Japan to learn Japanese methods of production, quality assurance and other management practices. Nearly 40 MUL employees were sent to Japan every year during 1982–88. Through the exchange and training of manpower, the company succeeded to effectively and smoothly transfer Japanese management systems to MUL, which in turn increased the overall productivity of MUL.

MUL adopted several practices of SMC. Everyone in the company wore common company uniform. Lunch was served for everyone in the same room. Morning Japanese exercise was introduced as part of the daily routine. Employees were encouraged to work in small teams throughout the factory. Company Union was formed the Japanese way to take care of employees' benefits and to provide a stable work environment in the factory.

The intensity and commitment of its investments across the Indian automobile industry is rather amazing. SMC not only invested capital in the Indian automobile industry, but also deputed its manpower in many of its joint ventures. It deputed nearly seven Japanese employees per year since 1987 to 1990 to work in MUL factory. Interestingly, SMC also deputed its employees in the factories of component manufacturers in India. FDI strategy of SMC on investing in local management was indeed unique and seems to have been effective.

Investment in distribution network, service centres and financing

In the 1980s, the car industry was in its infancy with an annual demand of only about 50,000 cars. Car dealers and service centres were limited to major cities and towns in India. Similarly, there were very few car service stations in the country. This deterred people from owning cars for personal use.

Since its entry in 1982, MUL has steadily developed an extensive dealer and service centre network in India. By 2003, it had 178 authorized dealers with 243 sales outlets and about 3,500 sales executives in 161 cities/towns across the country. There were 9 regional offices, 5 area offices and 187 sales and marketing personnel. MUL had 342 Maruti dealer workshops and 1545 Maruti authorized service stations in 898 cities. It also provided a 24-hour mobile service in 38 cities across the country. Every year the company trains thousands of dealers' sales personnel and thousands of technicians at its four training centres in Chennai, Kolkatta, Gauhati and Pune.

The company has multiple dealers and service stations in several towns and cities in India. Delhi has as many as 15 dealers and 19 car-service centres. Bombay has as many as 9 dealers and 13 service centres. Madras has 4 dealers and 10 service centres and Calcutta has 4 dealers and 4 service centres. In all, MUL has over 180 dealers and 1900 service centres in India.

The company also started car financing to assist potential buyers to purchase cars on credit. By 2004, it had three wholly owned subsidiaries, namely, Maruti Insurance Brokers Ltd, Maruti Insurance Distribution Services Ltd, and True Value Solutions Ltd and one associate company, Maruti Countrywide Auto Financial Services Limited to facilitate car financing. This pattern of investments of SMC in various complementary businesses in the Indian car industry is similar to the previous two cases discussed in the book.

Timings of investments

SMC, a relatively small car company in 1980s, had limited capital to invest in the huge undeveloped Indian car industry. With its limited capital, SMC however, has very carefully invested in its joint venture, MUL and in the ancillary and automobile component manufacturing partners in India. The timing of its investments shows the company's strategic choices to invest in its various complementary businesses in India.

Based on the criticality of a component, SMC prioritized its investments in the value chain of the Indian car industry. During the first three years (1983–85) of its operation, it invested in assembly line, car steering, car air-conditioning, and electric components. Subsequently, it invested in other parts or components. It invested in car seats, bumpers and front grills in 1986 and 1987, respectively. In 1988, it invested in automotive sheet metals and glass for car. Following a brief break, it invested in aluminium radiators in 1991 and then in car components in 1995. In recent years, it has promoted four companies that have been providing credit to customers to buy cars. The strategy to help customers easily obtain car loans seems to have also assisted the company into maintaining its lead in market share. In 2002, it invested in exhaust and door sashes (see Chart 6.2). The beginning of the shade in each column indicates the year when the investment in the area indicated on the top of the respective column was begun.

Attracting investments from other Japanese car component companies

In addition to making its own investments in the Indian car industry, SMC indirectly influenced a large number of Japanese car component manufacturers to invest in India. SMC persuaded many of its keiretsu[4] car component members in Japan to invest in India. A large number of Japanese car and car component manufacturers invested in India after 1982 (see Table 6.6).

Further, the high profits that SMC enjoyed from the beginning of its operation in India also attracted many Japanese companies to invest in India. SMC began to make profits from the very beginning as it received advance payments from many customers who wanted to place their orders for cars. This happened because the price of the proposed car was only about INR40,000 and the demand outstripped the production capacity of MUL. A large number of people especially in the middle-income group could afford to buy a car at that price. MUL earned an interest of 7 per cent on the advance payments that it received from the customers who placed their orders with MUL. Keiji Nakajima, General Manager, Sumitomo mentioned that many of the Japanese car companies were heavily motivated to invest in India on seeing the benefits that SMC enjoyed.

Product/ Year	Car Design & Assembly	Car Steering	Car Air Conditioning	Electric Component	Car Seats	Bumper & Front Grill	Autorr otive Sheet Metals	Glass for Car	Aluminium Radiator	Car Component	Car Finance	Exhaust & Door Sashes
1983												
1984												
1985												
1986												
1987												
1988												
1991												
1995												
1997												
2002												

Sources: The author has compiled the data from MUL Prospectus, 2003, SMC, Annual Report (1983–2002) and Toyo Keizai (1990, 1998).

Chart 6.2 Timings of investment in various complementary businesses

Table 6.6 Investment by Japanese companies in the Indian car industry, 1983–90

Year	*Japanese company*	*Parent equity (%)*	*Indian company*	*Amount (million INR)*
1983	Suzuki Motors	26	Maruti Udyog Ltd	894
	Mazda	15.6	Swaraj Mazda	105
1984	Suzuki Motors	25.97	TVS Suzuki	231
	Toyota Motors	26	DCM Toyota Ltd	150
	Nihon Gear	14	Limotorque India Ltd	5.5
	Nippon Denso	26	SRF Nippondenso Ltd	61.3
	Nippon Denso	13	Subros Ltd	37.5
1985	Honda Motors	26	Hero Honda Motors Ltd	157
	Honda Motors	26	Sriram Honda Power	75
	Honda Motors	33.33	Kinetic Honda Motors Ltd	99.9
	Mitsubishi Motors	10	Eicher Motors Ltd	100
	Yamaha	26	Birla Yamaha Ltd	80
	Kansai Painting	26	Goodlass Nerolac Paint Ltd	
	Sanwa	22.6	Rajasthan Exero Sanwa Midland	44.29
1986	Suzuki Motors	13.3	Bharat Seat Ltd	30
	Nissan Motors	15	Mahindra Nissan Allwyn Ltd	167
	Asahi Glass	12	Asahi India Safety Glass Co. Ltd	18.5
	Kokusan Electric	18.9	India Nippon Electricals Ltd	13.2
	Suzuki Motors	15.5	Machino Plastics Ltd	270
1987	Sumitomo Denso	24	Motherson Sumi Systems Pvt	15
	Sumitomo Denso	10	Accelerated Freeze Drying Co.	11.3
	Nihon Denchi	6.7	Willard India Ltd	50
	Honda Motors	10	TELCO	542
	Honda Motors	15	AMCO Batteries Ltd	33
	Honda Motors	40	Yokogawa Keonics Ltd	9.4
1988	Yamaha	13	Mi-Fujiyama Ltd	4
	Aibara Mfg.	40	Kirloskar Ever	10
1990	Mikuni Kogyo	26	Ulcal Fuel Systems Ltd	75

Sources: [8]The author has compiled this data from the Ministry of Finance, Government of Japan, (2003), and Toyo Keizai (1990 and 1998), Overseas FDI from Japan to Asia.

Prior to 1982, only two of the component manufacturers, namely Asahi Glass and Shimada Glass had investments in India. However, after SMC entered India many car component manufacturers such as Nihon Gear, Nippon Denso, Sumitomo Denso, Kokusan Electric, Mikuni Kogyo and others invested in India. In 1983, Mazda invested 105 million Yen in Swaraj Mazda. In 1984, Toyota Motors invested 150 million Yen in DCM Toyota. In the next three years, Mitsubishi tied up with Eicher Motors

Table 6.7 Group companies of MUL, 2003

Name of company	*% of Ownership*
Subsidiary companies	
1. Maruti Insurance Brokers Ltd	100
2. Maruti Insurance Distribution Services Ltd	100
3. True Value Solutions Ltd	100
Joint ventures	
4. J J Impex (Delhi) Private Ltd	49.13
5. Mark Exhaust Systems Ltd	44.37
Associate companies	
6. Bharat Seats Ltd	14.81
7. Caparo Maruti Ltd	20.0
8. Citicorp Maruti Finance Ltd	26.0
9. Climate Systems India Ltd	39.0
10. Denso India Ltd	10.27
11. Jay Bharat Maruti Ltd	29.28
12. Krishna Maruti Ltd	13.14
13. Machino Plastics Ltd	15.35
14. Mark Auto Industries Ltd	33.89
15. Maruti Countrywide Auto Financial Services Ltd	26.0
16. Nippon Thermostat (India) Ltd	10.0
17. Sona Koyo Steering Systems Ltd	7.85
18. Suzuki Metal India Ltd	49.0
Suzuki Group company	
19. Subros Ltd	–

Sources: MUL Prospectus, 2003 and MUL Annual Reports.

Ltd, Nissan Motors tied up with Mahindra Nissan Allwyn Ltd. In 1987, Honda invested 542 million Yen in TELCO (see Table 6.6). It is interesting to observe that among the various investments that came to India during this period, most of them were in the car industry.

The immediate success of SMC in India drew the attention of not only the Japanese car manufacturers but also the major car manufacturer from the UK, Germany, France, and Switzerland. Many started to perceive the high potential of the car market in India. George Fischer Ltd, Switzerland became a partner of TELCO in iron casting, Daimler Benz AG, Germany became a partner of Bajaj Tempo in diesel engines and Peugeot, France tied up with Mahindra and Mahindra.

The investments from the Japanese car companies, Japanese component makers and other foreign car companies in India increased the strength and vibrancy of the Indian car industry in general and these had a snowball effect on the growth of SMC. With the largest outfit in India, SMC benefited the most from all these developments.

Integrating business goals to host country's goals

Import substitution and exports

As per the joint venture agreement, SMC was to provide technical know-how, assistance and information for the manufacture of passenger cars in MUL. It was to train personnel in MUL and help develop local vendors so that the components for car manufacturing could be sourced from India and not imported (see Chart 6.1 for excerpts of joint venture agreement). Developing local suppliers helped SMC to meet this objective. Developing local suppliers reduced the cost of manufacturing cars affordable, which in turn increased the demand for cars in the Indian market. By 2003, MUL had 18 associate companies that were largely into car components, two joint ventures with J.J. Impex and Mark Exhaust and three subsidiary companies that were into insurance services. Subros Ltd was involved in the production network of MUL and remained a Suzuki Group company (see Table 6.7 for a list of vendors developed by SMC-MUL).

In the 1980s, the GOI encouraged and required large companies to earn foreign exchange through exports. In the initial years, MUL was a net borrower of foreign exchange to import important car components. However, it slowly contributed to the export earnings of the country when MUL was able to export its cars to other countries. Form a mere export earning of INR413 million in 1990, it has risen to INR9219 million in 2004. MUL's exports fluctuated after an initial growth but rose again after SMC increased its stake in MUL (see Figure 6.2). The tussle between SMC and the GOI began around 1997 and this affected the export performance of the company. It is argued that SMC lowered its rate of investment and reduced its export activity as a negotiating tool with the GOI. Once SMC gained control on the operations of MUL, the company again bounced back.

Investment in the social sector

MUL has also taken initiatives in the last few years to contribute to the social sector. It has taken the lead to improve the traffic safety in cities such as Delhi and Madras. In 1995, it set up vehicle interceptors (surveillance equipments) in Delhi. It provides information through FM radio channel on traffic congestion using these interceptors in Delhi and

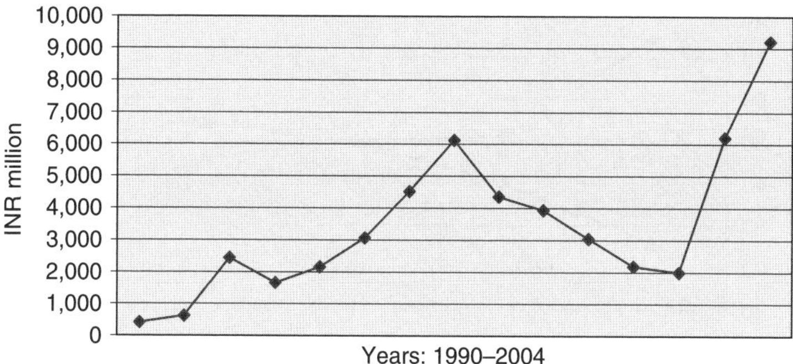

Sources: The author has compiled the data from Centre for Monitoring Indian Economy and MUL Annual Report, 2003 & 2004.

Figure 6.2 Export earnings of MUL

Madras. In 2000, it set up the Institute of Driving, Training and Research in Delhi. The company conducts blood donation camps and free eye check-up camps to promote safe driving. It provides educational benefits to underprivileged children and mothers of such children in Gurgaon, New Delhi, where its factory is located. It has also built a children's park in New Delhi to promote a clean and neat environment.

The company's involvement in the social sector seems to have been limited to a few activities that closely had links to the growth of the business of the company. Its involvement in corporate social responsibility also appears to be limited to operating the car business. The story of SMC in India is relatively new compared to the other two cases discussed. Moreover, many would contend that building the car industry in India and making personal transport possible in India itself has been the biggest social contribution of SMC.

Localization of ownership

Ownership of SMC in various businesses

In a short period of about 25 years, SMC has set up several group companies in India. It has stakes in car component manufacturing companies to car financing companies and insurance companies. SMC has three wholly owned subsidiary companies in the insurance and distribution services, namely Maruti Insurance Brokers, Maruti Insurance Distribution and True Value Solutions. It has two joint ventures with the Japanese car component manufacturers, namely J.J. Impex and Mark Exhaust.

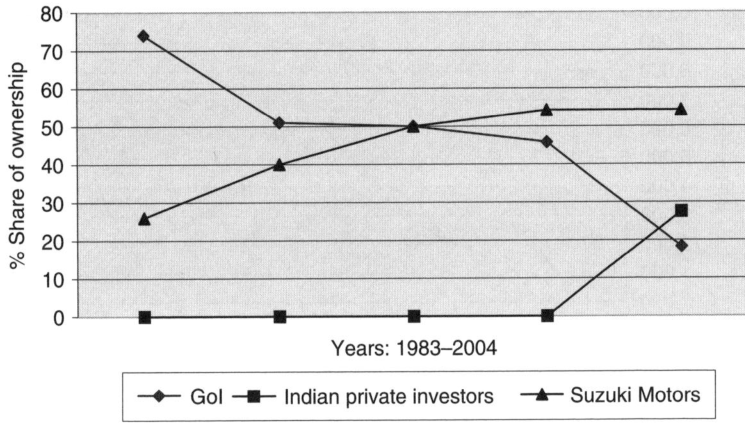

Figure 6.3 Ownership trends in MUL
Sources: The author compiled the data from MUL Prospectus, 2003 & MUL (1984–2004), Annual Report.

MUL has as many as 13 associate companies from Japan in the various car components businesses. (see Table 6.7).

In MUL, the GOI held 74 per cent and SMC held a 26 per cent stake in 1983. Over the years SMC has increased its stake in MUL. From 26 per cent in 1983, SMC increased its stake to 40 per cent in 1989 and then increased to 50 per cent in 1992. Today with a 54.2 per cent stake, SMC has the majority control in MUL. Indian private investors hold 27.5 per cent and the GOI holds the balance of 18.3 per cent equity. (see Figure 6.3). SMC seems to differ from the previous two cases with regard to its approach on ownership issues in India.

SMC experienced some difficult times with the GOI on the issue of management control and ownership in MUL. In 1997, when R.S.S.L.N. Bhaskarudu was appointed Managing Director by the government, SMC expressed its concern over the appointment. The problem continued till Bhaskarudu resigned in August 1999. During 1997–2001, the period of disagreement with the GOI, SMC reduced its level of investment in MUL. In 2000, SMC bargained hard with the government to increase its stakes in MUL. In 2002, SMC was successful in buying a part of GOI equity share.

Ownership advantages have been major motivators for foreign companies to invest in new markets across the world. Many foreign car firms were averse to investing in India because of the lower level of ownership that the GOI offered to its foreign partner. General Motors and Ford

Motors, who had been in India from 1928–30 to 1953, closed their operations when they were required to include local equity into their business in India. SMC appears to have largely looked for ownership advantages as it matured in the Indian market. While the ownership seeking behavior of SMC is similar to Unilever, it is quite different from BAT.

Performance indicators

Financials: sales, PBDIT, and PAT

The strategy to participate intensively in the Indian car industry has earned SMC a family brand name among the people in India. SMC has enjoyed the largest market share of passenger cars since its inception and until 1993, it enjoyed a virtual monopoly. It continues to be the leader among small passenger car manufacturers in India. MUL surpassed the production figure of SMC in Japan when it produced 100,000 cars per year in India. Its total production in 1999 was almost 400,000 cars, a figure twice what SMC had predicted in 1983.

MUL has maintained high profits all through its operation in India. Higher quality at lower prices generated a huge demand for cars in India. Customers paid money in advance to book their orders. MUL made a straight profit of 7 per cent on the interest earned on the money deposited by its customers. In addition to profits made on car sales, the additional profit through interest boosted its profit margins. MUL now exports cars to more than 70 countries worldwide, from Europe to South and Central America, Africa, Oceania and Asia. All these have contributed to increasing rise in its sales, PBDIT and PAT for SMC in India. From a modest beginning, the sales crossed INR11,000 million in 1990. Profit after tax grew significantly in 1995 reaching nearly INR2,500 million. Total profit after tax rose to INR4,276 million in 1996. It is interesting to note that the struggle for greater ownership and control by SMC began around this time. In 2001, MUL made a loss of INR2,696 million. However, MUL bounced back with profits after the SMC successfully gained majority control. In 2002, it made a profit after tax of INR1,045 million and reached an all time high after tax of INR5,421 million in 2004 (see Figure 6.4 and Table 6.5).

Market share

MUL has maintained a leading position among the car companies in India. Until 1990 it faced little competition and had a virtual monopoly in the Indian car market. Even with the increased competition since 1991, it has continued to have the highest market share in India. MUL

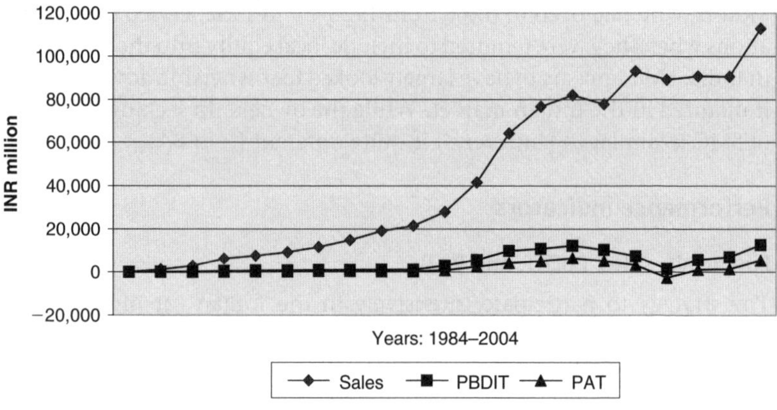

Source: MUL Annual Report (1984–2004).
Figure 6.4 MUL sales, PBDIT and PAT, 1984–2004

is far ahead of the major car companies of the world such as Honda Motors, Daewoo Motors, Hyundai, Peugeot and others. World players such as General Motors, Ford Motors, Toyota Motors, and Nissan Motors have been struggling to survive in the Indian market.

Despite their early entry in the 1930s, General Motors and Ford Motors ceased their operations in 1953 and returned to India only in the 1990s, when the market had been well entrenched by SMC. Today, Ford Motors expresses its commitment to India. While it has planned for high investments in India, its success is yet to be seen in the light of intense competition in the market. With the entry of Tata Motors in 1998, the competition in the passenger car market has increased further. Despite the increased competition in the recent years, MUL continues to dominate the Indian market.

MUL holds the maximum market share in each of the three passenger car segments in India. In segment A, it has almost 100 per cent market share. In segment B with over five players, it has about 35 per cent market share. In Segment C with over eight players, it holds 20 per cent of market share (see Table 6.8). MUL has added new car models such as Versa, Baleno and WagonR to keep pace with the competition (see Table 6.9).

Summary: FDI strategy of SMC

Despite its shorter presence in India, SMC has grown in size, strength and global presence through its timely and holistic investment pattern

Table 6.8 Segment volumes and market share of different car companies

Segment	*1999–2000*	*2000–2001*	*2001–2002*	*2002–2003*
Segment A	271,570	210,797	206,350	193,302
MUL	271,488	210,797	206,350	193,302
PAL	82	–	–	–
MUL market share in Segment A	100%	100%	100%	100%
Segment A share in overall market	44%	37%	36%	32%
Segment B	280,621	282,031	293,131	312,642
MUL	87,905	104,041	118,021	120,603
Fiat	16,178	7,205	20,379	23,317
Hyundai	69,449	64,877	67,909	82,892
Telco	54,499	43,797	64,037	72,713
Others	52,590	62,111	22,785	13,117
MUL market share in Segment B	31.3%	36.9%	40.3%	38.6%
Segment B share in overall market	45.7%	49.3%	50.8%	52.2%
Segment C	61,281	78,884	72,610	81,257
MUL	18,442	14,897	14,255	12,982
Fiat	4,567	2,149	898	2,615
Ford	7,988	18,024	14,650	14,954
GM	2,817	8,255	8,518	8,100
HM	8,545	7,783	6,589	5,105
Honda	9,698	10,009	9,600	12,000
Hyundai	6,215	16,083	17,700	19,152
Others	3,009	1,684	400	6,349
MUL market share in Segment C	30.1%	18.9%	19.6%	16%
Segment C share in overall market	10%	13.8%	12.6%	13.6%
Segment D & E	521	711	5,411	11,738
Total	613,993	572,423	577,502	598,939

Source: MUL Prospectus, 2003.

in India, a strategy that most of the major foreign car manufactures failed to adopt in India. SMC not only invested heavily in MUL, its Indian partner for manufacturing passenger cars, but also invested large amounts in many complementary businesses such as suppliers, dealers, and car service centres. It invested in various complementary activities like car steering, car air-conditioning, electric components, car seats, bumpers

Table 6.9 Manufacturers and models of cars in India

Manufacturer	*Name of model*	*Length-based classification*	*Price-based classification*
1. Daewoo Motors India Ltd	Cielo	A3	C
	Matiz	A2	B
2. Daimler Chrysler India Pvt Ltd	C Class	A4	E
	E 250	A5	E
	S Class	A6	E
3. Fiat India Automobiles Pvt Ltd	Fiat Palio	A2	B
	Fiat Siena	A3	C
	Fiat Uno	A2	B
	Palio Adventure	A3	C
4. Ford India Ltd	Escort	A3	C
	Ikon	A3	C
	Mondeo	A5	D
5. General Motors India Ltd	Opel Astra	A3	C
	Opel Corsa	A3	C
	Opel Swing	A3	C
	Corsa Sail	A2	B
6. Hindustan Motors	Ambassador	A3	B
	Contessa	A4	C
	Lancer	A3	C
7. Honda SIEL Cars India Ltd	Accord	A5	D
	City	A3	C
8. Hyundai Motor Company Ltd	Accent	A3	C
	Santro	A2	B
	Sonata	A5	D
9. PAL–Peugeot Ltd	118NE	A3	B
	Peugot 309	A3	C
10. Premier Automobiles Ltd	Premier-Padmini	A2	A
11. Skoda Auto India Pvt Ltd	Octavia	A5	D
12. Tata Engineering & Locomotive Company Ltd	Indica	A2	B
	Indigo	A3	C
13. Maruti Udyog Ltd	Maruti 1000	A3	C
	Maruti 800	A1	A
	Alto	A2	B
	Baleno	A3	C
	Esteem	A3	C
	WagonR	A2	B
	Zen	A2	B
	Versa	Utility vehicle	C
	Omni	Utility vehicle	A

Source: MUL Prospectus, 2003.

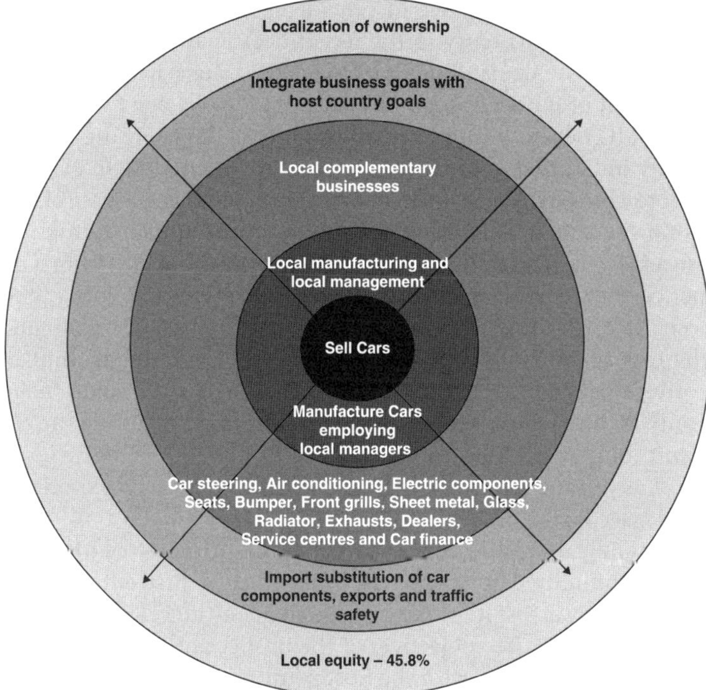

Figure 6.5 Holistic FDI pattern of Suzuki Motor Corporation, 1982–2004

and front grills, automotive sheet metals, glass, aluminium radiators, car components, car exhausts, door sashes and car-financing.

SMC also invested in local management. It transferred its production and management systems to MUL and many component suppliers in India. A large number of Japanese executives were sent to work with partner companies in India. Similarly, a large number of Indian executives from various partner companies including executives from MUL were trained in SMC's factories in Japan. In addition, SMC, either directly or indirectly, influenced many of the Japanese car component manufacturers to invest in India. It also indirectly attracted many global passenger car manufacturers to invest in India.

However, SMC's investments in the economic and social sector and the localization of ownership and management have been less compared to previous two cases, namely BAT and Unilever. The emphasis of SMC has been to develop the local car component industry, the dealer network and car service centres across the whole country. Recently, SMC also added a car-financing service to provide credit to potential buyers of cars. As a result of its entry in the recent decade and its direct venture with the GOI, the demand on SMC to add to others areas of economic development of India has been limited.

Since SMC began with a joint venture with the GOI, the company was fairly Indianized from the beginning. Employing Indian executives was more cost-effective than employing Japanese executives. The pattern of ownership has also been different from the other two cases. SMC has steadily raised its shareholding in MUL over the years. From a mere 26 per cent shareholding in 1982, it has raised its shareholding to 54.2 per cent in 2002. Although, the issue of ownership has been contentious in the case of SMC, it has followed a pattern of investment similar to the other two cases. SMC invested in all the layers of its value chain. It not only invested in car selling and manufacturing but also in the ancillary and component industry and aligned its business with the goals of the host government by local sourcing of components and exports of its products (see Figure 6.5).

In short, like BAT and Unilever (discussed in previous chapters), SMC has been committed to staying in India since it first entered. It has invested heavily across its industry value chain, astutely aligning its business objectives with the objectives of the host country, and sharing the management and equity with the host country. Statistical confirmation of the positive impact of investment in its main business activity and complementary businesses on the success of the company and the relevance of such a strategy to the success of a foreign firm in a developing host country like India is discussed in Chapter 7.

7
Statistics Support Intuition

This book is a result of testing a hypothesis that arose out of intuitive thinking about what made some foreign firms succeed in countries like India and let others fail. The framework of research was designed accordingly to test the intuition. The discussion in the book, so far, has been based on a large quantity of qualitative data in the context of India during the twentieth century. This chapter, however, shows the various statistical tests that were conducted to triangulate and confirm the explanations provided in the previous chapters, but especially in the last three chapters. The statistical test results confirm the proposition that complementary investments were crucial to the success of foreign firms in India. It also confirms that this strategy has worked across companies from all the three industries operating in different periods of the twentieth century.

Hypotheses tested

Two research hypotheses have been tested in this chapter. The hypotheses are:

1. Direct investment by foreign firms in complementary businesses contributed significantly to their success in India.
2. Determinants of success for foreign firms in India have been similar among successful cases across different industries.

The first hypothesis has been tested separately on BAT, Unilever and SMC. These three cases were chosen by a five-step sampling method and hierarchical clustering method, discussed in Chapter 4.

The second hypothesis has been inferred from the findings of individual statistical tests on these firms and by carrying out a statistical test using the aggregate data. The three firms represent three different industries (tobacco and cigarette, personal care and packaged food, and cars) and have operated in India for different lengths of time (from 1906, 1888 and 1982, respectively).

Variables, definitions and data

Independent variables:	investment in main business, complementary businesses and others
Dependent variables:	sales and PAT

Independent variables

Investment in Main Business (*MB*) constitutes the amount of Gross Block of the company. Since the dependent variables (sales and PAT) are usually influenced by the past cumulative investments of the company, 'Gross Block' was chosen as the independent variable. Investment in Complementary Businesses (*CB*) constitutes the investment made in subsidiary companies and related businesses. Investment in others (*O*) constitutes investments made in government securities and non-trade investments in stocks and bonds.

Dependent variables

Yearly Sales (*S*) and Profit After Tax (*P*) were used as dependent variables, as being good estimators of financial performance. They also represent profitability.

Nature of data and source

Data were obtained for the *Annual Reports* of the associate/subsidiary companies of BAT (1955–2004), Unilever (1955–2003), and SMC (1983–2004) operating in India.

Type of statistical tests

Multivariate dependency test, namely multiple linear regression analysis was used to verify both hypotheses. The data in the three cases being linear, linear regression was adopted for their individual analysis. For analysing their cumulative data, the aggregate data were first subjected to linear regression and then artificial neural networking (ANN) analysis. Details of ANN analysis are discussed in the respective section.

For multiple linear regression analysis, Software Program for Social Sciences (SPSS) 11 Version was used. '*Enter*' Method with a significance level of *0.05* was used to carry out the regression test. In each case two sets of regression tests were conducted with two different dependent variables, viz., *S* and *P* and the same set of independent variables, namely *MB*, *CB*, and *O*.

Check for multicollinearity in linear regression analysis

Two approaches were adopted to check for multicollinearity (Mason *et al.* 1975; Montgomery and Peck, 1982; Gujarati, 2003). First, for regression output with coefficient of determination (R^2) greater than 0.80, the number of significant *t values* were checked. In all cases, although the R^2 were found to be above 0.8, most of the *t values* were significant. Hence, the problem of multicollinearity was not envisioned. Secondly, it has also been observed that high R^2 can arise if the independent variables share a common trend, as is the case in the present analysis of *MB* and *CB*.

Regression analysis

Test 1 (Sales)

Dependent variable: sales
Independent variables: *MB*, *CB* and *O*

The output of the multiple linear regression analysis with coefficient of determination, coefficient of correlation (*R*), *F* statistics, *t* values, and coefficients of each independent variable along with its significance value are shown in Charts 7.1, 7.2 and 7.3 for BAT, Unilever and SMC, respectively. Each of these charts shows the variables entered, model summary of regression coefficients, analysis of variance (ANOVA), coefficients of independent variables with their significance level. Subscripts 1, 2, and 3 in the following equations stand for BAT, Unilever, and SMC respectively.

For BAT, R (=0.97) shows a strong and positive degree of association between *sales* and investments. The alpha (α) value for coefficient (β) of *MB* and *CB*, are significant suggesting that β of these variables are reliable but the alpha (α) value for *O* is not significant suggesting that the predictability of this variable will not be strong. Taking the variables and their coefficients, the following equation emerges.

$$S_1 = 54675 + 19.37\, MB + 38.21\, CB - 7.85\, O \qquad (7.1)$$

Variables Entered/Removed[b]

Model	Variables Entered	Variables Removed	Method
1	Others, Complementary Businesses, Main Business[a]		Enter

a. All requested variables entered.
b. Dependent Variable: Sales

Model Summary

Model	R	R Square	Adjusted R Square	Std Error of the Estimate
1	0.969[a]	0.938	0.934	86336.126

a. Predictors: (Constant), Others, Complementary Businesses, Main Business

ANOVA[b]

Model		Sum of Squares	df	Mean Square	F	Sig.
1	Regression	4.88E+12	3	1.627E+12	218.284	0.000[a]
	Residual	3.21E+11	43	7453926707		
	Total	5.20E+12	46			

a. Predictors: (Constant), Others, Complementary Businesses, Main Business
b. Dependent Variable: Sales

Coefficients[a]

Model		Unstandardized Coefficients		Standardized Coefficients	t	Sig.
		B	Std Error	Beta		
1	(Constant)	54674.660	14399.665		3.797	0.000
	Main Business	19.372	3.161	0.686	6.129	0.000
	Complementary Businesses	38.208	9.778	0.353	3.908	0.000
	Others	−7.850	6.806	−.069	−1.153	0.255

a. Dependent Variable: Sales

Chart 7.1 Output of multiple linear regression, BAT (*Sales*)

From the above equation (7.1), we can infer that for one unit increase in *MB* improved sales by 19.37 units, one unit increase in *CB* improved sales by 38.21 units, and one unit increase in *O* reduced sales by 7.85 units.

For Unilever, R (=0.997) shows a strong and positive degree of association between *sales* and investments. The alpha (α) value for *MB* and *CB*, are significant suggesting that the beta coefficient (β) of these variables are reliable but the alpha (α) value for *O* is not significant suggesting that

Variables Entered/Removed[b]

Model	Variables Entered	Variables Removed	Method
1	Others, Complementary Businesses, Main Business[a]		Enter

a. All requested variables entered.
b. Dependent Variable: Sales

Model Summary

Model	R	R Square	Adjusted R Square	Std Error of the Estimate
1	0.999[a]	0.997	0.997	1955.080091

a. Predictors: (Constant), Others, Complementary Businesses, Main Business

ANOVA[b]

Model		Sum of Squares	df	Mean Square	F	Sig.
1	Regression	5.85E+10	3	1.951E+10	5103.013	0.000[a]
	Residual	1.72E+08	45	3822338.162		
	Total	5.87E+10	48			

a. Predictors: (Constant), Others, Complementary Businesses, Main Business
b. Dependent Variable: Sales

Coefficients[a]

Model		Unstandardized Coefficients		Standardized Coefficients	t	Sig.
		B	Std Error	Beta		
1	(Constant)	57.656	373.581		0.154	0.878
	Main Business	4.647	0.252	0.783	18.436	0.000
	Complementary Businesses	13.589	1.103	0.512	12.325	0.000
	Others	−2.328	0.142	−0.327	−16.388	0.000

a. Dependent Variable: Sales

Chart 7.2 Output of multiple linear regression, Unilever (*Sales*)

predictability of this variable will not be strong. Taking the variables and their coefficients, the following equation emerges.

$$S_2 = 57.66 + 4.65\ MB + 13.59\ CB - 2.33\ O \tag{7.2}$$

From the above equation (7.2), we can infer that for one unit increase in *MB* improved sales by 4.65 units, one unit increase in *CB* improved sales by 13.59 units, and one unit increase in *O* reduced sales by 2.33 units.

Variables Entered/Removed[b]

Model	Variables Entered	Variables Removed	Method
1	Others, Main Business, Complementary Businesses[a]		Enter

a. All requested variables entered.
b. Dependent Variable: Sales

Model Summary

Model	R	R Square	Adjusted R Square	Std Error of the Estimate
1	0.967[a]	0.935	0.920	10537.8978

a. Predictors: (Constant), Others, Main Business, Complementary Businesses

ANOVA[b]

Model		Sum of Squares	df	Mean Square	F	Sig.
1	Regression	2.08E+10	3	6927983697	62.388	0.000[a]
	Residual	1.44E+09	13	111047290.6		
	Total	2.22E+10	16			

a. Predictors: (Constant), Others, Main Business, Complementary Businesses
b. Dependent Variable: Sales

Coefficients[a]

Model		Unstandardized Coefficients		Standardized Coefficients		
		B	Std Error	Beta	t	Sig.
1	(Constant)	9722.999	3925.886		2.477	0.028
	Main Business	1.284	.322	0.552	3.990	0.002
	Complementary Businesses	33.694	14.354	0.331	2.347	0.035
	Others	1.847	.642	0.224	2.875	0.013

a. Dependent Variable: Sales

Chart 7.3 Output of multiple linear regression, SMC (*Sales*)

For SMC, R (=0.968) shows a strong and positive degree of association between *sales* and investments. The alpha (α) value for *MB, CB,* and *O* are significant suggesting that the beta coefficient (β) of these variables is reliable for prediction. Taking the variables and their coefficients, the following equation emerges.

$$S_3 = 9723 + 1.33\ MB + 33.09\ CB + 1.75\ O \qquad (7.3)$$

From the above equation (7.3), we can infer that for one unit increase in *MB* improved sales by 1.33 units, one unit increase in *CB* improved sales by 33.09 units, and one unit increase in *O* improved sales by 1.75 units.

Test 2 (PAT)

Dependent variable: *PAT*
Independent variables: *MB, CB* and *O*

The output of the multiple linear regression analysis with coefficient of determination, coefficient of correlation (*R*), *F* statistics, *t* values, and coefficients of each independent variable along with its significance value are shown in Charts 7.4, 7.5 and 7.6 for BAT, Unilever and SMC, respectively.

For BAT, *R* (=0.997) shows a strong and positive degree of association between *PAT* and investments. The alpha (α) value for coefficient (β) of *MB* and *CB*, are significant suggesting that β of these variables are reliable, but the alpha (α) value for *O* is not significant suggesting that the predictability of this variable will not be strong. Taking the variables and their coefficients, the following equation emerges.

$$P_1 = -1001 + 2.59\ MB + 2.42\ CB + 0.43\ O \qquad (7.4)$$

From the above equation (7.4), we can infer that for one unit increase in *MB* improved *PAT* by 2.59 units, one unit increase in *CB* improves *PAT* by 2.42 units, and one unit increase in *O* improved *PAT* by 0.43 units.

For Unilever, *R* (=0.997) shows a strong and positive degree of association between *PAT* and investments. The alpha (α) value for coefficient (β) of *MB* and O, are significant suggesting that β of these variables are reliable, but the alpha (α) value for CB is not significant suggesting that the predictability of this variable will not be strong. Taking the variables and their coefficients, the following equation emerges.

$$P_2 = -132.97 + 0.39\ MB + 0.32\ CB + 0.42\ O \qquad (7.5)$$

From the above equation (7.5), we can infer that for one unit increase in *MB* improved *PAT* by 0.39 units, one unit increase in *CB* improved *PAT* by 0.32 units, and one unit increase in *O* improved *PAT* by 0.42 units.

Variables Entered/Removed[b]

Model	Variables Entered	Variables Removed	Method
1	Others, Complementary Businesses, Main Business[a]		Enter

a. All requested variables entered.
b. Dependent Variable: PAT

Model Summary

Model	R	R Square	Adjusted R Square	Std Error of the Estimate
1	0.997[a]	0.994	0.994	3037.3704

a. Predictors: (Constant), Others, Complementary Businesses, Main Business

ANOVA[b]

Model		Sum of Squares	df	Mean Square	F	Sig.
1	Regression	6.78E+10	3	2.262E+10	2451.504	0.000[a]
	Residual	3.97E+08	43	9225619.203		
	Total	6.82E+10	46			

a. Predictors: (Constant), Others, Complementary Businesses, Main Business
b. Dependent Variable: PAT

Coefficients[a]

Model		Unstandardized Coefficients		Standardized Coefficients	t	Sig.
		B	Std Error	Beta		
1	(Constant)	−1001.288	506.591		−1.977	0.055
	Main Business	2.585	0.111	0.799	23.248	0.000
	Complementary Businesses	2.418	0.344	0.195	7.030	0.000
	Others	0.428	0.239	0.033	1.786	0.081

a. Dependent Variable: PAT

Chart 7.4 Output of multiple linear regression, BAT (*PAT*)

For SMC, R (=0.917) shows a strong and positive degree of association between *PAT* and investments. The alpha (α) value for coefficient (β) of *O* is significant suggesting that β of this variable is reliable, but the alpha (α) value for *MB* and *CB* is not significant suggesting that the predictability of this variable will not be strong. Taking the variables and their coefficients, the following equation emerges.

Variables Entered/Removed[b]

Model	Variables Entered	Variables Removed	Method
1	Others, Complementary Businesses, Main Business[a]		Enter

a. All requested variables entered.
b. Dependent Variable: PAT

Model Summary

Model	R	R Square	Adjusted R Square	Std Error of the Estimate
1	0.997[a]	0.994	0.994	363.659596

a. Predictors: (Constant), Others, Complementary Businesses, Main Business

ANOVA[b]

Model		Sum of Squares	df	Mean Square	F	Sig.
1	Regression	1.05E+09	3	349816662.1	2645.151	0.000[a]
	Residual	5951174	45	132248.302		
	Total	1.06E+09	48			

a. Predictors: (Constant), Others, Complementary Businesses, Main Business
b. Dependent Variable: PAT

Coefficients[a]

Model		Unstandardized Coefficients		Standardized Coefficients		
		B	Std Error	Beta	t	Sig.
1	(Constant)	−132.974	69.489		−1.914	0.062
	Main Business	0.389	0.047	0.488	8.287	0.000
	Complementary Businesses	0.324	0.205	0.091	1.580	0.121
	Others	0.422	0.026	0.441	15.967	0.000

a. Dependent Variable: PAT

Chart 7.5 Output of multiple linear regression, Unilever (*PAT*)

$$P_3 = -335 - 0.01\, MB + 3.29\, CB + 0.56\, O \qquad (7.6)$$

From the above equation (7.6), we can infer with certainity the negative impact of *MB* and *CB* on *PAT* since their coefficients (β) are not significant. However, it is observed that one unit increase in *CB*, improves *PAT* by 3.68 units, suggesting the strong impact of CB on profit.

Variables Entered/Removed[b]

Model	Variables Entered	Variables Removed	Method
1	Others, Main Business, Complementary Businesses[a]		Enter

a. All requested variables entered.
b. Dependent Variable: PAT

Model Summary

Model	R	R Square	Adjusted R Square	Std Error of the Estimate
1	0.950[a]	0.902	0.880	−1151.1016

a. Predictors: (Constant), Others, Main Business, Complementary Businesses

ANOVA[b]

Model		Sum of Squares	df	Mean Square	F	Sig.
1	Regression	1.59E+08	3	53054487.81	40.040	0.000[a]
	Residual	17225453	13	1325034.840		
	Total	1.76E+08	16			

a. Predictors: (Constant), Others, Main Business, Complementary Businesses
b. Dependent Variable: PAT

Coefficients[a]

Model		Unstandardized Coefficients		Standardized Coefficients		
		B	Std Error	Beta	t	Sig.
1	(Constant)	−334.830	428.842		−0.781	0.449
	Main Business	−8.27E−03	.035	−0.040	−0.235	0.818
	Complementary Businesses	3.293	1.568	0.363	2.100	0.056
	Others	0.561	.070	0.764	8.001	0.000

a. Dependent Variable: PAT

Chart 7.6 Output of multiple linear regression, SMC (*PAT*)

Comparison across companies

Equations (7.1) to (7.6) are repeated here for ease of reference.

$$S_1 = 54675 + 19.37\, MB + 38.21\, CB - 7.85\, O \quad (7.1)$$

$$S_2 = 57.66 + 4.65\, MB + 13.59\, CB - 2.33\, O \quad (7.2)$$

$$S_3 = 9739.6 + 1.33\, MB + 33.09\, CB + 1.75\, O \quad (7.3)$$

$$P_1 = -1001 + 2.59\ MB + 2.42\ CB + 0.43\ O \qquad (7.4)$$

$$P_2 = -132.97 + 0.39\ MB + 0.32\ CB + 0.42\ O \qquad (7.5)$$

$$P_3 = -335 - 0.01\ MB + 3.29\ CB + 0.56\ O \qquad (7.6)$$

Observations

1. In all the three cases, *MB* and *CB* have had a positive effect on sales, with per unit investment in *CB* having a greater impact than per unit investment in *MB*, in the following ratios: 2:1 for BAT, 3:1 for Unilever, and 25:1 for SMC.
2. Similarly, in all the three cases, *CB* had a positive effect on *PAT* with similar degree of effect for BAT and Unilever. For SMC, *CB* had a much greater impact than *MB* on *PAT*.

Inferences

1. Direct investment in complementary businesses contributed significantly to sales and PAT in India.
2. Determinants of success for foreign firms in India have been similar across the three companies irrespective of the time in which they operated, with the degree of impact of each variable varying because of the type and nature of the industry and level of maturity of the business in the host economy. For instance, BAT has been in the Indian tobacco industry since 1906. Unilever has been in India since 1888 and it started direct investments in India from 1932. SMC entered the Indian car industry only in 1982.

Across industry analysis

This section makes an aggregate analysis of the impact of investments in main business, complementary businesses and others on sales and PAT taking the data of all three cases, namely BAT, Unilever and SMC. Deducing a single equation each for sales and PAT as dependent variables will simplify the understanding of successful FDI strategy in India across the three successful cases covering different periods.

The aggregate analysis involved two types of tests. First, multiple linear regression analyses of the aggregate data were carried out. Secondly, these aggregate data were tested through artificial neural network analysis (ANN) to recheck the degree of association of independent variables on the dependent variables, Sales and PAT of all three cases.

Unlike linear regression, ANN does not make prior assumption that a given set of data will follow a particular model whether linear or otherwise. ANN develops the best fit using the data themselves and then generates regression coefficients. Although each data set of the three cases was linear in nature, the aggregate data may not reflect the same linear nature as they are from different industries and from different time periods. Hence, the aggregate data of three cases were subjected to ANN analysis to ascertain the coefficient of correlations (R) between independent variables and dependent variables that were obtained through linear regression analysis.

For ANN analysis, the software Mathematics Laboratories (MATLAB), 6.5 Version was used. For running this program, a program specific to this study was written to train the dependent variables with the independent variables using all data from all three cases. Then, a randomly selected set of data of a few years was used to regress the actual values of dependent variables (sales and PAT) with the corresponding predicted values of these dependent variables for the same set of selected data.

Regression analysis (sales) – model based analysis

Dependent variable: sales
Independent variables: *MB, CB* and *O*

The output of the multiple linear regression analysis with coefficient of determination, coefficient of correlation, F Statistics, t values, coefficients of each of the independent variables along with their significance values are shown in Chart 7.7. It shows the variables entered, model summary of regression coefficients, analysis of variance (ANOVA), coefficients of independent variables with their significance level.

The coefficient of correlation ($R = 0.89$) shows a strong and positive degree of association between the dependent variable sales and independent variables of investments. The coefficients (β) of all the independent variables – *MB*, *CB* and *O* – are significant and hence are reliable. Using all the coefficients of independent variables, the following equation emerges on their cumulative effect on sales.

$$\text{Sales} = 16890.67 + 4.19\,MB + 89.79\,CB - 12.88\,O \quad (7.7)$$

From the above equation (7.7), we can infer that *MB* and *CB* had a positive impact on sales and *O* had a negative impact on sales. While one unit increase in *MB* improved sales by 4.19 units, one unit increase in *CB* improved sales by 89.79 units but one unit increase in *O* reduced sales by 12.88 units.

Variables Entered/Removed[b]

Model	Variables Entered	Variables Removed	Method
1	Others, Complementary Businesses, Main Business[a]		Enter

a. All requested variables entered.
b. Dependent Variable: Sales

Model Summary

Model	R	R Square	Adjusted R Square	Std Error of the Estimate
1	0.898[a]	0.806	0.801	106180.508

a. Predictors: (Constant), Others, Complementary Businesses, Main Business

ANOVA[b]

Model		Sum of Squares	df	Mean Square	F	Sig.
1	Regression	5.15E+12	3	1.717E+2	152.290	0.000[a]
	Residual	1.24E+12	110	1.127E+10		
	Total	6.39E+12	113			

a. Predictors: (Constant), Others, Complementary Businesses, Main Business
b. Dependent Variable: Sales

Coefficients[a]

Model		Unstandardized Coefficients		Standardized Coefficients	t	Sig.
		B	Std Error	Beta		
1	(Constant)	16890.674	11573.621		1.459	0.147
	Main Business	4.194	1.210	0.207	3.465	0.001
	Complementary Businesses	89.792	5.857	0.838	15.330	0.000
	Others	−12.879	2.892	−0.227	−4.453	0.000

a. Dependent Variable: Sales

Chart 7.7 Output of multiple linear regression of aggregate data of BAT, Unilever & SMC (*Sales*)

ANN analysis (sales) – data based analysis

The output of the neural network analysis confirms that there is a strong degree of association between the actual and predicted values of the dependent variable *sales*. The coefficient of correlation obtained through ANN analysis was $R = 0.90$ (see Figure 7.1). The ANN analysis further validated the value of R obtained through multiple linear regression analysis

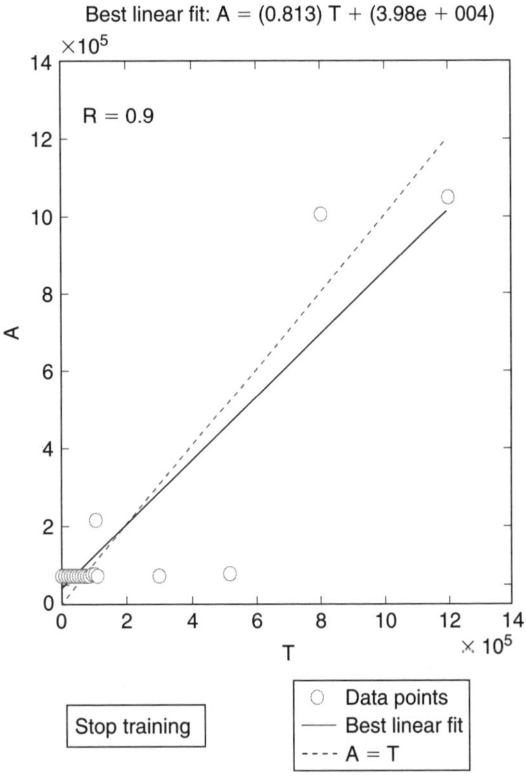

Figure 7.1 Actual sales data vs predicted sales data obtained from artificial neural network program on MATLAB 6.5

in the previous section. (see Charts 7.8–7.12 for ANN Program and ANN Data Sheet with details of training data, testing data, observation data and output data). Chart 7.8 refers to the ANN program. Chart 7.9 refers to data on investments and sales. Chart 7.10 refers to random selected input investment data of 33 years. Charts 7.11 and 7.12 refer to observed sales data of 33 years and predicted sales data for the corresponding years. Figure 7.1 shows the graphic output of the degree of association between the actual sales and predicted sales through the neural network analysis.

The test was undertaken with a configuration of 3:2:1. Here, 3 refers to number of input data, 2 refers to the number of nodal points in one hidden layer and 1 refers to the number of output data for corresponding set of input data. The architecture with 1 hidden layer was chosen as this gave a better result as compared to more number of hidden layers.

Artificial Neural Network Program for Training, Testing and Generating Output

```
format short g
load training.txt
data=training';
p=data(1:3,:);
t=data(4,:);
[pn,minp,maxp,tn,mint,maxt]=premnmx(p,t);
input_ranges=minmax(pn);
net=newff(input_ranges,[2 1],{'tansig','tansig'},'traingdm');
net.layers{1}.initFcn='initnw';
net.inputweights{1,1}.initFcn='initnw';
net.biases{1,1}.initFcn='initnw';
net.biases{2,1}.initFcn='initnw';
net=init(net);
net.trainParam.lr = 0.01;
net.trainParam.mc = 0.9;
net.trainParam.show = 100;
net.trainParam.goal = 0;
net.trainParam.epochs =5000;
netr=train(net,pn,tn);
load testing.txt
inpt=testing';
pnewn=tramnmx(inpt,minp,maxp);
outpt=sim(netr,pnewn)
outpt1=postmnmx(outpt,mint,maxt)
fid=fopen('outdat','wt');
fprintf(fid,'%f\n',outpt1);
load obs.txt
load1=obs';
[m,b,r]=postreg(outpt1,load1)
fclose(fid);
save rock netr;
```

Chart 7.8 ANN program 1

Literature on ANN also shows that architecture with 1 or 2 hidden layers is preferred for better generalization (Zhang *et al.*, 1998; Haykin, 2002; Bishop, 2004).

Regression analysis (PAT) – model based analysis

Dependent variable: *PAT*
Independent variables: *MB*, *CB* and *O*

The output of the multiple linear regression analyses with coefficients of determination, coefficient of correlation, *F* statistics, *t* values,

Data on Investments in Main Business, Complementary Businesses and Others and Sales for Training in Artificial Neural Network Program

35.5	0.41	2.97	2844
109.3	0.06	9.49	3036.4
113.1	0.06	11.22	3211.6
83	1.36	7.34	3261.2
83.9	1.33	3.24	342.04
86	0.37	7.25	3688.1
127	0.34	12.18	4280
129.5	0.32	4.25	4633
87.7	0.29	4.31	5041
91.4	0.27	0.63	5581
149.1	0.24	2.7	5980
156.7	0.22	1.08	6963
166.7	0.19	1.23	8220
180.7	0.73	1.13	10788
202.2	0.71	1.19	12626
219.8	2.98	0.68	14510
257.4	1.08	0.79	27442
310.1	1.11	0.99	32511
363.1	1.126	1.526	36116
445.3	1.061	1.518	36688
533.3	28.086	1.517	38467
575.1	39.005	1.607	42287
598.8	38.97	2.336	45880
656.9	42.17	3.263	43661
759.1	42.3	4.4	58862
1891.5	74.7	162.5	76593
1930.2	56.6	466.7	69818
1980.8	57.8	482.1	81198
2289.3	88.9	482.5	94239
2362.2	94.21	378	106516
2524.3	101.21	12.5	120044
2638	101.3	0.4	106764
2988	131.3	371	182730
3509.9	366.51	371.3	231638
4535.8	472.2	371.7	301708
5622.8	840	280	380967
7119	1995.1	565.8	428015
8297.9	2536.6	779.2	470930
9436.4	2660.9	779.1	518786
12741.5	3260.6	275.2	599060
14386.3	3895.8	273.1	692375
17183.1	9845.7	1019.6	770096
21454.9	10113.6	26.7	806937
26680.8	10310.8	26.3	882711

Chart 7.9 ANN data sheet 1

40818.5	8308.4	62.6	998246
44156.1	7071.8	6738.1	1119447
50546.8	9178.2	19257.9	1203992
27.9	3.32	0	40.36
35.1	1.03	0	277.777
34.4	1.03	0	336.156
36.1	0.004	0	372.082
37.3	0.003	0	422.97
38.6	0.003	0	461.186
43	0.003	0	499.182
46.7	0.003	0	538.542
60.6	0.103	0	595.474
69.4	0.103	0	618.701
77.7	0.582	0	714.801
85.3	0.732	0	846.681
84.6	0.807	0	932.815
81.7	0.807	0	925.875
84.5	0.807	0	1087.91
86.8	0.807	0	1192.099
89.7	0.807	0	1341.029
266.8	0.807	0	1404.379
267.3	0.807	0	1328.811
278.3	0.807	0	1457.288
304	1.282	0	2059.884
325.8	1.282	0	2129.922
364.9	1.286	0	2616.827
484.2	0.986	0.911	3010.362
574.9	0.94	1.215	3226.333
629	0.94	1.215	3999.039
978.8	0.94	1.215	4807.842
1067.9	1.24	1.215	4572.394
1667.6	1.24	1.215	5011.732
1144.1	0.783	2.978	5389.982
1471.5	0.765	2.978	6179.486
1634.1	0.815	1.215	7145.719
1971.9	0.508	10.095	7953.703
2096.5	15.106	18.7	8454.063
2265.6	58.762	20.365	10081.654
2673.5	58.762	26.423	12011.48
2977.4	59.562	16.422	15065.831
3304.7	104.973	13.636	17570.28
3655.9	180.82	328.67	20631.674
4917.9	691.827	1222.64	28264.825
5638.4	858.785	369.49	33669.474
9542.3	2131.19	1156.6	66001.079
10358.2	2621.09	2694.6	78197.084

Chart 7.9 (Continued)

13841.3	3118.78	4176.3	94818.486
14810.6	2991.48	7389.6	101424.884
16687.4	4403.46	13918.9	106037.896
19358.7	3526.01	13163.3	109719
19943.6	4422.94	19554.5	103394
21417.2	4272.95	21778.5	105982
2188.1	6.82	0.012	6303.3
2313.8	14.47	0.012	7665.5
2460.7	35	606.5	9257.7
2596.9	35.7	1255.5	11770.1
3281.5	35.7	2092.4	14885.6
4126.1	98.4	317.1	19137
6325.1	116.4	0.003	21500.5
9580.9	131.8	1140.8	27929
11638.3	166	8302.5	41494
15757.8	196.8	9105.2	64130
16470	270.8	4074.6	76803
18172.2	838.7	8856.3	82066
23637	986	3858	77814
34999	732	3242	93151
38657	671	284	89287
43847	684	284	90809
45138	835	197	90636
45667	853	15920	112840

Chart 7.9 (Continued)

coefficients of each of the independent variables along with their significance values are shown in Chart 7.13. The chart shows the variables entered, model summary of regression coefficients, analysis of variance (ANOVA), coefficients of independent variables with their significance level.

The coefficient of correlation ($R = 0.891$) shows a strong and positive degree of association between the dependent variable sales and independent variables of investments. The alpha (α) values for coefficient (β) of *MB, CB and O* are significant suggesting that β of these variables are reliable. Using all the coefficients of independent variables, an equation can be constructed to show how *PAT* was affected by *MB, CB* and *O* taken together.

$$\text{PAT} = -1595.83 + 0.37\ MB + 9.69\ CB - 0.69\ O \tag{7.8}$$

From the above equation (7.8), we can infer that while *MB* and *CB* had a positive impact on *PAT, O* had a negative impact. Further, while one unit increase in *MB* increased *PAT* by 0.371 units, one unit increase in

Randomly chosen 33 sets of data on Investments in Main Business, Complementary Businesses and Others for Testing

35.5	0.41	2.97
83	1.36	7.34
127	0.34	12.18
149.1	0.24	2.7
180.7	0.73	1.13
310.1	1.11	0.99
533.3	28.086	1.517
656.9	42.17	3.263
1930.2	56.6	466.7
2524.3	101.21	12.5
4535.8	472.2	371.7
9436.4	2660.9	779.1
21454.9	10113.6	26.7
50546.8	9178.2	19257.9
37.3	0.003	0
60.6	0.103	0
84.6	0.807	0
84.5	0.807	0
89.7	0.007	0
304	1.282	0
574.9	0.94	1.215
1667.6	1.24	1.215
1971.9	0.508	10.095
2977.4	59.562	16.422
5638.4	858.785	369.492
10358.2	2621.09	2694.565
14810.6	2991.48	7389.645
21417.2	4272.95	21778.523
2313.8	14.47	0.012
4126.1	98.4	317.1
15757.8	196.8	9105.2
34999	732	3242
45667	853	15920

Chart 7.10 ANN data sheet 2

CB increased PAT by 9.69 units and one unit increase in *O* decreased it by 0.69 units.

ANN analysis (PAT) – data based analysis

The output of the neural network confirms that the there is a strong degree of association between actual and predicted values of the dependent variable, *PAT*. The coefficient of correlation obtained through ANN analysis was $R=0.907$ (see Figure 7.2). The ANN analysis further

Observed Sales data for the 33 years that were randomly chosen for testing purpose

2844
3261.2
4280
5980
10788
32511
38467
43661
69818
120044
301708
518786
806937
1203992
40.364
595.474
932.815
1087.91
1341.029
2059.884
3226.333
5011.732
7953.703
15065.831
33669.474
78197.084
101424.884
105982
7665.5
19137
64130
93151
112840

Chart 7.11 ANN data sheet 3

validated the value of *R* obtained through multiple linear regression analysis in the previous section. For ANN data sheets on training, testing, observed data and predicted data, (see Charts 7.14–7.17). The program, the configuration and the architecture of ANN for this test were same as in the previous ANN analysis for sales.

Chart 7.14 refers to data on investments and *PAT*. Chart 7.15 refers to random selected input investment data of 27 years. Charts 7.16 and 7.17 refer to observed *PAT* data of 27 years and predicted *PAT* data for the corresponding years. Figure 7.2 shows the graphic output of the degree

Predicted Sales Output for corresponding 33 years

71312.272475
71312.713132
71312.851821
71312.784320
71312.982209
71313.656336
71318.859006
71321.699378
71339.273987
71341.553172
71444.682831
73550.628125
1005148.802367
1047078.265484
71312.171174
71312.296958
71312.516071
71312.515595
71312.540391
71313.636283
71314.908816
71320.302823
71321.857658
71336.916857
71579.297211
74070.728904
78721.103789
214777.025224
71325.633166
71356.392690
71774.154640
72234.441488
68979.224571

Chart 7.12 ANN data sheet 4

of association between the actual *PAT* and predicted *PAT* through the neural network analysis.

Across industry effect

From the aggregate analysis equations (7.7) and (7.8) were obtained, as follows:

$$\text{Sales} = 16890.67 + 4.19\ MB + 89.79\ CB - 12.88\ O \qquad (7.7)$$

$$\text{PAT} = -1595.83 + 0.37\ MB + 9.69\ CB - 0.69\ O \qquad (7.8)$$

Variables Entered/Removed[b]

Model	Variables Entered	Variables Removed	Method
1	Others, complementary Businesses, Main Business[a]		Enter

a. All requested variables entered.
b. Dependent Variable: PAT

Model Summary

Model	R	R Square	Adjusted R Square	Std Error of the Estimate
1	0.891[a]	0.794	0.788	12034.9260

a. Predictors: (Constant), Others, Complementary Businesses, Main Business

ANOVA[b]

Model		Sum of Squares	df	Mean Square	F	Sig.
1	Regression	6.14E+10	3	2.047E+10	141.326	0.000[a]
	Residual	1.59E+10	110	144839444.6		
	Total	7.73E+10	113			

a. Predictors: (Constant), Others, Complementary Businesses, Main Business
b. Dependent Variable: PAT

Coefficients[a]

Model		Unstandardized Coefficients		Standardized Coefficients		
		B	Std Error	Beta	t	Sig.
1	(Constant)	−1595.827	1311.801		−1.217	0.226
	Main Business	0.371	0.137	0.167	2.708	0.008
	Complementary Businesses	9.688	0.664	0.822	14.594	0.000
	Others	−0.685	0.328	−0.110	−2.091	0.039

a. Dependent Variable: PAT

Chart 7.13 Output of multiple linear regression of aggregate data of BAT, Unilever and SMC (*PAT*)

Observations

On an aggregate level, *MB* and *CB* had a positive impact and *O* a negative impact on both sales and *PAT*. *CB* had 20 times the impact than *MB* on both sales and *PAT*. One unit increase in *CB* improved sales by 89.79 units; one unit increase in *MB* improved sales by only 4.19 units. Similarly, one unit increase in *CB* improved *PAT* by 9.69 units, one unit increase in *MB* improved PAT by only 0.37 units.

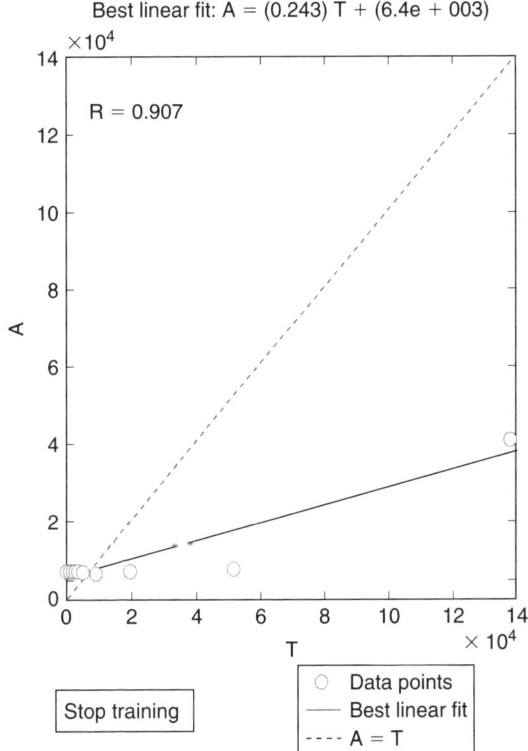

Figure 7.2 Actual profit after tax vs predicted profit after tax from artificial neural network program on MATLAB 6.5

Inference

The above findings establish that the strategy of successful foreign firms in India, across the three cases in three different industries and over different time periods have been similar. The strategy of making direct investment in complementary businesses contributed significantly to their success in India.

Summary

A summary of all the statistical indicators obtained from the multiple linear regression analyses for the three cases and aggregate regression analyses of three cases are shown in Table 7.1. We find some important

Data on Investments in Main Business, Complementary Businesses and Others and PAT for Training in Artificial Neural Network Program

35.5	0.41	2.97	168.9
109.3	0.06	9.49	186.7
113.1	0.06	11.22	137.9
83	1.36	7.34	132
83.9	1.33	3.24	115
86	0.37	7.25	141.6
127	0.34	12.18	188
129.5	0.32	4.25	146
87.7	0.29	4.31	180
91.4	0.27	0.63	99
149.1	0.24	2.7	162
156.7	0.22	1.08	206
166.7	0.19	1.23	206
180.7	0.73	1.13	266
202.2	0.71	1.19	359
219.8	2.98	0.68	323
257.4	1.08	0.79	392
310.1	1.11	0.99	266
363.1	1.126	1.526	359
445.3	1.061	1.518	323
533.3	28.086	1.517	357
575.1	39.005	1.607	403
598.8	38.97	2.336	233
656.9	42.17	3.263	392
759.1	42.3	4.4	777
1891.5	74.7	162.5	2447
1930.2	56.6	466.7	1458
1980.8	57.8	482.1	1514
2289.3	88.9	482.5	4312
2362.2	94.21	378	4394
2524.3	101.21	12.5	2479
2638	101.3	0.4	2920
2988	131.3	371	5262
3509.9	366.51	371.3	7752
4535.8	472.2	371.7	22166
5622.8	840	280	15531
7119	1995.1	565.8	20632
8297.9	2536.6	779.2	26164
9436.4	2660.9	779.1	26108
12741.5	3260.6	275.2	34690
14386.3	3895.8	273.1	52620
17183.1	9845.7	1019.6	62342
21454.9	10113.6	26.7	79244
26680.8	10310.8	26.3	100626

Chart 7.14 ANN data sheet 5

40818.5	8308.4	62.6	118972
44156.1	7071.8	6738.1	137135
50546.8	9178.2	19257.9	159285
27.9	3.32	0	8.96
35.1	1.03	0.00	10.40
34.4	1.03	0.00	10.02
36.1	0.00	0.00	12.86
37.3	0.00	0.00	20.84
38.6	0.00	0.00	24.95
43	0.00	0.00	22.55
46.7	0.00	0.00	23.49
60.6	0.10	0.00	14.75
69.4	0.10	0.00	16.49
77.7	0.58	0.00	17.15
85.3	0.73	0.00	22.11
84.6	0.81	0.00	20.01
81.7	0.81	0.00	23.94
84.5	0.81	0.00	27.50
86.8	0.81	0.00	22.77
89.7	0.81	0.00	30.06
266.8	0.81	0.00	36.65
267.3	0.81	0.00	32.46
278.3	0.81	0.00	34.25
304	1.28	0.00	47.72
325.8	1.28	0.00	69.50
364.9	1.29	0.00	78.22
484.2	0.99	0.91	93.09
574.9	0.94	1.22	175.96
629	0.94	1.22	165.28
978.8	0.94	1.22	207.24
1067.9	1.24	1.22	221.97
1667.6	1.24	1.22	185.64
1144.1	0.78	2.98	216.76
1471.5	0.77	2.98	325.58
1634.1	0.82	1.22	390.72
1971.9	0.51	10.10	464.95
2096.5	15.11	18.70	487.77
2265.6	58.76	20.37	538.11
2673.5	58.76	26.42	658.51
2977.4	59.56	16.42	802.02
3304.7	104.97	13.64	984.76
3655.9	180.82	328.68	1272.71
4917.9	691.83	1222.6	1899.63
5638.4	858.79	369.49	2392.21
9542.3	2131.20	1156.6	4142.62
10358.2	2621.09	2694.6	5603.71

Chart 7.14 (Continued)

13841.3	3118.79	4176.3	8057.11
14810.6	2991.49	7389.6	10699.40
16687.4	4403.46	13918.9	13100.93
19358.7	3526.02	13163.3	15409.50
19943.6	4422.95	19554.6	17697.40
21417.2	4272.96	21778.5	17717.90
2188.1	6.82	0.012	102.3
2313.8	14.47	0.012	222.8
2460.7	35	606.5	264.7
2596.9	35.7	1255.5	419.4
3281.5	35.7	2092.4	481.2
4126.1	98.4	317.1	290.7
6325.1	116.4	0.003	365.8
9580.9	131.8	1140.8	861
11638.3	166	8302.5	2476
15757.8	196.8	9105.2	4276
16470	270.8	4074.6	5101
18172.2	838.7	8856.3	6519
23637	986	3858	5230
34999	732	3242	3301
38657	671	284	−2696
43847	684	284	1045
45138	835	197	1464
45667	853	15920	5421

Chart 7.14 (Continued)

observations and therefore can make some important conclusions thereof.

First, all coefficients of *MB* and *CB* for sales and *PAT* in all three cases and aggregate data except for PAT of SMC are statistically significant.

Secondly, as intuition would suggest, the Y intercept (*C*) for sales is positive and Y intercept (*C*) of *PAT* is negative for all cases including aggregate data. This confirms that while there will be some positive sale from the first year of investment and production, profits will accrue only after the gestation period of investment.

Thirdly, Investment in main business and investment in complementary businesses had positive impact on both sales and profits. Investment in other unrelated businesses was inconsistent.

Fourthly, investments in complementary businesses had significantly more impact on sales and profits that investment in main business had on sales and profit.

Fifthly, impact of investment in complementary business on sales and profit was more prominent across the industry data, implying that factor for success were similar for individual cases and across the three industries.

Randomly chosen 27 sets of data on Investments in Main Business, Complementary Businesses and Others for Testing

35.5	0.41	2.97
87.7	0.29	4.31
166.7	0.19	1.23
257.4	1.08	0.79
533.3	28.086	1.517
759.1	42.3	4.4
2289.3	88.9	482.5
2988	131.3	371
7119	1995.1	565.8
14386.3	3895.8	273.1
40818.5	8308.4	62.6
37.3	0.00	0.00
60.6	0.10	0.00
84.6	0.81	0.00
89.7	0.81	0.00
304	1.28	0.00
574.9	0.94	1.22
1667.6	1.24	1.22
1971.9	0.51	10.10
2977.4	59.56	16.42
5638.4	858.79	369.49
14810.6	2991.5	7389.65
2313.8	14.47	0.012
4126.1	98.4	317.1
15757.8	196.8	9105.2
34999	732	3242
45667	853	15920

Chart 7.15 ANN data sheet 6

In other words, our intuition and explanation that direct investment by foreign firms in complementary businesses contributed significantly to their success in India and that the determinants of success for foreign firms in India have been similar across successful cases or companies have been vindicated through statistical tests.

Observed PAT data for the 27 years that were randomly chosen for testing purpose

168.9
180
206
392
357
777
4312
5262
20632
52620
118972
20.84
14.75
20.01
30.06
47.72
175.96
185.64
464.95
802.02
2392.21
10699.40
222.8
290.7
4276
3301
5421

Chart 7.16 ANN data sheet 7

Predicted PAT Output for corresponding 27 years

7176.519238
7176.534068
7176.546482
7176.579295
7176.976557
7177.217270
7179.427343
7179.963258
7252.531667
7624.181026
41352.917972
7176.508486
7176.515621
7176.530125
7176.531430
7176.591912
7176.660132
7176.946403
7177.036420
7178.071112
7196.076463
7837.127520
7177.276205
7179.691521
7241.156141
7231.235815
7194.714918

Chart 7.17 ANN data sheet 8

Table 7.1 Summary of statistical indicators of all multiple linear regression analyses

Dependent Variable of the Case		R^2	R	F	B			
					C	*MB*	*CB*	*O*
BAT	Sales	0.94	0.97	218.28	54675	19.37*	38.21*	−7.80
	PAT	0.99	0.99	2451.50	−1001.29	2.59*	2.42*	0.43
Unilever	Sales	0.99	0.99	5103.01	57.66	4.65*	13.59*	−2.33*
	PAT	0.99	0.99	2645.15	−132.97	0.39*	0.32	0.42*
SMC	Sales	0.94	0.97	70.07	9739.64	1.33*	33.09**	1.75**
	PAT	0.84	0.92	24.71	−335	−0.01	3.29	0.56*
Aggregate data of BAT, Unilever and SMC	Sales	0.80	0.90	152.29	16890.67	4.19*	89.72*	−12.88*
	PAT	0.79	0.89	141.33	−1595.83	0.37**	9.69*	−0.68**

Notes: * $P < 0.01$, ** $P < 0.05$.
R^2 = coefficient of determination, R = coefficient of correlation, F = F Statistic from ANOVA, B = coefficient of independent variable, C = constant, MB = investment in main business, *CB* = investment in complementary businesses, *O* = investment in others

8
Complementation – the Winning Strategy

Investing directly in a developing host country can be highly problematic. Host country context, alternate global space, and the firm itself are the three major constraints for appropriate firm strategy in a developing host country.

The nature and characteristics of a typical developing country poses the biggest threat for returns on investment. Poor basic infrastructure of transport, communication and utilities, industry structure with poor coordination, undeveloped ancillary and support industry, unclear regulatory and governance mechanisms, and undeveloped financial institutions and market pose severe problems for a new investment trying to take off.

Lack of superstructure across the boundaries of host countries throws open a large number of alternate host locations in which a firm could invest. The large number of options for investment location with highly attractive offers from different host countries is often a distraction from focusing on a particular host country.

Each of the first two dimensions pose both a high opportunity and high risk depending on how one looks at these. This phenomenon throws the decision-maker in the firm out of balance and out of focus. Often comprehending the host country and the alternating global space can be confusing and firms may spread their investment thinly instead of committing deeply to any particular host country.

The winning strategy proposed in this chapter has to be read within the above context. This chapter summarizes the holistic investment strategy of three multinational enterprises, namely British American Tobacco, Unilever and Suzuki Motor Corporation in India. It discusses the overwhelming significance of investing in the complementary businesses that promote the success of a foreign firm in a developing country such as India, an issue that most foreign firms in India and other developing countries have failed to understand. Finally, the chapter provides a few windows for future research that can advance the frontiers of FDI strategy.

Holistic investment pattern

BAT, Unilever and SMC made *holistic investment*, in India. They invested in selling, main business, and complementary businesses. They also ingeniously integrated their business goals to India's national goals and strategically diluted their equity with Indian equity.

First, they invested not only in their main businesses but also in complementary businesses. For instance, BAT invested in tobacco leaf growing, paper and paperboard, packaging, filters, and machinery for rolling cigarette. Unilever invested in fine chemicals, industrial chemicals, catalysts, dairy plants, oil extraction from forest produce such as sal, neem and karanj, and dehydration of peas. SMC invested in several car components: steering, electric components, air-conditioning, dashboards, and car seats. In other words, these firms internalized those market functions that had not developed in their respective industries in India. By investing in their downstream activities they created a stable local supply system and thereby reduced the cost of their products.

Secondly, they were committed to invest in India. This commitment meant developing the various undeveloped market functions of their industries in the country. Most foreign companies feared to commit huge amounts of direct investments in building Indian industries, especially when the initial market demand for their products was low. But the three companies studied strategically timed their investments. Based on the criticality of a market function each of these companies timed its investment and made optimal use of its limited capital.

Thirdly, while many large foreign companies feared the demands of the GOI to invest in the country's priority areas, they ingeniously integrated the host country's national goals with their business objectives. When GOI restricted imports to control foreign exchange, Unilever began developing import substitutes. When GOI demanded large companies to invest in core sectors where it did not invest, BAT invested in paper, paperboard, and hotels. Under the policy of the GOI to indigenize local industries, SMC locally developed 65 per cent of its car components in a period of five years. Developing import substitutes helped the companies to reduce cost and meet export targets. Investing in greenfield ventures helped these companies qualify for various incentives from the host government and generate extra revenue.

Fourthly, these companies included Indian equity as a strategy to localize their businesses. Localizing equity and sharing ownership with the host country has been the most difficult aspect for foreign companies in India. SMC gradually raised its ownership in its subsidiary in India from 26 per cent in 1983 to 54.2 per cent in 2002. Unilever diluted its equity from 100 per cent in 1955 to 51 per cent in 1980, maintaining that level ever since. BAT has truly localized ownership of the company. From 100 per cent ownership, BAT gradually reduced its ownership to 32.5 per cent and allowed Indian institutions and public hold more than 50 per cent of the equity. Figure 8.1 provides a diagrammatic

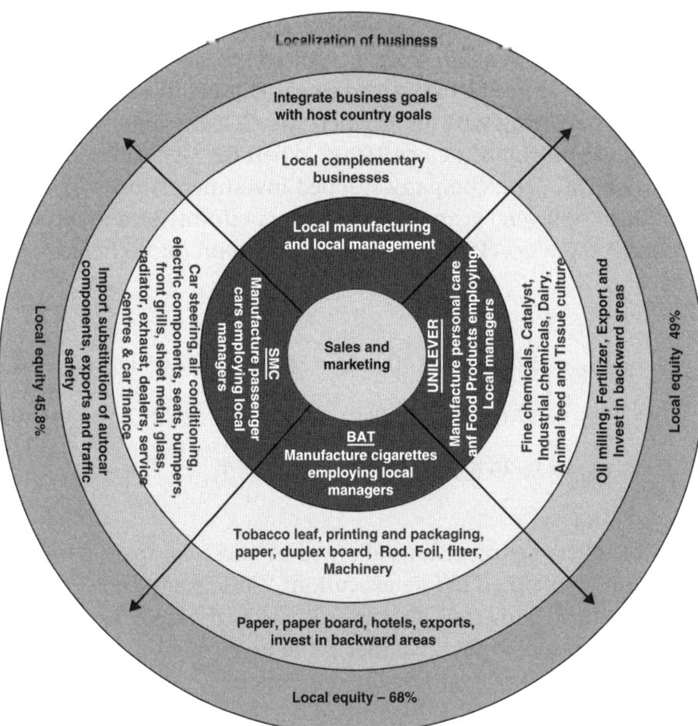

Figure 8.1 Holistic FDI strategy of successful foreign firms in India, 1906–2004

representation of the investment pattern and the direction of investment adopted by the three companies.

Significance of complementation as a strategy

Direct investment by foreign firms in complementary businesses contributed significantly to their success in terms of their sales and PAT in India. In all the three cases, investments in complementary businesses have had much greater effect on sales than investment in the main business, in the following ratio: BAT 2:1, Unilever 3:1, and SMC 25:1. As regards PAT as well, investments in complementary businesses have had a positive effect. For BAT and Unilever, investments in complementary businesses and the main business have had a similar degree of positive effect on PAT. For SMC, investments in complementary businesses had a much greater impact on PAT than investment in the main business.

In the case of SMC, investment in the main business showed a negative coefficient, but since the regression output for this case shows that this value is not significant at 5 per cent level of significance, the negative coefficient cannot be fully ascertained. This could also be attributed to the SMC's fighting with its partner, the GOI for higher equity and management control in the late 1990s. When the GOI did not heed the demands of SMC, the company stopped investments in its main business in MUL for several years and also under performed leading to losses. Equations 7.1–7.6 developed in Chapter 7 are reproduced here for quick reference.

$$S_1 = 54675 + 19.40\, MB_1 + 38.2\, CB_1 - 7.85\, O_1 \tag{7.1}$$

$$S_2 = 57.66 + 4.65\, MB_2 + 13.59\, CB_2 - 2.33\, O_2 \tag{7.2}$$

$$S_3 = 9739.6 + 1.33\, MB_3 + 33.09\, CB_3 + 1.75\, O_3 \tag{7.3}$$

Not all the strategic decisions adopted by these companies were well thought out or planned before execution. While some decisions might have been arrived at by trial and error, others might have been a result of necessity and not of choice. Neither is the investment pattern followed by any case studied perfect nor the dimensions of holistic investment. However, in retrospect, the investment decisions followed by the three cases studied show a move towards a winning strategy of FDI in a developing country context.

$$P_1 = -1001 + 2.59\ MB_1 + 2.42\ CB_1 + 0.43\ O_1 \quad (8.4)$$

$$P_2 = -132.97 + 0.39\ MB_2 + 0.32\ CB_2 + 0.42\ O_2 \quad (8.5)$$

$$P_3 = -335 - 0.01\ MB_3 + 3.29\ CB_3 + 0.56\ O_3 \quad (8.6)$$

Where *S* represents sale, *P* represents PAT, *MB* represents investment in main business, *CB* represents investment in complementary businesses and *O* represents investment in others. Subscripts 1, 2, 3 in the above equations represent BAT, Unilever and SMC, respectively.

Determinants of success

First, all the three successful cases have followed a holistic investment pattern in India. BAT, Unilever and SMC graduated from investing in selling to investing in their respective main businesses and respective complementary businesses. They also imaginatively integrated their business goals to India's national goals and strategically diluted their equity with Indian equity.

Secondly, the determinants of success for foreign firms in India have been similar across industries and across time. This can be inferred from equations (8.1)–(8.6). In all the three cases investment in complementary businesses had a more positive effect than investment in the main businesses. The variations in the degree of impact of each variable in each case have been because of the type and nature of the industries and level of maturity of the businesses in the host economy.

Thirdly, in the aggregate analysis, we find that investments in main businesses and complementary businesses had a positive impact, and investment in others had a negative impact, on both sales and PAT. Investments in complementary businesses had a far greater impact, about 20 times more, than investment in main business on both sales and PAT. These can be inferred from equations (7.2) and (7.8) developed in Chapter 8.

$$\text{Sales} = 16890.67 + 4.19\ MB + 89.79\ CB - 12.9\ O \quad (7.7)$$

$$\text{PAT} = -1595.83 + 0.37\ MB + 9.69\ CB - 0.69\ O \quad (7.8)$$

In sum, the key determinants of success for foreign firms in India had more to do with their internal strategy. More than a myopic strategy to seek resource, market or efficiency, a holistic investment strategy, including investment in both the main business and, more importantly, investment in complementary businesses of a foreign firm was critical to the success of foreign firms in India.

Major learnings

We can make a few important observations from the analysis in this book. The research findings add new perspectives to the literature on FDI in general and factors that determine the success of foreign firms in India.

First, it contributes to an important strand of FDI literature that has not been sufficiently studied, namely, FDI strategy and performance of investing firms. Although the determinants of FDI have been studied extensively the impact of FDI on host country, host country policies that attract FDI, the area of FDI strategy and performance have been relatively less explored.

Secondly, it identifies an FDI strategy that has worked across three companies irrespective of their industry, country of origin, and duration of their operation in India. This throws open the argument whether the proposed strategy is a solution to companies of all industries in India and in developing countries in general.

Thirdly, it establishes that investment in complementary businesses has been critical to the success of foreign firms in a developing host country like India. While this has not only been observed in each of the three cases, the argument was sharper and stronger for the aggregate data of investments and performance indicators for all cases taken together.

Fourthly, this study provides a few critical factors that managers of foreign companies should look into while investing in developing countries. It establishes that a holistic investment strategy, with emphasis on investment in complementary businesses, can lead to consistent performance over a period of time. We can compare the strategy of Suzuki Motors with that of General Motors and Ford Motors and work out why Suzuki has a much stronger market power than either of the two car giants.

Fifthly, this study also provides a methodology for researchers in FDI strategy. It presents a sampling method for selecting cases prior to undertaking a case study method of research. Since the issue of FDI strategy is highly contextual, the sampling method used in this research might be appropriate for research in the area of FDI strategy.

Sixthly, the study analyses critically the FDI history in India during the 1900s–2000. Although there have been a large number of studies on FDI in India, especially in the 1990s, the contextual history of FDI in India has not been properly documented. The current study has been able to provide a historical perspective to the evolution of FDI in India during the last hundred years.

Windows for future research

While this book has explored some aspects of FDI in India, there are indeed a number of issues that could be studied in the future. Future studies could look into issues that can't be addressed here because of the limitations of this book.

First, the present analysis is limited to the Indian context and hence cannot generalize on successful FDI strategy across developing countries unless empirically tested in other developing countries.

Secondly, this study has not looked into cases of failures in FDI, the causes of which are highly varied. Studying failures would also require defining failure first and then sampling cases based on that definition.

Thirdly, this study has been based on the manufacturing sector and not the non-manufacturing industries. FDI in the non-manufacturing sector constituted only a small portion of the FDI in India and it has gained importance during the last decade only.

Fourthly, direct investment data of the subsidiaries of BAT and Unilever have been limited to the last 50 years, beginning in 1955. Prior to 1955, both these companies operated in India through a number of subsidiaries. However, since 1955, they have reorganized their subsidiaries through various mergers and acquisitions.

Future research on determinants of successful FDI strategy can look into the following five potential research issues, among many others:

1. Using the research methodology adopted in this study, FDI strategy of successful foreign multinational enterprises in other developing countries in Asia, Africa, South America and Eastern Europe could be explored.
2. The investment strategy of foreign firms that failed in India could be examined. Although obtaining data for cases that have failed may be difficult, such analysis can help compare and contrast the methods and strategies adopted by different companies and the power of their respective strategies.
3. It could be investigated whether the holistic FDI strategy suggested for a developing country like India holds true in industrially developed countries. An industrially advanced country could be chosen and it

could be seen if the suggested strategy is of any relevance in such a country.

4. Whether successful FDI strategy in the manufacturing industry differs from that in the non-manufacturing industry and hence one could investigate whether holistic FDI strategy is also a winning strategy for multinational enterprises in the non-manufacturing sectors like information services, financial services, etc.
5. Impact of FDI on the host country could be explored. Although this study has looked at how the company invested in various areas within India, including the social sector, future research can also look into the impact of each of the three successful foreign companies in India, namely BAT, Unilever and SMC, on the economy of India.

Notes

2 Evolution of FDI, 1900s–2000

1. Investments from foreign sources may be FDI and Foreign Portfolio Investments (FPI). Reserve Bank of India guidelines have an additional category, namely the issue of a global depository receipt (GDR), which is the Euro issue by Indian companies. The present study focuses on FDI. In the colonial period there was no clear distinction between FDI and FPI. GDR is a recent development (Krishnan 2003).
2. With independence India's regulatory framework changed.
3. Department of Commercial Intelligence and Statistics, a department of the British Government in India.
4. Kuwahara, Tetsuya (Seminar discussions, 2000) and Manuscript of Mitsui Bussan Kaisha '100 Years', vol. 1, 1978 (unpublished) provide details about the historical roots of Japanese business in India. Mitsui Bussan sent Yasukawa to India in December 1892, who set up a purchase office in Bombay in February 1893. Nihon Menka followed suit within a few months. Gosho was another large trading house that set up its office in India. Many smaller trading houses like Itochu and Marubeni also started trading in raw cotton and yarn with India.
5. Discussing the case study of Kanegafuchi Cotton Spinning Company and the role Sanji Muto played in building high productivity and efficiency of Japanese textile spinning companies, Tetsuya Kuwahara (2000) mentions how this had a great influence in the overall development of international competitiveness of Japanese textile and textile-related companies in the early 1900s.
6. D.K. Fieldhouse (1978) discusses the local government introduction of high import duties during the 1930s. B.R. Tomlinson (1989) and A.K Bagchi (1972) also highlight the issue of import duties.
7. Under FERA (1973) all foreign companies holding more than 40 per cent equity in their Indian operations were required to get the permission of the Reserve Bank of India to continue business in India. Section 2 of the Act required foreign firms to include local equity. Depending on the nature of business, companies were also allowed to own 51 per cent or even 74 per cent of equity (Roy 1973).
8. The MRTPA (1970) was introduced to ensure diffusion of economic power and minimize restrictive trade and monopolistic practices. The Act especially put controls on the size of operations and pricing of products of both domestic and foreign companies.
9. FDI data from India Investment Centre, GOI, shows that FDI from many Asian and South East Asian countries have significantly increased in the recent years. The largest investor in India in 1999 has been Mauritius. Korea and Australia have also significantly increased their share of investments in India.

3 Analytical Framework

1. *Success* here is defined by a firm's consistency in terms of annual sales, profit-generating ability or profit before depreciation, interest and tax (PBDIT) and profit sharing ability or PAT.
2. *Holistic investment* means investing in main business, complementary businesses, and certain areas such that the firm's goals become gets aligned with the host country's national goals, and localization of management and ownership.
3. *Complementary businesses* include all the directly and indirectly related economic activities in the value chain of a firm's business line. These could be in the downstream or upstream of the vertical value chain or in some support activities in the horizontal value chain. For instance, the value chain of a company selling cars will include assembling, engine manufacturing, component making, distribution network, service centre network, and financing.
4. Investment in *other areas* includes investment in government securities and other unrelated activities.
5. Although USA has been a major contributor of FDI to India in the last several decades, American companies have not been consistent in their performance. BAT, however, has its roots in USA. It was registered in UK in 1905 with 70 per cent equity from American Tobacco Company, USA and 30 per cent equity from Imperial Tobacco Company, UK.
6. For Unilever, data for 2004 were not available.

4 British American Tobacco, 1906–2004

1. Most of serving executives I met with seemed to see ITC as an Indian company. They were surprised to know how the transition has come about from BAT to ITC.
2. According to Ajit N. Haksar, former Chairman, ITC, the company lacked expertise in sea fishing and could not monitor the fish catch by its trawlers. The trawlers were subsequently sold off at a huge loss.
3. ITC's former Chairman Samir Ghosh mentioned this aspect during my interview with him.
4. Ajit N. Haksar mentioned, during my discussion with him, that the top company management tried to integrate its business objectives with the objectives of the government but had to convince BAT, the parent company of ITC, about the need for such company strategy.
5. Choupal in Hindi means a place where the villagers gather for discussion and recreation.
6. A mandi is a government mandated market place where farmers sell their crops.
7. T. Thomas, the then Chairman of HLL wanted to meet Ajit N. Haksar, then Chairman of ITC to discuss the issue and make a joint representation to the Government of India. The meeting, however, did not take place because Haksar strongly differed with him on the issue. Company sources revealed this during interviews.

8. Samir Ghosh, who closely worked with Ajit N. Haksar and who later became Chairman of ITC reasoned that because of BAT's experience of political pressure for national control in several of the 55 countries where it operated, BAT was quick to adopt the guideline of the GOI to dilute its equity in India by including the local equity.
9. Enforcement Directorate is an enforcement body appointed by the central government for the purposes of foreign exchange regulation.

5 Unilever PLC, 1932–2004

1. HVMC had a capital of INR1,00,000 with unit share price of INR10. The objects of the company were (a) to carry on the business of manufacturing of vegetable products, margarine and all types of fat and oleaginous emulsions, (b) to carry on the business of manufacturing of soap, soap powders, detergents and toilet requisites, and (c) to carry on the business of manufacturing pharmaceuticals and general chemists and druggist, manufactures of and dealers in glycerine and all kinds of toilet requisites and many other areas of business. (Source: HVMC, MOU). United Traders had a capital of INR300,000 with unit share price of INR10. The company was registered with the following objects: (a) to carry on the business of merchants and of importers and exporters of merchandise of all kinds, (b) to establish and carry on the business of manufacturers of soap, soap-powder, detergents and toilet requisites, and to buy, sell, manufacture, refine, prepare and deal in all kinds of oils and oleaginous and saponaceous substrates, and all kinds of unguents and ingredients, and (c) to carry on the business of pharmaceuticals, food of all kinds, oil, cattle food, manure, and many other areas of business.
(*Source*: United Traders Limited, MOU).
2. With brands like OK, 501, Burnol, TOMCO was a major competitor of HLL in the personal care products in the Indian market.
3. Brooke Bond Lipton India (BBLIL) was formed with the merger of Brooke Bond and Lipton India. These were in the business of tea and coffee. The merger of BBLIL with HLL strengthened the food business of HLL and helped Unilever to hold both its businesses of personal care and packaged food under a single umbrella.
4. Ponds India Ltd was in the business of lotion and personal care before it was merged with HLL. Ponds, a US company, started its production in India in 1977. It was a competitor of HLL for several years until it was finally merged with HLL.
5. The investment data have been compiled from various Annual Reports (1955–2003) of the company.
6. N.C.B. Nath, during a discussion with the author, mentioned that the Indian managers were carefully selected and trained. They work in the Head Office of the parent company or in a subsidiary outside India under observation of senior executives from the parent company before they were assigned greater responsibilities in the company.
7. Chairman's Annual Speeches, HLL; interview with Irfan Khan and S. Varadharajan.

8. FERA 1973 Guidelines allowed foreign companies engaged in the manufacture of high-technology products and exported a minimum of 60 per cent of their products to retain a majority of shareholding. Synthetic detergents, fine chemicals and industrial machinery of HLL were part of core sectors; soap, vanaspati, and toothpaste were not. The Government approved HLL's application to retain 51 per cent majority share on the ground that it was exporting more than 10 per cent of its product value, and was producing 60 per cent in sophisticated product lines. Some of the executives interviewed by the author were not sure how the Government came to this conclusion.
9. Irfan Khan, former General Manager, Corporate Communications, HLL mentioned during the author's discussion with him that Unilever was willing to forgo its control on its subsidiary as long as it earned profits from its investment. The Indian managers of the company, however, were of the opinion that India would gain the most by allowing Unilever to retain majority of the shareholding in HLL, in terms of getting technology and capital for growth and expansion. T. Thomas, the then chairman of HLL, spearheaded this movement, speaking to managers at all levels and in every interaction on this subject.

6 Suzuki Motor Corporation, 1982–2004

1. In an interview with Keiji Nakajima, General Manager-Sumitomo, India, the dynamics of how SMC improved its financial situation were mentioned. Nakajima closely worked with SMC in its early years of operation in India.
2. The future potential of cars in India was clearly visualized by Osamu Suzuki. Osamu Suzuki's perspective of huge potential for cars in India was reiterated by Keiji Nakajima, General Manager-Sumitomo and by Junzo Sugimori, Director of SMC and Joint Managing Director of MUL during interviews with each of them separately.
3. Many of the senior and top executive like Junzo Sugimori, Joint Managing Director, R.C. Bhargava, former Managing Director of MUL and Keiji Nakajima, General Manager-Sumitomo expressed that the top management in MUL were very open to the introduction of management practices of SMC, Japan. This practice was also appreciated by the young managers in the company.
4. Keiretsu is a Japanese term for business group in Japan. The business units with in such a group are tied to each other through cross-holdings of equity. There is a rich flow of information across the members and a lot of cooperation among the members of a business group. A keiretsu is usually supported financially by a major Japanese Bank.

Bibliography

All Japan Cotton Spinners Association (1949), *Cotton Statistics of Japan, 1903–1949*, Osaka: Japan Cotton Spinners' Association.

Anand, J. and Delios, A. (1996), 'Competing globally: how Japanese MNCs have matched goals and strategies in India and China', *The Columbia Journal of World Business*, autumn: 50–62.

Andersson, U., Forsgren, M. and Pedersen, T. (2001), 'Subsidiary performance in multinational corporations: the importance of technology embeddedness', *International Business Review* 10: 3–23.

Athreye, S. and Kapur, S. (1999), 'Foreign controlled manufacturing firms in India – long-term trends', *Economic and Political Weekly*, 27 November.

Axelsson, Bjorn and Johanson, Jan (1994), Foreign market entry – the textbook vs the network view, in Johansson & Associates (eds), *Internationalization, Relationships and Networks*, Stockholm: Uppsala University, Norstedts Tryckeri AB, ch. 16.

Bagchi, A.K. (1972), *Private Investment in India, 1900–1939*, New York: Cambridge University Press.

Barlett, C.A. and Ghosal, S. (2002), *Managing Across Borders: The Transnational Solution*, Boston, Mass.: Harvard Business School Press.

Basu Champaka (1988), *Challenge and Change, The ITC Story: 1910–1985*, Calcutta, Orient Longman.

Birkinshaw, J. and Hood, N. (2000), 'Characteristics of foreign subsidiaries in industry clusters', *Journal of International Business Studies* 31(1): 141–54.

Birkinshaw, J.M. and Morrison, A.J. (1995), 'Configurations of strategy and structure in subsidiaries of multinational corporations', *Journal of International Business Studies*, 4th quarter: 729–53.

Bishop, C.M. (2004), *Neural Networks for Pattern Recognition*, New Delhi: Oxford University Press.

Bjorkman, I. and Osland, G.E. (1998), 'Multinational corporations in China: responding to government pressures', *Long Range Planning* 31: 436–45.

Brewer, T.L. (1992), 'Effects of government policies on foreign direct investment as a strategic choice of firms: an expansion of internalization theory', *The International Trade Journal* VII(1): 111–27.

Buckley, P. and Casson, M. (2001), 'Strategic complexity in international business', in Rugman, A.M. and Brewer, T.L. (eds), *The Oxford Handbook of International Business*, New York: Oxford University Press, ch. 4.

Campbell, A., Goold, M. and Alexander, M. (1995), 'Corporate strategy: the quest', *Harvard Business Review*, March–April: 120–32.

Carlsson, J., Nordegren, A. and Sjoholm, F. (2005), 'International experience and the performance of Scandinavian firms in China', *International Business Review* 15: 21–40.

Carr, E.H. (1994), *International Relations Between the Two World Wars 1919–1939*, London: Macmillan.

Centre for Industry and Economic Research, *Industrial Databook* (1986), New Delhi.

Centre for Monitoring Indian Economy (1955–2004), Database, Mumbai, Centre for Monitoring Indian Economy.

Chakrabarti, A. (2001), 'The determinants of foreign direct investment: sensitivity analysis of cross-country regressions', *Kyklos* 54: 89–114.

Chakraborty, C. and Basu, P. (2002), 'Foreign direct investment and growth in India: a cointegration approach', *Applied Economics* 34: 1061–73.

Chandler Alfred, Jr (1969), *Strategy and Structure: Chapters in the History of the American Industrial Revolution*, Boston, Mass.: MIT Press.

Chandrapalert, A. (2000), 'The determinants of U.S. direct investment in Thailand: A survey on managerial perspectives', *Multinational Business Review*, autumn: 82–7.

Chandra, B. (1991), *India's Struggle for Independence 1857–1947*, New Delhi: Penguin Books.

Chang, Ha-Joon (2002), *Kicking Away the Ladder: Development Strategy in Historical Perspective*, London: Anthem Press.

Chang, Ha-Joon (2004), *Kicking Away the Ladder: Development Strategy in Historical Perspective*, London: Anthem Press.

Chen, H. (1999), 'International performance of multinationals: A hybrid model', *Journal of World Business* 34(2): 157–70.

Choe, J. (2000), 'Japanese foreign direct investment in electrical machinery and appliances in the United States: a combined theory approach', *Asian Economic Journal* 14(3): 301–13.

CIER (Centre for Industrial and Economic Research) (1986), *Industrial Data Book*, New Delhi: Government of India.

Cieslik, A. and Ryan, M. (2002), 'Characterising Japanese direct investment in Central and Eastern Europe: a firm level investigation of stylized facts and investment characteristics', *Post-Communist Economies* 14(4): 523–5.

Cooper, Donald R. and Schindler, Pamela S. (1999), *Business Research Methods*, New Delhi: Tata McGraw Hill.

Davenport, R.P., Hines, T. and Judy, S. (1992), *Glaxo: A History to 1962*, Cambridge University Press.

Debroy, Bibek (1996), *Beyond the Uruguay Round: The Indian Perspective on GATT*, London: Sage.

Deolakikar, A.B. and Evenson, R.E. (1989), 'Technology production and technology purchase in Indian industry: an economic analysis', *The Review of Economics and Statistics* 71(4): 687–92.

Department of Commercial Intelligence and Statistics (DCLS) (1924, 1929, 1931, 1939, 1941, and 1951), *Report on Joint Stock Companies, 1928–29*, New Delhi: Government of India.

Desai, A.R. (1990), *Social Background of Indian Nationalism*, Bombay: Popular Prakashan.

Dooley David (1997), *Social Research Methods*, New Delhi: Prentice-Hall of India.

Dunning, J.H. (1988), *Explaining International Production*, London: Unwin, Hyman, 13–40.

Dunning, J.H. (1998), 'Location and the multinational enterprise: a neglected factor?', *Journal of International Business Studies* 29(1): 45–66.

Dunning, J.H. (2000), 'The eclectic paradigm of international production: a personal perspective', in Pitelis C.N. and Sugden, R. (eds), *The Nature of the Transnational Firm*, New York: Routledge, 119–39.

Dunning, J.H. (2003), 'Some antecedents of internalizing theory', *Journal of International Business Studies*, vol. 34, no. 2, pp. 108–15.

Eisenhardt, Kathleen, M. (1989), 'Building theories from case study research', *Academy of Management Review*, 14.

Eisenhardt, Kathleen, M. (1991), 'Better stories and better constructs: the case for rigor and comparative logic', *Academy of Management Review*, 16:3.

Ellis, C.J. and Fausten, D. (2002), 'Strategic FDI and industrial ownership structure', *Canadian Journal of Economics* 35(3): 476–94.

Encarnation, D. (1989), *Dislodging Multinationals, India's Strategy in Comparative Perspective*, Cornell University Press.

Ericsson, J. and Irandoust, M. (2001), 'On the causality between foreign direct investment and output: A comparative study', *The International Trade Journal* XV(1): 20–2.

Fieldhouse, D.K. (1978), *Unilever Overseas, The Anatomy of a Multinational, 1895–1965*, London: The Hoover Institution Press.

Five Year Plans, Planning Commission, Government of India (accessed 30 September 2004), at http://planningcommission.nic.in/plans/planrel/fiveyr/welcome.html

Franko, L.G. (1989), 'Use of minority and 50–50 joint ventures by United states multinationals during the 1970s: the interaction of host country policies and corporate strategies', *Journal of International Business Studies*, Spring 1989.

Frost, T. and Zhou, C. (2000), 'The geography of foreign R&D within a host country: an evolutionary perspective on location-technology selection by multinationals', *International Studies of Management & Organization* 30(2): 10–43.

Galego, A., Vieira, C. and Vieira, I. (2004), 'The CEEC as FDI attractors: A menace to the EU periphery?', *Emerging Markets Finance and Trade* 40(5): 74–91.

Ganesh, S. (1997), 'Who is afraid of foreign firms? current trends in FDI in India', *Economic and Political Weekly*, 31 May.

Ghemawat, P. (1991), *Commitment*, New York: Free Press.

Ghemawat, P. (2001), 'Tool kit. Distance still matters – The hard reality of global expansion', *Harvard Business Review*, September: 137–47.

Ghoshal, S. and Moran, P. (2005), 'Towards a good theory of management', in Birkinshaw, J. and Piramal, G. (eds), *Sumantra Ghoshal on Management*, Great Britain: Pearson Education Ltd.

Gordon, James (2002), 'Foreign direct investment and exports, presentation at Indian Institute of Foreign Trade', New Delhi.

Government of India (GOI), (2000–2001), *Industrial Data Book: 2000–01*, New Delhi.

Green, P.E., Tull, D.S. and Albaum, G. (1999), *Research for Marketing Decisions* (5th edn), New Delhi: Prentice-Hall of India.

Gujarati, Damodar, N. (2003), *Basic Econometrics*, (4th edn), New Delhi: Tata McGraw-Hill: 341–70.

Hair, J.F., Anderson, R.E., Tatham, R.L. and Black, W.C. (2003), *Multivariate Data Analysis*, Delhi: Pearson Education.

Haksar, Ajit, N. (1993), *Bite the Bullet, Thirty-four Years with ITC*, Viking, Penguin India.

Hamel, Jacques, Dufuor, S. and Fortin, D. (1993), *Case Study Methods Qualitative Research Methods Series 32*, New Delhi: Sage.

Haykin, S. (2002), *Neural Networks: A Comprehensive Foundation*, 2nd edn, Delhi: Pearson Education.

Hennart, J. (2000), 'Transaction costs theory and the multinational enterprise', in Pitelis, C.N. and Sugden, R. (eds), *The Nature of the Transnational Firm*, New York: Routledge: 72–118.

HLL (1955–2003), *Annual Reports*, Bombay: Hindustan Lever Limited.

HLL (1959–2004), *Chairman's Annual Speech*, Bombay: Hindustan Lever Limited.

HLL, History of Unilever in India (accessed March 2001), at http://www.hll.com

Hunter, J.B.K. and Keir, D. (unpublished, 1969) manuscript of the Coats' History.

HVMC (1931), Memorandum of association of The Hindustan Vanaspati Manufacturing Co., Ltd. with Articles of Association. Bombay: Hindustan Vanaspati Manufacturing Company Limited.

India Investment Centre (1967–1990), *Foreign Business Investments in India* (monthly newsletter), New Delhi: India Investment Centre, Government of India.

India Investment Centre (2003), Net Flow of FDI to India, 1991–2002 (accessed 19 November 2003), at http://www.iic.nic.in

India Investment Centre (accessed March 2000), at http://www.iic.nic.in

India Investment Centre (1991–2000), *FDI Data: 1991–2000*, New Delhi: Government of India.

India Investment Centre (2000), *Foreign Direct Investment Approved by the Government of India, 1990–2000*, New Delhi: Government of India.

International Investment Position of India (accessed 13 November 2003), at http://www.finmin.nic.in

ITC Ltd (1955–2004), *Annual Reports*, Calcutta: ITC Ltd.

Johnston, Westley J., Leach, Mark, P. and Liu, Annie, H. (1999), 'Testing theory using case studies in business-to-business research', *Industrial Marketing Management* 28(3).

Johri, L.M. (1983), *Business Strategies of Multinational Corporations in India: Case Study of Drug and Pharmaceutical Industry*, New Delhi: Vision Books.

Jones, G. (1996), *The Evolution of International Business: An introduction*, London: Routledge.

Jones, G. (2000), *Merchants to Multinationals, British Trading Companies in the Nineteenth and Twentieth Centuries*, London: Oxford University Press.

Khanna, T. and Palepu, K. (1997), 'Why focused strategies may be wrong for emerging markets', *Harvard Business Review*, July–August: 41–51.

Kidron, M. (1965), *Foreign Investments in India*, London: Oxford University Press.

Krishnan, R. (2003), *Commercial's Handbook on Foreign Collaborations and Investments in India, Law, Practice and Procedures*, New Delhi: Commercial Law Publishers (India).

Kumar, K. (2003), 'Has India Inc failed in playing the leadership role?', *Vikalpa* 28(3) (July–September).

Kumar, N. (1990), *Multinational Enterprises in India – Industrial Distribution, Characteristics, and Performance*, New York: Routledge.

Kumar, S. (1996), *Foreign Direct Investment in India*, Delhi: BR Publishing Corporation.

Kurian, M.K. (1966), *Impact of Foreign Capital on Indian Economy*, New Delhi: People's Publishing House.

Kuwahara, Tetsuya, (2000), Seminar discussions, Graduate School of Business, Kobe University, Japan.

Lall Sanjaya (1999), 'India's manufactured exports: comparative structure and prospects', *World Development* 27(10), Elsevier Science Limited (accessed 20 November 2003), at http://www.sciencedirect.com

Luo, Y. (1998), 'Timing of investment and international expansion performance in China', *Journal of International Business Studies* 29(2): 391–408.

Malairaja, C. and Zawadie, G. (2004), 'The "black box" syndrome in technology transfer and the challenge of innovation in developing countries: the case of international joint ventures in Malaysia', *International Journal of Technology Management and Sustainable Development* 3(3): 233–51.

Mason, R.L., Gunst, R.F. and Webster, J.T. (1975), 'Regression analysis and problems of multicollinearity', *Communications in Statistics A*, 4(9).

Mason Robert (1995), *Qualitative Researching*, Thousand Oaks, CA: Sage.

Milner, C. and Pentecost, E. (1996), 'Locational advantage and US foreign direct investment in UK manufacturing', *Applied Economics* 28: 605–15.

Ministry of Finance, Government of Japan, FDI from Japan to India (accessed March 2000). at http://www.mof.go.jp/english/e1c008.htm

Ministry of Finance, Government of India, Sectoral distribution of FDI (accessed November 2003), at http://www.finmin.nic.in

Mintzberg, Henry (1994), *The Rise and Fall of Strategic Planning*, New York: Free Press.

Montgomery, Douglas and Peck, Elizabeth (1982), *Introduction to Linear Regression*, New York: John Wiley.

Moon, C.W. and Lado, A.A. (2000), 'MNC–host government bargaining power relationship: a critique and extension within the resource-based view', *Journal of Management* 26(1): 1–30 (accessed 18 February 2005), http://web35.epnet.com/citation.asp?tb=1&_ug=sid+C3C049B6%2DEF07%2D49E8%2D9.

Mudambi, R. (1999), 'Multinational investment attraction: principal–agent considerations', *International Journal of the Economics of Business* 6(1): 65–9.

MUL (1984–2004), *Annual Report*, New Delhi: Maruti Udyog Limited.

MUL (2003), Maruti Udyog Limited, Prospectus, Dated 25 June 2003, 100% Book Building Offer, New Delhi: Maruti Udyog Limited.

Myneni, S.R. (2000), *World Trade Organization*, Hyderabad: Asia Law House.

Nair-Reichert, U. and Weinhold, D. (2001), 'Causality tests for cross-country panels: a new look at FDI and economic growth in developing countries', *Oxford Bulletin of Economics & Statistics* 63(2): 153–68.

Narayanan, K. (2005), 'Globalization and competitive capabilities in Indian automobile industry', Third International Conference, Academy of International Business – India Chapter, Indian Institute of Technology, Kharagpur, 11–13 January.

Narula, R. and Dunning, J.H. (2000), 'Industrial development, globalization and multinational enterprises: 'new realities for developing countries', *Oxford Development Studies* 28(2): 158–63.

Nayak, Amar, K.J.R. (2002), 'Foreign investments in India: disequilibria in extraction-manufacturing and conservation of natural resources', International Conference on New Environmental Technologies, by BORDA, Germany & NISWASS, Bhubaneswar, India, 7–8 October.

Nayak Amar, K.J.R. (2003), 'Impact of trade and investment policies of GATT/WTO on India, 1955–2000', Indian Academy of Social Sciences, XXVII Indian Social Science Congress, Indian Institute of Technology, Kharagpur, India, 3–7 December.

Nayak, Amar, K.J.R. (2004), 'Globalization process in India: a clash of developmental objectives of host with growth objectives of foreign companies', Academy of International Business – India: Second International Conference, Loyola College, Chennai, India, 14–16 January.

Nayak, Amar K.J.R. (2005a), 'FDI Model in Emerging Economics: Case of Suzuki Motors in India, *The Journal of American Academy of Business*, Cambridge, Vol.6, No. 1.

Nayak, Amar, K.J.R., Chakravarti, Kalyan and Rajib, Prabina (2005b), 'Globalization process in India: a historical perspective since independence, 1947', *South Asian Journal of Management*, Vol. 12, Issue 1.

Ng, L.F.Y. and Tuan, C. (2002), 'Building a favourable investment environment: evidence for the facilitation of FDI in China', *World Economy*, Blackwell Publishers: 1095.

Ok, S.T. (2004), 'What drives foreign direct investment into emerging markets?', *Emerging Markets Finance and Trade* 40(4): 101–14.

Oliva, Maria-Angels and Rivera-Batiz, Luis A. (2002), 'Political Institutions, Capital flows, and developing country growth: an empirical investigation', *Review of Development Economic* Vol. 6, Issue 2.

Panneerselvam, R. (2004), *Research Methodology*, New Delhi: Prentice-Hall of India.

Park, B. and Lee, K. (2003), 'Comparative analysis of foreign direct investment in China: firms from South Korea, Hong Kong, and the United States in Shandong province', *Journal of the Asian Pacific Economy* 8(1): 57–84.

Park K.H. (2003), 'Patterns and strategies of foreign direct investment: the case of Japanese firms', *Applied Economics* 35: 31739–46.

Patwardhan, M.S. (1986), *OIL and Other Multinationals in India*, Bombay: Popular Prakashan.

Penrose, Edith (1995), *Theory of the Growth of the Firm*, 3rd edn, Oxford: Oxford University Press.

Porter, M.E. (1980), *Competitive Strategy: Techniques for Analyzing Industries and Competitors*, New York: The Free Press: ch. 10.

Porter, M.E. (1985), *Competitive Advantage: Creating and Surfacing Superior Performance*, New York: The Free Press: ch. 2.

Poynter, T.A. (1986), 'Managing government intervention: a strategy for defending the subsidiary', *Columbia Journal of World Business*, winter: 55–65.

Pradhan, S. (2000), 'Foreign direct investment: risk, return and host country's strategy', *Journal of Management Research* 1(1): 18–30.

Prahalad, C.K. and Hamel, G. (1990), 'The core competence of the corporation', *Harvard Business Review*, May–June: 79–90.

Principal Exports from India (accessed 13 November 2003), at http://www.finmin.nic.in

Principal Imports from India (accessed 16 November 2003), at http://www.finmin.nic.in

Qian, J.L.G., Lam, K. and Wang, D. (2000), 'Breaking into China: strategic considerations for multinational corporations', *Long Range Planning,* 33: 673–87.

Rajib, P. *et al.* (2003), 'MNC de-listing in India: is it a fair deal?: a case of Sandvik Asia Ltd', Strategic Management Forum, Xavier Labour Relations Institute, Jamshedpur, India, 24–26 April.

Ramirez, M.D. (2000), 'Foreign direct investment in Mexico: a cointegration analysis', *The Journal of Development Studies* 37(1): 155–7.

Rangan, S. and Drummond, A. (2004), 'Explaining outcomes in competition among foreign multinationals in a focal host market', *Strategic Management Journal*, 25: 285–93.

Reserve Bank of India (RBI) (1976, 1977, 1978, 1980, 1981, 1985, 1991), *Annual Reports,* Bombay: Government of India.

Reserve Bank of India (accessed January 2000) at <http://www.rbi.org.in>

Reserve Bank of India, (online), (cited January, 2000) at <URL: http://www.rbi.org.in

Reserve Bank of India, (2003) Government of India, (online), (cited 17 November, 2003) at <URL: http://www.rbi.org.in>

Resmini, L. (2000), 'The determinants of foreign direct investment in the CEECs: new evidence from sectoral patterns', *Economics of Transition* 8(3): 665–89.

Rivoli, P. and Salorio, E. (1996), 'Foreign direct investment and investment under uncertainty', *Journal of International Business Studies*, 2nd quarter: 335–57.

Rolf, R.J., Ricks, D.A., Pointer, M.M. and McCarthy, M. (1993), 'Determinants of FDI incentive preferences of MNEs', *Journal of International Business Studies*: 335–54.

Roy, S.K. (1973), *Foreign Exchange Regulation Act, 1973*, Calcutta: Kamal Law House.

Roy, S.K. (2000), *Foreign Exchange Management Act, 2000*, Calcutta: Kamal Law House.

Rugman, A.M. and Verbeke, A. (2001), 'Location and competitiveness', in Rugman, A.M. and Brewer, T. (eds), *The Oxford Handbook of International Business,* New York: Oxford University Press; 150–77.

Rugman, Alan, M. and Verbeke (2002), 'Edith Penrose's contribution to the resource-based view of strategic management', *Strategic Management Journal,* 23: 769–80.

Rumelt, P., Schendel, D.E. and Teece, D.J. (1994), *Fundamental Issues in Strategy,* Boston, Mass.: Harvard Business Press.

Sahoo, D. and Mathiyazhagan, M.K. (2003), 'Economic growth in India: does foreign direct investment inflow matter?', *The Singapore Economic Review* 48(2): 151–71.

Sanna-Randaccio, F. (2002), 'The impact of foreign direct investment on home and host countries with endogenous R & D', *Review of International Economics* 10(2): 278–98.

Sara, T.S. and Newhouse, B. (1995), 'Transaction costs and foreign direct investment in developing countries', *International Advances in Economic Research* 1(4): 317–25.

Sarkar, S. (1996), *Modern India 1865–1947*, Madras: Macmillan.

Schaffer, Marvin Baker, Speculations about geopolitics in the 21st century, Elsevier Science Limited (accessed 11 November 2003), at http://www.sciencedirect.com

Sharma, Kishore (2000), Export growth in India, has FDI played a role? Discussion Paper, Yale University, Economic Growth Center (accessed November 2003), at http://www.econ.yale.edu/~egcenter

Slaveski, T. and Nedanovski, P. (2002), 'Foreign direct investment in the Balkans', *Eastern European Economics* 40(4): 83–99.

SMC (1983–2000), *Annual Reports*, Hamamatsu, Japan: Suzuki Motor Corporation.

SMC (1990), *70 Years of Suzuki Motor Corporation*, Japan: Suzuki Motor Corporation.

SMC, 'History: Suzuki Motors, 1909–2001' (accessed January 2000), http://www.suzuki.co.jp/cpd/kobe_e/6-1.htm

Stiglitz, Joseph, E. (2002), *Globalization and Its Discontents*, London: Allen Lane.

Taggart, J.H. (1999), 'MNC subsidiary performance, risk, and corporate expectations', *International Business Review,* 8: 233–55.

Tahir, R. and Larimo, J. (2004), 'Understanding the location strategies of the European firms in Asian countries', *The Journal of American Academy of Business*, September: 102–8.

Tang, L. (2002), 'Measuring the intensity of vertically integrated multinational enterprises', *Review of Development Economics* 6(3): 478–91.

Tomlinson, B.R. (1989), 'British Business in India, 1860–1970', in Davenport-Hines, R.P.T. and Geoffrey, J. (eds), *British Business in Asia Since 1860,* New York: Cambridge University Press.

Toyo, Keizai (1990 and 1998), *Overseas FDI from Japan to Asia*, Tokyo: Toyo Keizai.

Trevino, L.J., Daniels, J.D., Arbelaez, H. and Upadhyaya, K.P. (2002), 'Market reform and foreign direct investment in Latin America: evidence from an error correction model', *The International Trade Journal* XVI (4): 367–89.

Trivedi, P. (2004), Role of the State in globalizing India, Second International Conference, Academy of International Business – India Chapter, Loyola College, Chennai, 14–16 January.

Tufano, Peter (2001), HBS-JEE Conference volume: Complementary research methods, *Journal of Financial Economics* 60(2, 3).

UNCTAD X Press (2000), Asia's Share of Global FDI doubles in 1990s, Bangkok, 17 February.

United Traders Limited (1935), *Memorandum and Articles of Association,* Bombay: United Traders Limited.

US Department of Commerce (1961), *Investment in India: Basic Information for United States Businessmen, 1961*, Washington: Government of United States of America.

Varghese, K.V. (1993), *Indian Economy: Problems and Prospects*, New Delhi: Ashish.

Venkataramani, R. (1990), *Japan Enters Indian Industry: The Maruti–Suzuki Joint Venture*, New Delhi: Radiant.

Vernon, R. (1966), 'International investment and international trade in the product cycle', *Quarterly Journal of Economics,* 80: 190–207.

Vernon, R. (1971), *Sovereignty at Bay: the Multinational Speed of U.S. Enterprises*, New York: Basic Books.

Walkenhorst, P. (2004), 'Economic transition and the Sectoral patterns of foreign direct investment', *Emerging Markets Finance and Trade* 40(2): 5–26.

Welch, C., Piekkari, R.M., Pettinen, H. and Tahvanainen, M. (2002), Corporate elites as informants in qualitative international business research', *International Business Review* 11(5).

Wilkins, M. (1994), 'Comparative Hosts', in Geoffrey, J. (ed.), *The Making of Global Enterprise*, London: Frank Cass and Company Limited.

William, J. Goode and Hatt, Paul K. (1981), *Methods in Social Research*, London: McGraw Hill.

World Bank Report (2003), India at a glance, *Development Economics*, 25 August.

Wright, J.T. (1965), *The New Corporate Strategy*, New York: John Wiley: ch. 7.

Yaffe David (2003), 'Globalization – a redivision of the world' (accessed 20 November), at http://www.Imperialism.html

Yamin, M. (2000), 'A critical re-evaluation of Hymer's contribution to the theory of the transnational corporation', in Pitelis, C.N. and Sugden, R. (eds), *The Nature of the Transnational Firm*, New York: Routledge; 57–71.

Yang, J.Y.U., Groenewold, N. and Tcha, M. (2000), 'The determinants of foreign direct investment in Australia', *The Economic Record* 76(232): 45–54.

Yeung, Henry Wai-Chung (1995), 'Qualitative personal interview in international business research: some lessons from a study of Hong Kong transnational corporation', *International Business Review* 4(3): 313–39.

Yin, Robert K. (1994), *Case Study Research: Design and Methods*, Thousand Oaks, CA: Sage

Zhang, G., Patuwo, B.E. and Hu, M.Y. (1998), 'Forecasting with artificial neural networks: the state of the art', *International Journal of Forecasting*, 14: 35–62.

Zhang, K.H. (2001), How does foreign direct investment affect economic growth in China?', *Economics of Transition* 9(3): 679–93.

Zhao, H. and Levary, R.R. (2002), 'Evaluation of country attractiveness for foreign direct investment in the E-retail industry', *Multinational Business Review*, Spring: 8–9.

Subject Index

t – table, f – figure, c – chart, n – note

Name Index